AF292337

The Tooting Tragedy

The Tooting Tragedy

Cholera, Cruelty and Children of the Victorian Poor

William Ellis-Rees

First published in Great Britain in 2026 by
Pen & Sword History
An imprint of Pen & Sword Books Limited
Yorkshire – Philadelphia

ISBN 978 1 03614 524 8

A CIP catalogue record for this book is
available from the British Library.

Typeset by Mac Style
Printed in the UK by CPI Group (UK) Ltd, Croydon, CR0 4YY.

The Publisher's authorised representative in the EU for product
safety is Authorised Rep Compliance Ltd., Ground Floor,
71 Lower Baggot Street, Dublin D02 P593, Ireland.
www.arccompliance.com

For a complete list of Pen & Sword titles please contact:

PEN & SWORD BOOKS LIMITED
47 Church Street, Barnsley, South Yorkshire, S70 2AS, England
E-mail: enquiries@pen-and-sword.co.uk
Website: www.pen-and-sword.co.uk
or
PEN AND SWORD BOOKS
1950 Lawrence Road, Havertown, PA 19083, USA
E-mail: uspen-and-sword@casematepublishers.com
Website: www.penandswordbooks.com

For Karen, Tom and Anna

Contents

Acknowledgements

My thanks to the staff of the British Library, the Guildhall Library, the Hampshire Record Office, the London Archives, the London Library, the National Archives, the Surrey History Centre and the Wandsworth Heritage Service.

Thanks also to Liz Buchanan, the Operations Director at St Nicholas Church in Tooting, for some useful extra information about burials in the graveyard and for permission to use an image of a page from the burial register. Wendy Hawke, the Senior Archivist at the London Archives, kindly supplied a scan, for which I am duly grateful. Thanks also to Emma Anthony, the Wandsworth Borough Archivist, for her help in finding material, and to Philip Bradley, Chair of the Tooting History Group. Philip generously sent me a copy of the photograph of the 1920s Tooting Public Baths and gave me permission to use it in the book.

I would also like to thank Sarah-Beth Watkins and Laura Hirst at Pen & Sword for guiding me through the publishing process, Alan Murphy for his editorial insights and illuminating suggestions, and Jon Wilkinson for his striking jacket design.

Last but not least, I would like to thank my family for their patience throughout the Drouet years, as they have come to be known. Above all, I would like to thank my wife, Karen, who has been more supportive and encouraging during the research and writing stages of this project than she will ever know.

Prologue

Friday, 13 April 1849 was a chilly spring day in London, and the rain was already falling as crowds began to gather in Old Bailey, a narrow street with Sessions House and the granite mass of Newgate Prison on its east side, and on its west side a jumble of shops, public houses and coffee rooms. A contingent of the City police had been dispatched to keep order on the pavements, and to prevent jostling and confusion when the doors of the court were opened shortly before nine o'clock and spectators were admitted to the public gallery. Admission was restricted to those who had managed to buy a ticket signed by an under sheriff, a system used at high-profile trials to deal with the problem of excessive demand, although it was not unknown for disappointed and desperate members of the public to get into the courthouse illicitly by offering officials generous bribes.

Four cases would be heard that morning in the Old Court, and the fourth would continue until late the following day. The defendant was a middle-aged man by the name of Bartholomew Peter Drouet. He was neither tall nor short, he was grey-haired and stout, and he had the ruddy complexion that betokened his failing health, his problematic heart, and maybe also the quick, blustering temper for which he was renowned.[1] He considered himself respectable, and in line with the fashion of the day, he would have been wearing a frock coat and long trousers, a waistcoat, a high-collared shirt and a cravat. Throughout January he had been one of the most talked about men in England, and no doubt there would have been a number of spectators who had come to the Old Bailey for no other reason than being drawn to the latest media sensation. They had read the newspaper reports and knew all the details. Now they were anxious to see the infamous Drouet in the flesh.

The atmosphere in the courtroom was charged. There was a sense of anticipation, not to say excitement, which would only have been heightened by the delay of an hour while the preliminary cases were tried. These were run-of-the-mill robberies, two of which involved breaking and entering. In the first of these, two robbers had helped themselves to two pairs of trousers to the value of 10s.[2] In the second, another two robbers had run off with a clock worth 15s.[3] In the third case, a pocket had been picked, and its owner robbed of a half crown, a sixpence and a farthing.[4] It is unlikely that anyone would have had much interest in the fate of the defendants, the five young men who stood in a morose group in the dock as their sentences were handed down. Between them, they were to be transported for a total of twenty-seven years.

The moment all had been waiting for was when Drouet finally entered the courtroom at a few minutes before ten o'clock.[5] Accompanied by the four men who had put up his bail, he took his place in the dock. Then he relinquished his freedom and handed himself over to the court to be tried. Opposite him was the judges' bench, with the gilded sword of justice hanging above the principal chair. To his left were the seats for the jurors and the witnesses, to his right those for the magistrates and the reporters, while below him was the sunken cockpit where the barristers and the attorneys sat at tables strewn with papers and books. Up above, behind him and to his right, ran the public gallery. Although the light from the three windows above the jurors' box was dismal, Drouet was lit by two gas lamps fixed to the front of the dock, one on either side. In this way he could be studied by the judges and the jury and identified by witnesses taking the stand. He was centre stage, with his face and the play of his emotions fully on display.[6]

The drama that was about to begin had its origins in a terrible tragedy. Drouet was the owner of Surrey Hall, a house in what was then the village of Lower Tooting, where he ran a residential school. But this was not a school in the ordinary sense of the word, and it was definitely not dedicated to the task of cultivating young minds. His charges were workhouse children who had been sent to him in large numbers by the parish authorities in every part of the metropolis. Naturally, the parishes had to pay for Drouet's services, and he made a handsome profit. His critics worried that the children taken to Lower Tooting became invisible; and indeed they did, until the early weeks of 1849 when cholera tore through Surrey Hall.

This book is the story of that tragedy: its deep roots, its shocking details, its immediate and distant consequences. It is the story of a shameless Victorian entrepreneur who took advantage of the plight of destitute children to line his own pockets. But it is also the inspiring story of good people who sought to right these wrongs, and of the children themselves, many of whom found the courage to speak openly about their ordeal when the opportunity arose.

Chapter One

Elizabeth Frost

Elizabeth Frost was nine years old. Although her life went largely unrecorded, which was the reality for countless Victorian children born to poor parents, she has left some clues. It is known, for example, that she was born in May 1839, that her parents were called Henry and Elizabeth, and that in early June they bundled her up and took her to be baptised in the parish church of Islington, St Mary the Virgin, which stood a few streets from where they lived in Adelaide Square.

Henry Frost was a plasterer, and Elizabeth a laundress, and their neighbours in Adelaide Square were working-class men and women engaged in occupations similar to theirs. The men were employed in manual trades, and although some, like Henry, had definite skills and worked as carpenters or masons, others had the less impressive job title of general labourer. The women – if caring for their children left them time and energy for paid work – followed Elizabeth's example by taking in washing.[1] This was a world of dirt and decay, of pavements covered with refuse of every description, of dark and twisting alleys leading the unwary away from the relative safety of the streets into the menacing enclaves or 'courts' where many people were afraid to enter. Often these were no-go areas, and they were avoided where possible, even by officers of the law.

Life in these squalid surroundings was primitive, and the large families that made up much of the population of Islington had to endure particular miseries as, more often than not, they had to squeeze into cramped rooms in teeming and run-down tenements. The censuses provide stark evidence of their plight. In June 1841, two years after Elizabeth's birth, the enumerator was confronted with twelve premises that between them housed no fewer than 132 men, women and children, all jostling for space in a way that stripped them of their dignity. Ten years later, in the census of March 1851, the same number of premises housed well over 200 individuals. In No. 1 Adelaide Square alone four families with a combined total of twenty-four members lived cheek by jowl, while in No. 7, which was shared by another four families, a carpenter and his wife were struggling to bring up eight children ranging in age from three to sixteen.[2]

Not surprisingly, then, Adelaide Square had acquired an unenviable reputation as 'a square only in name'; that is to say, it was a clutter of densely populated houses lacking every desirable feature.[3] There were no wide pavements to give the residents a sense of space, no trees to add dashes of colour to their drab and dreary environment, and no grassy areas to contribute to their general physical and mental wellbeing. So unhealthy was Adelaide Square that in 1859 it was reckoned that the mortality rate was twice that of other parts of Islington, and roughly in line with that of Naples, a comparison many would have found shocking in view of the notoriety of nineteenth-century Neapolitan slums.[4]

In the 1840s, the decade in which Elizabeth Frost lived her short life, the residents of Islington were mostly poor, and they were given mixed reviews by those who were fortunate enough to live in more salubrious areas. A contemporary writer, Samuel Lewis, drew attention to 'the masses that are crowded in our courts and alleys'. His attitude towards this sizeable underclass was not entirely sympathetic, and he was at pains to point out that it had a decidedly 'heathen' element, which, when measured against that familiar yardstick of nineteenth-century morality, namely attendance at church, fell so short of the mark that the process of evangelisation could only be achieved by 'aggressive' and 'penetrating' efforts.[5]

On the other hand, as Lewis recognised, the provision of places of worship had not kept pace with the rapid growth of the population, a woeful state of affairs that prevailed more in the impoverished districts than in the well-heeled. Also conspicuous by their absence were public baths and washhouses, which were, of course, of vital importance in areas where many people lived in unhygienic and insanitary conditions. Furthermore, there was no model housing of the sort that had been built elsewhere to alleviate the miseries of the metropolitan slums. Lewis considered the absence of these amenities 'a signal disgrace to a parish of a hundred thousand inhabitants'. Islington was 'far below' many other parts of the capital 'in respect of public spirit'.[6]

Although there seems to have been no eyewitness account of the tenements in Adelaide Square, they cannot have differed much from those in other deprived areas of the capital. An unsparing description of Charlotte's

Buildings in Holborn, published in 1853, is a reasonable basis on which to imagine the conditions the Frosts would have lived in. Fifteen dilapidated houses stood round a filthy court off Gray's Inn Lane, a mile or so to the south of Adelaide Square and in all respects as dismal as its Islington counterpart. The writer of the piece, a reporter from the *Builder* who went into this dangerous area with a police escort, did not mince his words: 'During the day, and particularly in the evening up till about ten or eleven o'clock, the narrow area is filled with strange-looking and ragged figures, whose dresses and complexion harmonise with the grey, mouldy and dingy-looking walls of the buildings.'[7]

When the reporter stepped warily into one of the houses, which had been chosen at random, he was horrified at what he found. The walls had cracks running through them, the floorboards were rotten, and plaster was crumbling from the ceilings. The rooms had little or nothing in the way of furniture, but there was no shortage of washing, and it had been strung in drooping festoons over the fire grates to dry. In a room on the ground floor there were sad little tokens of a life that might have been but never was: a looking glass about three inches high dangling above the mantel, torn prints of the Crucifixion, pieces of broken crockery in a cupboard without doors. Even sadder were the occupants, the wretches who scratched a living of sorts by chopping firewood, which the children took out into the streets to sell. Some of the men had paid employment as bricklayers' labourers, while others resorted to more desperate ways of keeping the wolf from the door, either 'working at the carrion heaps' that festered in the streets of the neighbourhood, or begging.[8]

Elizabeth would surely have resembled the children who lived in Charlotte's Buildings or in any of the mean tenements and low lodging houses described for the horrified middle classes in the *Builder*, in the novels of Charles Dickens, and in the journalism of Henry Mayhew, who went among the poor of the capital in search of material for the articles he published in the *Morning Chronicle* in 1849 and 1850. Here, there and everywhere in the work of writers who ventured into the metropolitan slums, either on foot or in their imagination, are the street urchins, the crossing sweepers, both male and female, the dust-yard scavengers and the flower sellers. Mayhew interviewed some of these London children, and they spoke as Elizabeth would have spoken, their unrefined speech coarsened with London vowels and turns of phrase.[9] And so it is not too difficult to 'hear' Elizabeth, nor indeed to 'see' her as one of the many bedraggled little girls in Gustave Doré's haunting images of Orange Court in Drury Lane, Wentworth Street in Whitechapel, and Dudley Street in Seven Dials.[10] Her clothes would have been shapeless, worn and torn, in all likelihood cast-offs or hand-me-downs. Her face would have been that of all undernourished London children, her skin pallid, her eyes sunken and lifeless. Her hair would have been wild and straggly, unwashed and unloved, lank and matted, and probably infested with lice.

In common with the children of Charlotte's Buildings, she was born into a world of constant hardship. Her earliest experiences would have been of unrelenting discomfort, of gnawing hunger, of penetrating cold in the winter months as winds blew through broken windows. Even though by the time she was two years old the family had moved out of Adelaide Square and settled a few streets away in Ward's Place, nothing much would have changed. She would still have had to endure the same cramped conditions, which almost certainly meant sharing a bed at night with her two older brothers, and also with her sister, who was born two years after her.

It was not unusual for the children of poor parents to have to sleep in a shared bed. When the reporter from the *Builder* went into a gloomy room in another Holborn lodging, in Plumtree Court in Shoe Lane, he was able to make out, with the help of the policeman's lantern, a bed that 'seemed to have heads all round it' and turned out to be occupied by nine women and children, a second bed in which a man and a boy were sleeping, and a closet occupied by another three people. Overcrowding on this scale was made worse by poor ventilation, as the visitors discovered when they stepped into the room only to be momentarily driven back by the rank smell of fourteen human beings living in close proximity, with neither the means nor the incentive to maintain even a modest level of hygiene. Conditions in Ward's Place would undoubtedly have been similar to those in Plumtree Court. Less extreme, perhaps, but not by that much of a margin.[11]

Elizabeth and her parents and her many siblings were typical of the labouring classes towards whom Samuel Lewis directed his critical gaze. But the needs of indigent families like the Frosts were to some degree recognised and catered for, and one of the most prominent landmarks in their corner of Islington, and a fine example of nineteenth-century enlightenment, was the ragged school built at no great distance from Adelaide Square and Ward's Place in Elder Walk. The school came too late for Elizabeth, as it opened in the late summer of 1848, by which time she had been sent to Tooting, but it was designed for children in the same circumstances as her, children whose parents were too poor to provide moral or religious, or indeed any sort of, education. 'They had been lying about the courts and alleys of the Lower Road,' the *Ragged School Union Magazine* said of these fledgling scholars, 'or else crowding in the dirty and miserable hovels with which the neighbourhood abounds.'[12] Up to a hundred bedraggled children would be herded into the school every day to be cared for and instructed by its one paid and eight voluntary teachers. Many came without shoes or stockings, and their pinched features and hunched shoulders made it all too obvious that their most basic needs were not being met. One cannot imagine that Elizabeth would have been in any way different from these destitute pupils of the ragged school in Elder Walk.[13]

* * *

There is no reason to suppose that the Frosts, for all that they were poor, were not a close and loving family. The fact that Henry and Elizabeth had their children baptised, and that they handed down their own names to the first-born son and daughter, is perhaps an indication of the sort of old-fashioned values that helped poverty-stricken Victorians stay afloat in the choppy waters of adversity and privation. What is more, Henry, as a plasterer, had a skill that made him eminently employable at a time when the building of houses was going on at a furious pace. At only a slight risk of wishful thinking, he can be pictured arriving home at the end of the day, tired out by his labours and spattered with daubs of plaster. He would be greeted by his wife and children, the oldest of whom, Henry and John, might have understood that they too would be going out to work before too long. Elizabeth, who was hardly more than a baby, would simply be gazing fondly up at her father. But all that would change in the autumn of 1843, when, at the age of thirty-one, Henry fell seriously ill and did not recover.

It was recorded on his death certificate that he had been suffering from 'brain fever'. This is the term the nineteenth-century medical profession gave to illnesses that have now been identified as either encephalitis or meningitis, so it can be inferred with a degree of confidence that his illness would have taken the form of a steady, irreversible and distressing decline. The first sign of danger would have been a stiffness in his neck, which Henry might well have dismissed out of hand, attributing it to the long hours and physical demands of his work as a plasterer. He is less likely to have ignored subsequent symptoms, such as severe headaches, which were often debilitating. Then, as the illness tightened its grip, an obvious change would have come over him, and those with whom he had close contact would have noticed patterns of abnormal behaviour. He might have begun by losing his patience over the slightest matter and snapping testily at his family. In time, though, this relatively mild loss of control would have made way for more violent outbursts. These unmistakable signs of deterioration, quite apart from filling Henry with a sense of shame, could not have failed to frighten his wife and children. At this point the picture of the proud working man providing for his family must be redrawn. Henry would now have been bedridden, burning up with fever and only just clinging on to life. When he finally gave up the ghost, his wife Elizabeth was at his side, and it was Elizabeth who walked over to Halton Street to report the death to the registrar, marking the certificate with an X, which was her only form of signature and was required of a person who had never been taught to write.[14]

For the younger Elizabeth, who was only four years old, and indeed for her mother and siblings, the death of Henry Frost was a double tragedy. In addition to inflicting personal loss on the family, it pushed them down into the lowest and most humiliating of social categories as dependants on the parish. Even when Henry was in good health and bringing home a wage, his wife would have been struggling to bring up children in the depressed surroundings of Adelaide Square and Ward's Place. That was at the best of times, but now widowhood had proved to be the final straw, and Elizabeth would eventually choose what for many women in her position would have been the only chance of survival by taking herself and her children into the workhouse. She was certainly there in 1847. Moreover, in July 1845, almost two years after Henry's death, she had given birth to another daughter, named Emma. At the time, she was residing a few streets from Ward's Place in Windsor Street, presumably with the man with whom she was sharing her life, and her bed. Nothing about him is known: even his name is a mystery. However, it is recorded that Elizabeth had her daughter baptised as a Frost, which further suggests that her liaison with the girl's father was not officially recognised, whatever promise of emotional or financial support it held out.

The Islington workhouse was at the corner of Liverpool Road and Upper Barnsbury Street, and a print dated 1819 shows that in those earlier times it had been a stark and cheerless edifice, several storeys high, with a row of houses directly behind it and in front of it a patch of ground where cattle grazed. What alterations, if any, were made in the years following the Poor Law Amendment Act of 1834 is not clear, but a report on the state of the infirmary published in the *Lancet* in the mid-1860s gives at least some idea, in spite of the passage of twenty years, of the gloomy and forbidding environment in which the Frosts found themselves when they entered the workhouse as inmates. 'It is an example of a thoroughly bad edifice,' the report stated, 'with wards ill built, too small, too low, badly lighted and badly ventilated, rambling in plan, and closets opening into the wards.' For all its damning assessment of the facilities, the report was generous in its praise of the work that went on in the infirmary. Thanks to the efforts of the medical officer, who was properly supported by the guardians and the master and matron of the workhouse, some sense had been made of a building riddled with defects.[15]

Even a cursory search through the newspapers of the day reveals that conditions in the Islington workhouse were as harsh in the 1840s as they were in the 1860s. As well as the many deaths of inmates who had been ground down and weakened by chronic poverty, there were accusations of access to relief being denied, obvious cases of destitution, and bizarre tragedies such as the one that befell a seventy-year-old man who choked to death on a piece of beef.[16] A girl as young as Elizabeth Frost could not have been unaffected by being thrown into the company of children who were the victims of extreme adversity, some of whom were being cared for against all the odds by a parent or parents struggling with poverty, while others had simply been neglected, or orphaned, or abused. It was not uncommon for a child to be brought into the workhouse by a policeman, having been found wandering alone in the streets, unable to remember an address or even a name. One little unfortunate had been found lying in a stone-yard by the Regent's Canal half-dead with cold. She was eighteen months old, and all her clothes had been stolen from her with the exception of her socks.[17]

If sights like these were not harrowing enough, there were the noises that echoed through the corridors of the workhouse as the shouted orders of the staff vied for supremacy with the upsetting cries of 'lunatic' inmates who had fallen prey to mental illness or the ravages of drink. And for all the regimentation and the strict rules by means of which the inmates were kept in check, disorder continually threatened to break out. One such incident, which became briefly notorious, involved a large group of vagrants. It would appear that these men were all able-bodied and therefore not in need of relief, but this did not stop them laying siege to the workhouse and forcing the authorities to give them lodgings for the night. The newspapers, always ready to pounce on the worst examples of pauperism, made it obvious that in their view the behaviour of the vagrants was outrageous. 'One stout ruffianly-looking fellow, named Baines,' declared the *Essex Herald*, 'who described himself as a labourer out of work from Brentwood, kept the house in a continual uproar during the whole of the night by his bawling, swearing, and abusing the officers.' The rioting had also spilled out into the streets around the workhouse, and the local residents, understandably, were badly shaken.[18]

*　*　*

The Liverpool Road records make it clear that the Frost children, although admitted frequently in the years following their father's death, were only ever in the workhouse itself for a day or two.[19] One reason for these short stays was that they had been sent off to the infant poor house around eight miles north of Islington, at Ford's Green in Edmonton, which, in accordance with Hanway's Act of 1767, kept the youngest children in the healthier countryside on the fringes of the city and at a safe distance from the workhouse with its attendant evils. An institution of this kind, dedicated to the care of the young, could in principle provide the moral education and the industrial and domestic training that would make future employment achievable. Moreover, and importantly, it would make looking for paid work in the outside world a more attractive prospect than relying on the parish, which filled decent Victorian society with disgust and disdain.

The fear that pauper children would be irremediably corrupted by the example of their feckless elders was universal, though in some quarters it went hand in hand with a natural compassion, and also perhaps with a belief that it was necessary to consider the interests and wellbeing of the most defenceless members of society. The author of *The Poor Laws Unmasked*, for example, published in 1859, was guided as much by his heart as by his head. Although he did not reveal his name, he claimed that he had been a relieving officer for many years, and that in this capacity it had been his responsibility to assess those trying to gain entry to the workhouse and decide who qualified for indoor and who for outdoor relief. The job must have given him experience of the entire spectrum of dependency, from playing the system at one end to being genuinely destitute at the other. In any event, he approved of those boards of guardians who had the good sense, and the common decency, to place children in 'suburban localities' well away from the 'foetid air of our workhouses in the town districts', whatever the expense.[20]

This last matter was not unimportant. The cost of sending inmates to private establishments such as the infant poor house at Ford's Green was a burden that ultimately had to be shouldered by the parish ratepayers. The late relieving officer maintained that even so it was a sacrifice that had to be made. 'Money,' he insisted, 'should never be placed in the scale against human life.'[21] And what would the ratepayers' money buy for these unhappy creatures? In the first place, the physical conditions that all children, whatever their station in life, have need of: clean air, space to exercise, enough to eat. But there was a further advantage in that the infant poor house, built in a suitable spot and run by humane adults, would provide to a degree what the workhouse child lacked, namely a family and a home. To be deprived of these fundamental necessities was the worst possible injury that could be inflicted on the young. To have a loving family and a home, whatever form they assumed, made everything else more or less bearable. Even the child in the slums might find the nastiness of their surroundings 'in some measure mitigated by the general happiness experienced from being "at home" receiving the caresses of their parents, and the society of their friends'. Children like Elizabeth Frost had none of these comforts.[22]

Given its location and its composition, the infant poor house at Ford's Green would appear to have been exactly the sort of child-friendly establishment the anonymous author of *The Poor Laws Unmasked* was pushing for. At the time of the 1841 census, there were only twenty boys and sixteen girls on the premises, all aged seven or under, and cared for by an elderly schoolmistress, three nurses, and four domestic staff. The head of the operation was the matron, Frances Cable Hartley, a widowed mother in her early forties, who, one would like to think, kept a kindly eye on the children and ensured that their needs were met.[23] The most important of these was food, and the children were fed a diet of bread and milk, beef, mutton, broth and potatoes.[24] Of course, the reality might not have been so benign, and nothing prevents us from wondering if Mrs Hartley's establishment was in fact rather closer to the 'farm' in Chapter Two of *Oliver Twist*. Here, the juvenile inmates 'rolled about the floor all day, without the inconvenience of too much food or too much clothing', while the elderly Mrs Mann, who was Dickens's fictitious version of the real Mrs Hartley, directed her 'wisdom and experience' more to skimming off a tidy sum from the fees extracted from the parish than to observing her responsibilities as the children's principal carer.[25]

Furthermore, although the location of the infant poor house, in the midst of fields and no great distance from the green slopes of Winchmore Hill, was inevitably more conducive to good health than the back streets of Islington, the children brought with them all the medical complications that thrived in any workhouse population. A number of the reports of the workhouse medical officers who visited Ford's Green have survived, and it is evident, for example, that the highly infectious complaint known as ophthalmia was rife among the children, even spreading to the cook and to more than one of the nurses. Ophthalmia would have caused the intense discomfort of inflamed eyes, a tormenting irritation, and a sensation of burning beneath the eyelids, and if left untreated it might have resulted in the permanent loss of sight. One has to fear for those children who had 'weak' eyes as a lasting reminder of the inflammation they had already suffered.[26]

There seemed to be no consensus on how to treat children whose eyesight had been affected by ophthalmia. Some officers from the workhouse proposed that they be given meat on a daily basis. Their thinking may have had less to do with an understanding of eye conditions than with their reaction to the sight of children who were generally unhealthy, principally because they were undernourished, which strongly suggests that the diet for the inmates of the infant poor house was not as generous in reality as it was in its official publicised form.[27]

Another problem to be contended with was scabies. At the time, scabies was commonly referred to as 'itch', and with good reason. It was the work of a merciless parasite burrowing under the skin, and it broke out in burning red patches, or unsightly pustular eruptions, over its victim's ribs, back, legs and arms. It would spread through a community of unwashed children like wildfire, moving by contact from one child to the next in the shared beds and jam-packed schoolrooms and in the rough and tumble of the yard. The sensation its name so accurately described caused untold misery, and it is recorded that a father in one of the London workhouses, on seeing his little daughter's ravaged skin, described her as being 'eaten up' by the disease.[28]

Itch crops up so often in the reports the medical officers submitted from Ford's Green that one has to assume that it had become endemic. But the more worrying concern was the poor state of the children's general health. The problem, it was believed, started in the home with their parents. Where the parents were in poor health, they were liable to communicate diseases to their offspring. As a result, the infant poor house was populated by children who were eminently susceptible to medical problems. The ailments and disorders from which they suffered were many and varied, and ranged from diarrhoea and fever to influenza and convulsive fits. There are scattered references in the reports to children whose lives were clearly hanging in the balance.

Taking all these written reports into consideration, it would be little short of a miracle if the Frost children had not suffered from such complaints in the time they spent at Ford's Green. Even if they remained relatively healthy, they had to submit to being shuttled from one temporary home to another, which meant an uncomfortable journey along the roads and lanes of Middlesex in a 'van' or horse-drawn wagon in the company of other children from the workhouse. Nothing in their lives seemed permanent now. In May 1847, after only four days in Ford's Green, they were carted back down to Islington, probably at the insistence of their mother, who discharged herself from the workhouse the next day and took her family home with her.[29] This yo-yoing happened again later in the year, in September, when Elizabeth and her children once again went into the workhouse, and after a stay of forty-eight hours went home only to be readmitted the following day.[30] What emerges is a picture of a widowed mother who was desperate to keep her family together but was unable to cope, either because she lacked the necessary resources, or because her health, or short periods of paid work as a laundress, presented too much of an obstacle.

Then, in June 1848, four of the five Frost siblings were driven down to Surrey to the pauper establishment in Lower Tooting.[31] Elizabeth, who had only recently turned nine, was one of them, and must have experienced considerable turmoil. In her short life she had been faced with the death of her father, periods of separation from her mother, the harsh realities of her status as an inmate of the workhouse, and a series of relocations that would inevitably have had a destabilising effect, leaving her feeling rootless, worthless, and unloved. Her existence had become one of constant unwelcome surprises: another day, another journey, and once again the rough adult voices ordering her to clamber into or jump down from yet another van. Probably no one ever told her where she was being taken, let alone why, and on that journey to Lower Tooting, which would be her last, she cannot have been anything other than bewildered, unhappy and fearful of what lay ahead. But then no one at the establishment, not even the proprietor, Bartholomew Peter Drouet, could have had the faintest idea what lay ahead.

She would have been one of many workhouse children who huddled together on the benches of the van as it trundled down Liverpool Road, bound for Surrey. For the past few days there had been almost constant rain. Although it was now the third week in June, the air was still cool, and the city sat under a sky weighed down with dark clouds. The horses hauled the van through the hustle and bustle of Clerkenwell and Farringdon and skirted round the great meat market at Smithfield before crossing over London Bridge. On the south side of the river, in a world Elizabeth knew nothing of, was the sprawl of Borough and Newington. But this soon gave way to the greener stretches of Kennington and Clapham, which led in turn to the fields and meadows of Balham and Upper Tooting. From there, as the ground fell gently away, the village of Lower Tooting was only a short distance further on.

*   *   *

At any other time, Lower Tooting would have been a welcome change from any of the places where Elizabeth had lived, Adelaide Square and Ward's Place included. A directory of Surrey published in 1839 by Pigot & Co. praised the village for its pleasant situation, its ample street lighting, its cleanliness and its general air of respectability. Standing at the crossing point of two roads, one running from the city down to Worthing, the other from Mitcham to Wimbledon, Lower Tooting was visited not only by the traffic of the local tradesmen's carts but also by that of the mighty passenger carriages, which had already travelled about seven miles from the capital and were now thundering on their way through Surrey in the direction of the south coast. The village was still unspoilt by industry and it was yet to be touched by the relentless southward march of an ever-expanding city.[32]

The dwellings identified by Pigot & Co. as tasteful villas and handsome mansions were dotted around Lower Tooting's rural setting. They housed the well-to-do, many of whom had made money in mercantile occupations and now had the leisure to enjoy a peaceful environment where they might fill their lungs with the invigorating air for which the area was known. Images exist of some of the village's buildings. A fine view of St Nicholas Church places it in a spacious setting beneath a calm and expansive sky. A group of two women with a boy and a girl, a strolling couple, and other figures standing round the church add to the scene's charm and tranquillity.[33] A view of the Angel Inn in the High Street shows another side of Lower Tooting life. The inn is quietly magnificent with its steeply pitched roofs and overhanging upper floors, its shuttered windows, and its tavern sign in a carved frame held aloft on a tall wooden post. There are people engaged in various tasks, a man and a woman walking with a child, and a carriage waiting outside with its team of horses.[34]

The Surrey Hall establishment was a red-bricked, two-storey Georgian mansion standing at the centre of the village. In front of the house, and facing the main road and the village green, were iron fences and a crescent-shaped gateway with wrought-iron gates, and beyond these a coach house and stabling. There was a playground behind the house, but it was little more than a long, narrow, roughly paved yard. It was bounded on one side by Garratt Lane, the road running west through Summerstown and then north to Wandsworth, and on the other side by fields. There were gardens and an orchard as well, but the most distinctive feature of this part of the property was an assortment of scruffy outbuildings serving as workshops, laundries and storerooms. Some of these unappealing structures, which extended about halfway along the upper boundary of the yard and all the way along the lower boundary with Garratt Lane, had obviously been made on the cheap, with schoolrooms at ground level and dormitories on the floor above.

It would have needed only a quick glance inside the schoolrooms, where the ceilings were low and the furniture crude and utilitarian, to see that they had been designed and fitted out with scant concern for the convenience of teachers and pupils. The dormitories were just as rudimentary, and nothing about them suggested that the occupants, who were boys at the lower end of the age range, were deserving of a proper night's sleep. The older boys had been allocated a row of 'cottages' at the far end of the yard, where they enjoyed no more comfort than their younger counterparts and had to put up with the suffocating smells that wafted over them from an open sewer running alongside their accommodation. The girls were spared the worst. The younger ones slept in the hall under the watchful eye of Drouet and his family, and the older ones in an adjoining building known as the White House.[35]

It would not have been easy to distinguish Elizabeth among the multitude of children who resided at Surrey Hall. When she arrived in the early summer of 1848, they numbered well over 1,000,[36] but in the months that followed, and for reasons that will become clear in due course, the population increased at a rapid rate, with dramatic consequences. They were at every stage of childhood: some were well into adolescence while others were barely out of infancy. All they had in common was that they had been sent to Lower Tooting from one of the many workhouses that had business arrangements with Drouet. They might have come down from Islington, like Elizabeth, or from another of the metropolitan sinks of deprivation, such as St Pancras or Holborn. Or they might have been more local, from Newington, for example, or Wandsworth. But they were equal in one important respect: they found themselves at the very margins of Victorian society. They had all, without exception, got off to the worst possible start in life.

The care and management of this mass of lost souls called for a virtual army of adults. The resident surgeon, William James Kite, reckoned that there were fifty-seven nurses alone, roughly one to every twenty-five children, which he seemed to think was the ratio required in all pauper establishments.[37] But the nurses were only one part of the roll call. There were also the domestic servants, the kitchen and laundry staff, and the employees with occupations calling for specific skills. Examples of this last category were the two schoolmasters, Samuel Harding and Joshua Brown, and the two schoolmistresses, Sarah Shambler and Sarah Goat. They may have had other colleagues to help them in the schoolrooms, though none are known by name with the exception of John 'Johnny' Kerr, a young man of about nineteen years of age. He had once been one of Drouet's children, then at the age of twelve, having made a favourable impression as a classroom monitor, he was taken on as a school assistant. He supervised the younger boys at mealtimes and kept an eye on them in the dining hall. He must have been full of youthful ardour, as he once made a boy run away, having pulled his ears painfully.[38]

Other identifiable individuals who are on record as working for Drouet had essential trades such as tailoring and shoemaking. Their employment was twofold: they manufactured, on the premises, the items of clothing and footwear worn by the children, and they also provided the boys with the industrial training that would help them gain a foothold in the world of work once they graduated from Surrey Hall. For the girls, the equivalent training was in needlework, and they spent long hours at this arduous and soul-destroying activity, which, if nothing else, would have made them familiar with its demands by the time they were old enough to earn their living. Records also show that Drouet had basket makers, tinplate workers and gardeners on his books, and there are grounds to believe that boys were given hands-on experience of agricultural work by being put at the disposal of a local landowner for the summer haymaking, probably without being paid.[39]

Drouet, who was fifty-four years old in late 1848, shared the running of his operation with a half-brother, Richard, and his son, William Charles, who were thirty-one and twenty-six respectively. While both have crawled into the vast archive of documents that chronicle the history of Surrey Hall, it is fair to say that of the two Richard was the more significant, and it is indisputably the case that by virtue of his appalling behaviour he had the more profound impact on the lives of the children. As will become all too apparent, the shadow he cast over the establishment was very dark indeed, although up to a point his malign influence would have been offset by the milder management style of the matron and her assistant.

The matron was Drouet's wife, Maria, and her partnership with her husband at the helm of Surrey Hall was something of a convention in pauper establishments. She was evidently a very capable woman, but the responsibilities that came with her position would have been onerous, and it is perhaps no surprise that her health was poor, so much so that at the beginning of October, when she was still only forty-six, she died. All the while her assistant, a Whitechapel woman in her late thirties by the name of Sarah Jane Day, was making herself indispensable, and although she was technically a servant, it would appear that Drouet thought very highly of her, to the point where questions might legitimately be asked about the nature of the relationship that bound them together. They are questions that are unlikely ever to be answered, but they remain an intriguing aspect of the complex and ultimately tragic story of Surrey Hall.

Chapter Two

Bartholomew Peter Drouet

Bartholomew Peter Drouet, the second of the eight children of William Henry Drouet and Elizabeth Oram, was born on 28 November 1794. The exact address where his parents were living at the time is not known, but he was baptised shortly after, on 4 December, in the church of St Luke's in Finsbury. In all likelihood the Drouets resided in the area lying between Old Street and City New Road, beyond which, to the north, the dense mass of London petered out, leaving large tracts of land that had yet to be developed. Not far off stood the theatre at Sadler's Wells. There were also a number of buildings of a more mundane sort that give some idea of the character of London life in the late eighteenth century, amongst which were factories, hospitals and workhouses.

Drouet's father was a customs officer at the Port of London, and documents dating from the time when his son would have been approaching young adulthood make it quite clear what his work entailed. He was employed on the north bank of the Thames at the Waterside for Foreign Business Outwards as a searcher, and as such he was empowered to board any ship heading out of the port in order to ensure that the goods being loaded for export tallied with the cargo manifest, and to verify that the necessary dues had been paid.[1] Although his position at Custom House invested him with an air of respectability, and encouraged him to style himself a 'gentleman' on official documents, his would not have been the most genteel of occupations. It would not be surprising if his accounts of his dealings down at the wharves with sea-hardened sailors and ship's captains, over whom he exercised his power in a none too friendly manner, predisposed his son to work of an authoritarian nature.

Although he would eventually forge a career in the world of pauper institutions, the younger Drouet initially found employment in connection with the river. He was a chip off the old block, and in 1809, when he was fourteen or fifteen, he started work with Messrs Mallough & Co. at Fresh

Wharf on Lower Thames Street. The Malloughs were lightermen, ferrying cargo between the ships and warehouses on flat-bottomed barges. One of their men, William Boak, took Drouet on as an apprentice soon after he turned seventeen.[2] It was a long apprenticeship, and he would not gain 'freedom of the river' until he was almost twenty-five. For a time he remained at Fresh Wharf, working directly for the owner, John Knill.[3]

However, he would not have been doing the heavy and dangerous work of the lightermen, who took great risks as they rode the powerful Thames currents. He had a reasonable level of education, as demonstrated by the many letters that have survived from the later years of his career, written in a clear and confident hand. As likely as not, he was employed in Knill's offices, drawing up lists of cargo and keeping records of the payment of dues. Either that or he was entrusted with the management of the crews who operated the lighters, or of the unskilled men who laboured on the wharves and in the warehouses. At this point it might have seemed that he was destined to follow in his father's footsteps, and it is a sobering thought that had he carried on in this line of work, the horrors that are to be chronicled in later chapters of this book would not have taken place. There would have been no 'school' at Surrey Hall in Lower Tooting. There would have been no suffering, no scandal, and no deaths.

On reaching his thirties, Drouet moved down to the Hampshire coast to take up a position in the workhouse at Alverstoke, which was in the borough of Gosport. He had resigned from Knill's firm for no more mysterious reason than that there was not enough money in it: money was then, and would always be, the main driving force in his working life. He must have seen profitable opportunities in pauper administration, and it is not as if he was moving into an entirely unrelated environment. He certainly believed that his experience of managing the lightermen and dockside labourers down by the Thames had prepared him for the responsibilities he would subsequently shoulder in organising workhouse inmates. And so began a series of events that would lead, many years later, to tragedy.

Once Drouet was installed at Alverstoke, and his work as a 'contractor', or provider of services and goods to the workhouse, was up and running, he emerged from the shadows, as it were. From this point on, a great deal is known about him, and also about his brother, William Leonard Drouet, who was about eighteen months older. William's significance lies in the fact that he held the contract for the Alverstoke workhouse prior to Bartholomew's arrival, and if an impression is beginning to emerge of a family of businessmen operating in the pauper industry, it is not far from the truth, because there was also a half-brother, Alfred Charles Drouet, who would make money in this way.

William was himself no stranger to pauper institutions. In partnership with another contractor, Charles Mott, he worked at Alverstoke and also at the Newington workhouse in South London, or Surrey as it was then, where Mott was both provisioner and master. Indeed, they were already provisioning for Alverstoke when, early in 1823, they tendered for the contract to oversee the running of the workhouse, which was properly known as the House of Industry. They saw off the competition with a proposal to set their rate at 2s. 9d. per head per week, reduced to 2s. 6d. for boys aged fifteen and below and girls aged sixteen and below. Drouet, still in partnership with Mott, took up the position of master of the establishment, while his wife, Rebecca, was appointed matron.[4]

Along with their experience of managing the inmates at Newington, which would have given them impressive credentials, Mott and Drouet both had backgrounds in retail. Mott, who was based in Limehouse in the East End, sold the cheap and shoddy clothing known as slops, and Drouet, in partnership with a Joseph William Snuggs, dealt in ale and porter from premises in Lime Street in the City, at least until 1816, when he filed for bankruptcy. Given that weak beer was routinely drunk by adults and children alike as a safe substitute for water, it is almost inconceivable that Drouet was not selling his liquid merchandise to at least one of the London workhouses.[5]

Having followed William down to Alverstoke, Bartholomew soon made his mark, and by 1826 he had replaced his brother as assistant to Mott at the House of Industry. There is good reason to believe that the transfer of power had come about in a less than amicable fashion, seeing as William competed unsuccessfully against Bartholomew for the 1827 contract, and having failed to outbid his younger brother, went off to Gosport to run the Crown Inn. At the same time, Rebecca Drouet was replaced as matron by Maria Fraiser, who was Bartholomew's partner and also the mother of his son William Charles. Although she would remain unmarried for another year, Maria presented herself as 'Mrs' Drouet, as the master and matron of a workhouse were, as a rule, husband and wife.[6]

Although one brother had gone, and another had taken his place, what had not changed was the issue of money. The new partnership of Charles Mott and Bartholomew Peter Drouet pushed for an increase in their rates, employing the tried and trusted argument that the rising cost of supplies, over which they naturally had no control, looked set to leave them out of pocket. To make matters worse, a fall in the number of inmates, caused in part by children leaving the workhouse for employment, made it harder to achieve economies at the point of purchase by buying in bulk.[7] These arguments, backed by the spurious claim that they, the contractors, would willingly maintain their original low terms if it made good business sense to do so, must have had some traction as the parish agreed to a rise in their rate from 2s. 9d. to 3s. per head per week in the period 1826 to 1827[8]. Nevertheless, Mott and Drouet had to reckon with market forces, and in their tender for the following year's contract they dropped their rate to 2s. 6d.[9]

Aside from their continuing attempts to charge as much for their services as they could get away with, the new partners' abiding concern was the absurdity, as they saw it, of the poor of the parish being more comfortably off in the workhouse than they would be on the outside. When asked for evidence by the Royal Commission that was set up in 1832 to inquire into the operation of the Poor Laws, Drouet asserted that he had witnessed these outrages with his own eyes while doing the rounds with parish officials, knocking on doors to collect rates from indigent householders. 'I have seen a very poor rate-payer dining on potatoes, and that for days together,' he stated, 'and I have gone back to the workhouse and helped to serve the paupers there with meat and with dinners comparatively sumptuous.' He was armed with other equally disturbing anecdotes. A poor agricultural labourer would go off to do a day's work with only a small piece of gritty bread to sustain him. During the day he drank water, and in the evening, if he had milk with his supper, he would have been given it by a neighbouring farmer. 'The man in the house gets more meat,' Drouet insisted, 'more food of every sort.' The 'man in the house' had a hot breakfast and a hot dinner, neither of which he had to prepare himself. He was better clothed and he enjoyed better accommodation and better sleep. He did less work for less time. These advantages inevitably sapped the will: 'When a poor family has once been driven into the workhouse, the proof they give of its being better is that they never can be got out of it.' Drouet had heard new inmates regretting not entering the workhouse sooner. Even those who had previously stayed out of it, who pitied those in it and hoped never to share their misfortune, would change their tune once they were forced across its threshold. Seduced by its 'superior comfort', they would persuade other members of their family to follow them in.[10]

Mott, also contributing to the inquiry, went even further than Drouet by drawing convicts into the argument. He proposed a hierarchy of privilege with the convict at the top, the pauper beneath the convict, and, most shamefully, the poor ratepayer beneath the pauper. An example of the problem was the soldier employed at the prison as a guard: on any given day he received one ounce of meat less than the convicts he guarded. Mott had no reason to doubt the truth of this because he heard it from any number of the people he talked to in Gosport. Nor was that all. The convicts taunted the guards, who had to stand over them, bellies rumbling, as they ate their meals. 'What next, I wonder!' the convicts would say in front of the guards when given some unpleasant task. 'Damn it, we shall soon be as bad off as soldiers.' One soldier, so the story went, asked a convict if he would change places with him. The convict replied that he would only do so for £25, which would make a very large hole in the pocket of a soldier paid the traditional shilling a day.[11]

*   *   *

Mott and Drouet were still clinging to these uncompromising views when in 1830 they switched operations from Hampshire to South London, where they had won the contract for the workhouse in St Mary Lambeth. Only scraps of information about the early Lambeth years have survived, such as that Drouet was now living in Prince's Road, where the workhouse stood, and that in December 1831 he entered a twenty-four-week-old half-China pig – which he had bred himself, feeding it on barley meal and scraps from his kitchen – into the Smithfield Club Cattle Show.[12] Rumour had it that he was also employed at the workhouse as a porter, and that Maria Drouet was the cook, a slur against the character of any entrepreneur who aspired to the status of gentleman. This rumour needs to be discounted as it surfaced only in 1849, when events in Lower Tooting had made Drouet public enemy number one and an easy target for scandalmongers.[13] Far more significant is the fact that he was not only contractor for the Lambeth workhouse but master as well, with his wife as matron, which was exactly the arrangement that had obtained at Alverstoke. He held this post until 1838, by which time, as a result of the passing of the Poor Law Amendment Act in 1834, St Mary had been joined by five other districts to form the Lambeth Union. The workhouse of the new union was regulated by a board of twenty elected guardians, with whom Drouet had constant dealings, more often than not in connection with finances.

In Lambeth, quite as much as in Alverstoke, Drouet was troubled by the spectre of pauperism. He visited the homes of the poor, where, much to his annoyance, he discovered that life was harder than it was in the workhouse. He thought that the chasm separating the poor man from the pauper was even wider than it had been in Alverstoke. When questioned, he would mention the superior diet the Lambeth inmates enjoyed, which included not only a more generous allowance of meat but also extended to beer, butter and sugar, and included a pea feast, a bean feast, two mutton feasts and a plum pudding feast every year. He made a sharp distinction between the 'deserving poor' with useful skills and the 'born and bred paupers'. While the former were generally appreciative of what they were given, the latter were impossible to satisfy.[14]

Drouet's dislike of pauperism can only have deepened as a direct consequence of the problems he faced as master of the workhouse. A source of constant discontent was the lack of a system of classification rigorous enough to identify and isolate undesirable inmates. 'We have the worst of characters in the house,' he complained. The house provided a hiding place for thieves. Indeed, he believed that there were thirty ex-convicts on the register, who attracted unwelcome attention from the police whenever they went out into the streets of Lambeth. In addition, there were at least twenty, and maybe as many as thirty, known prostitutes lurking inside the workhouse. According to Drouet, the problem was that these criminal characters were able to mix freely with other inmates: 'We cannot prevent the thief speaking to the young, or keep the prostitute from the young girl who has not been corrupted.' He spoke from experience. Only recently he had dragged a male inmate before the magistrate for teaching the workhouse boys to 'star the glaze', a slang expression for taking panes of glass out of shop windows noiselessly. Previously, he had been obliged to deal with the case of seven girls so criminalised by an eighth girl, whom he was able to name, that they all ended up in prison. This, however, was no disincentive. 'We live as well there as in the workhouse,' the inmates would say.[15]

Drouet had a number of suggestions for solving these problems, and they are interesting in that they reveal how far he was prepared to go, in principle, to achieve the desired control of the inmates. He would happily have deprived them of many basic rights. Preventing young males and females from communicating with one another, whether face to face or by the more desperate use of signs and signals, was one such measure, achievable by issuing exeats on different days or by dividing the yard with a wall. Since the yard was a shared space, partitioning it in this way would effectively create two independent workhouses, the only catch being that such a costly, and therefore unpopular, project was not one that any parish officer would want his name attached to. Beyond that, the problem of indiscipline could be solved by cracking down harder on offenders, especially if they were young. 'I think that we should have more ready means of sending them to a prison,' Drouet argued, 'where the boys might be whipped and the girls kept for a time in solitary confinement.'[16]

There is very little information about Drouet's actual dealings with inmates until 1834. One exception is the oddly appropriate fact that he was not unaffected by the cholera epidemic that broke out in October 1831: cases in the Lambeth workhouse, some of them fatal, were recorded.[17] More can be discovered about him in the years that followed the passing of the Poor Law Amendment Act, the implementation of which generated a good deal of paperwork. It is known, for example, because he said as much in a letter to the Poor Law Commissioners, that he had real difficulty with an inmate by the name of Maria Hunt, who was incorrigibly demanding and abusive. There was nothing he or anyone else could do with her, and he was at his wits' end.[18] Other information can be found in newspapers, which frequently published accounts of unfortunate incidents in workhouses, often in great detail.

One such incident concerned an inmate by the name of Thomas Ottewell, a shoemaker aged about seventy, who, as a resident of some two or three years standing, had permission to go out whenever he wanted. On one occasion, at some point in the evening, he had been found slumped on a footpath in Kennington and was escorted by a policeman back to the workhouse, where Drouet, assuming that he was drunk, had him taken to the men's ward to sleep it off. The next day, although he was seen by a doctor, who recognised the symptoms of a stroke, Ottewell died. The circumstances of his death were reported in a number of newspapers, along with an account of the inquest, at which the parish officers were accused before the Surrey coroner, William Carter, of wilful negligence in having been slow to provide medical assistance. Although Carter ruled that he would take the matter no further on the grounds that misdiagnosing a stroke as being 'in liquor' was excusable, Drouet was still rebuked. It transpired that it was not he who had called for the inquest, as one might expect, but an acquaintance of the dead man. The coroner made it plain that the master of the workhouse, in deciding that an inquest was not needed, had appointed himself a judge in the matter. Drouet was guilty of gross impropriety.[19]

Drouet must have been humiliated, as the newspapers, by identifying him as the master of the Lambeth workhouse, had placed him before the gaze of the public. In the same way, when a manic depressive hanged himself from the handrail of a staircase, Drouet was named as the master who had 'employed him in the washing-rooms' to punish him for his violent behaviour.[20] Even when he was not directly named, he was found guilty by association, as in the truly shocking case of Henry Bailey, a boy in the workhouse who died after being brutally beaten by a schoolmaster and a nurse. Such cruelty could hardly fail to damage the reputation of the master on whose watch it had been perpetrated.[21]

Drouet would not have welcomed this sort of scrutiny. In the end, though, the people whose opinion of him mattered most were not the readers of newspapers but those who were in a position to help or hinder his career. Principally, he had the support of Mott, who, in the Royal Commission's inquiry, held him up as 'a person of respectability' and 'a remarkably active man, who resides in the house and devotes his whole time and attention to the management'.[22] Mott's enthusiasm is especially telling in the light of the fact that he had a loud enough voice in powerful circles to be appointed an assistant Poor Law Commissioner in 1834, the Commission being a government department that had been established to implement the policies enshrined in the Act. In this capacity, he asked Drouet to inspect and report on a number of workhouses outside the metropolitan area, and as a result of the inspections carried out in Buckinghamshire, it was decided to close the establishment in Chesham, which was judged to be not fit for purpose.

Although the inmates were to be accommodated in the workhouse in Amersham, local feelings ran high because it was feared that shopkeepers would lose income and paupers would be separated from their families. Drouet was drafted in to help with the removals, and when things turned nasty, he slipped away. He was wise to do so as he might not have escaped the rioting unscathed.[23]

* * *

If the Chesham riots illustrated forcefully the problems associated with the Poor Law Amendment Act, so too did the behaviour of the guardians, which, perhaps rather surprisingly, did not always meet the highest standards of sobriety and decorum. In his correspondence Mott expressed a particularly low opinion of the Lambeth guardians with whom he had dealings in 1838. Their weekly meetings were held in the evening, which was apparently too late an hour for 'respectable men of business' to attend, and they were dominated by 'furious pot valiant champions' who 'set all law & decency at defiance'. In case his meaning was still not clear, Mott characterised these evening meetings as little more than slanging matches that invariably ended in 'quarrels and drunken broils'. The consequences were deplorable: the proper evening routine of the workhouse was interrupted and the reputation of the parish was damaged.[24]

On the face of it, Drouet's experience of the Lambeth guardians did not tally with Mott's damning comments. It would seem that by the time his contract had run its course in 1838, he had earned their respect. They organised a farewell dinner at the Plough, a riverside tavern in Blackwall, where, according to a local newspaper, the chairman of the board presented him with 'a handsome piece of plate' inscribed with a message bearing witness to his professionalism in the discharge of his duties and to his attentiveness to the needs of the inmates.[25] But Drouet felt that there was unfinished business, and in a pungent letter to the Poor Law Commission he complained that the Lambeth board of guardians had failed to reimburse him fully for his many services.[26]

Drouet's contract with Lambeth had come to an end because the master of a workhouse, under the stipulations of the 1834 Act, was to be a paid officer appointed by the relevant Poor Law Union, whereas a man who simply held a contract did not fit this definition. He had a *de facto* authority granted contractually by the parish but not sanctioned legally by the Union. He had a power to discipline inmates, which might manifest itself in unreasonable and even illegal methods. And since he controlled the purchase of provisions and services, he was ideally placed to act dishonestly, either by presenting the parish with inflated demands for reimbursement or by favouring tradesmen with whom he had a private understanding. The contractor was still essential to the running of a workhouse, of course, but his role was strictly that of supplier of food and drink, or clothes, or the expertise and manpower to carry out running repairs. His contract with the workhouse was a straightforward business arrangement that had been won by competitive tendering.

For several years, Drouet was able to renew his contract thanks to the intervention of the Lambeth board with the Poor Law Commissioners. The argument the guardians put forward was that abandoning the current system of management was undesirable at a time when an extensive building programme, the purpose of which was to facilitate the separation of inmates, had already been set in motion.[27] But in 1837 Drouet was informed that his contract would run only for another year. Questioned about this at a later date, he insisted that 'a change of guardians' had been the determining factor.[28] Presumably, he was making a political point: he no longer had legitimacy in the eyes of a newly elected board keen to adhere to the terms of the 1834 Act. Ironically, the man who replaced him as master of the workhouse, George Sanglier, was a disaster, and after only a few months he was dismissed for drunkenness. He was also accused, possibly unfairly, of embezzling workhouse funds and sentenced at the Central Criminal Court to seven years' transportation.[29]

However, long before his contract at Lambeth expired, Drouet had been developing other business interests. At the beginning of 1834, through a newspaper advertisement, he offered to receive workhouse children into 'a respectable Establishment' where they would be clothed, maintained, educated, and prepared for apprenticeships or employment as servants.[30] Although he did not name his establishment, he was referring to Grove House in Brixton, which he operated in conjunction with its owner, his sister-in-law Rebecca. Realising that in a climate of reform he must find a new direction, or simply identifying profitable opportunities, Drouet had begun the process of turning fully private.

The origins of the Grove House operation are in some respects obscure. It is at least possible, though, that Drouet's move was facilitated by inside contacts, given that when the Lambeth Union was eventually formed at the end of 1835, Brixton was one of its constituent districts. Then again, Mott had his finger in many pies, and it was even said of him, rather tantalisingly, that he had at one time kept 'an establishment for the reception of Infant Paupers at Brixton'.[31] If that was indeed the case, then the obvious conclusion would be that he had passed the management of Grove House on to Drouet when his appointment to the Commission put an end to his activities as a contractor.

Either way, Drouet would have realised that Grove House, which stood just off Brixton Rise on the Clapham side, was ideally situated. Every half hour a coach from one of several pick-up points in London, heading down through Surrey, stopped only a short walk from the premises at the White Horse public house. The White Horse was itself an attraction, and it is easy to imagine guardians who had travelled down from the workhouses ensconced in one of its rooms and discussing their findings, or families who were visiting the children eating and drinking before undertaking their journey home. What is more, when it came to touting for business, Drouet offered much. A striking example is the approaches he made by letter to the administrators of the workhouse in Newington, who in 1835 were planning to farm out their children. He assured them that 'the comforts' of 'the little inmates' were of paramount importance.[32] These were evidently not just physical, and he had a standing agreement with the parish church, St Matthew's, that it would open its doors to the pauper children from Grove House. Furthermore, he professed himself flexible in his arrangements for schooling and willing to adopt whatever system of education Newington recommended.

Indeed, claiming to be flexible was a key tactic, and Drouet resorted to it again in satisfying the terms of Hanway's Act. These required that pauper children be sent to locations in the country where those aged between two and six would be no less than three miles, and those under two no less than five miles, from the city. Being about four miles from the city, Grove House passed only the first of these tests, but by way of a solution Drouet proposed that he would hire 'a cottage' at the required distance for the under twos, and at no extra cost to Newington. Not only was he master of the relevant law, but he understood how to do business with boards of guardians, whose decisions were dictated more often than not by the state of their balance sheet.[33]

Drouet also understood that reputation mattered, and he offered Newington the Lambeth guardians as witnesses to his character and sound practices. In fact, all the parishes with which he was working would have only good things to say about his treatment of their children, and his supporters included three medical men, who had examined Grove House and its grounds and signed a certificate of satisfaction. One of these gentlemen, Dr David Uwins, was physician to Peckham House, a fine old mansion in verdant surroundings and a private lunatic asylum. Given that the asylum had been co-founded in 1826 by none other than Mott, it is not clear just how disinterested Uwins's report on Grove House can have been. Another medical man in Mott's circle, Peter Armstrong, who was one of three superintendents of Peckham House, stood surety for Drouet when he finally entered into a contract with Newington. It is a curious fact that a rival contractor, Joseph Cox, had been trying to interest the Newington guardians in a former boarding school in about eight acres of land that had come up for sale in Tooting. Almost certainly, Cox was referring to Surrey Hall, and in view of later events it is surely to be regretted that he failed to secure the contract.[34]

Drouet's overtures to the Newington board were remarkably shrewd. In the first place, he offered to fix his rate for up to three years. But this was just the start, and he also undertook to adopt the diet already in place at the workhouse, even forgoing the widespread practice of reducing quantities in line with the lesser nutritional needs of the smaller children. A further undertaking, which at first glance might appear tasteless in the context of a business proposal but was actually dictated by nineteenth-century realities, was to bury children who died in his establishment at no extra cost. Then, being wise to a possible ruse whereby a penny-pinching workhouse sent him sickly children on the verge of death, he added the proviso that children only qualified for a free burial after being with him for four weeks.[35]

The list of promises was seemingly inexhaustible. He would create more space for schoolrooms and dormitories in order to effect separation of the children by sex and by parish. He would employ teachers. He would arrange regular visits by a doctor, who would be pleased to discover that not a single bed had more than two occupants. He would not take adult paupers while there were Newington children on the premises, and he would allow the children to be removed by the parish, if the parish so wished, at a month's notice. He would relieve new arrivals of their drab workhouse costume, dressing boys in corduroy or fustian, girls in gingham frocks, and both in 'brown stuff' on Sundays. As a final touch, he would ensure that any child, on being discharged, was sent home with a new set of clothes. For their part, the guardians had no grounds for complaint, and they noted with satisfaction that Drouet would be saving the Newington ratepayers in the region of £300 a year.[36]

*   *   *

It must have been around 1836 that Drouet came into possession of Surrey Hall, but he was still the proprietor of Grove House, and it would appear to be the case that he divided his time between the two establishments. Although there is no evidence at this date that Maria Drouet was involved in these arrangements, it is clear that Rebecca Drouet was, and that she took on the role of matron at Grove House, where she was assisted by two of her three daughters. It might be expected that William Leonard Drouet worked alongside his wife in Brixton, but there is every indication that he was still busy as a publican. After running the Crown Inn in Gosport, he moved to the George Commercial Inn in Andover, and from there to the Angel Inn in Marlborough.[37] In 1837 he sold the lease on the Angel, and it is safe to say that at this point he must at least have been planning to rejoin Rebecca, because from 1840 on it is he and not Bartholomew who was routinely named as proprietor of the Brixton establishment.

There is no getting away from the fact that Grove House was scandalously mismanaged. In 1845 guardians from the Kensington workhouse went down to Brixton without prior arrangement in response to concerns raised by parents. When they entered the premises, the children ran up to them, begging to be taken away. The little creatures were half-starved, and it was obvious why, as the soup on which they were being fed consisted of little more than the liquor from boiled meat, thickened with oatmeal and peas. The guardians were further horrified to discover that the children were not allowed to sit to eat. Instead, they had to stand in an outbuilding that was all but open to the elements, their ill-shod feet chafed by the rough brick floor.[38] When the guardians' report was leaked to the press, William Leonard

Drouet took immediate steps to silence his detractors, publishing a robust defence of his managerial philosophy, which he insisted had been wilfully misrepresented, and quoting verbatim the comments of other guardians who had given Grove House the stamp of approval. He added that the doors of the establishment were always open to the press and the public alike, as if to prove that he had nothing to hide.[39]

To see that Drouet was attempting a cover-up, and that in reality there was a good deal to hide, it is only necessary to consider the fate of two boys who were the subject of an earlier scandal in 1837, when Grove House was still being run by Bartholomew, his brother. They were being punished for bad behaviour, each having a wooden log attached to one of his legs at the end of a chain measuring between four and five feet, secured with a padlock. The log weighed around ten pounds, and for several days each boy would have to drag it behind him wherever he went, hoisting it on to his shoulder if he needed to climb stairs, and sleeping at night with it lying on the floor beside his bed. The peculiar horror of this macabre technique was that it combined humiliation with physical discomfort and the danger of injury. If it is asked who could do such a thing to children, then the answer is that the old schoolmaster, Henry Lawson, who in his younger days had served in the army as an artillery captain, certainly seemed happy to do so. But he was not the only villain of the piece as he took his orders from Rebecca Drouet.[40]

The cruelties practised at Grove House came to light when a young schoolmistress, Jemima Jennings, resigned her post in protest. Jemima was nineteen years old and had been sent to the Drouets only three weeks previously from the Home and Colonial Infant School Society, a teacher training establishment in Gray's Inn Road.[41] She was set on making a formal complaint, and so, having handed in her notice, she went back to the Society's offices, where she was interviewed by Dr James Kay, an assistant Poor Law Commissioner. Kay also questioned Rebecca Drouet and Henry Lawson, along with another schoolmistress, Elizabeth Rogers, a resident needlewoman, Harriet Thomas, and the two boys who had been punished with the log, George Roberts and William Ryan. To her consternation, Jemima found herself facing determined opposition, not only from Mrs Drouet, who not unnaturally countered her allegations, but also from the other three adults, who sought to undermine her as a gesture of loyalty to their employers. When she voiced criticisms of the food, for example, they simply praised it. In their eyes she was an outsider, a newcomer to Grove House who had made up her mind to attack the way it was managed, believing she had nothing to lose.[42]

In the course of these interviews, other disgraceful practices emerged. Many of these were methods of punishment, although none was as grotesque as the log. Lawson freely admitted to Kay that he beat children with a ferule or a cane, adding, rather gratuitously, that the cane he used was the sort 'you buy a penny a yard'. He would respond to the severest provocation with two or three swipes on the shoulder. On the other hand, Elizabeth Rogers claimed that she did not often have recourse to punishment, her rationale being that it hardened the children, but she still swore by the cane, which only had to be applied lightly to have the desired deterrent effect. She justified this on the grounds that the children generally, and the boys in particular, were difficult. Harriet Thomas said the same about the boys, even though, as a needlewoman, she had nothing to do with them. But the worst of the adults was Mrs Drouet. According to Jemima, she was very unkind to the children. 'She used to beat them for every little offence with her hand,' she told Kay. When beating children, she would unleash a torrent of foul language, and when not beating children, she might still punish them by stopping their evening meals. These accusations were either explained away or flatly denied by Mrs Drouet and her defenders.[43]

The children must have found Grove House constantly teetering on the brink of chaos. They may have created the unruliness of the classroom but they also suffered from it, and Lawson appears to have spent as much time maintaining order as delivering the curriculum. He did not even attempt to teach some boys with educational difficulties or refractory natures: they were employed instead in picking bristles or plaiting straw. He had no one to assist him in the classroom other than a child acting as a monitor. Only recently, though, a boy accused of talking had attacked first the monitor and then Lawson himself. No wonder the schoolmaster was conscious that he was struggling. 'I have never half an hour to myself,' he complained to Kay. There was no respite even after the school day ended: he slept in the same room as the boys and had to keep them quiet all night.[44]

The boy who attacked Henry Lawson was William Ryan. The schoolmaster caned him and banished him to a corner of the room, and Mrs Drouet ordered him to be punished with the log. It was in this sorry state that the Assistant Commissioner discovered him, along with George Roberts, whose offence was not recorded. They were unhappy boys. George's mother was dead, and his father had recently been ill in St Bartholomew's Hospital. William had been an orphan for about four years. He had been at Grove House for eleven months, having previously spent time in the union workhouse in Stepney. But the life stories of George and William would not have been especially unusual in that company of broken children. Indeed, a number of them, damaged before they came to Grove House, found that they could not submit to the Drouet regime, and ran away. Lawson was under orders to punish these runaways with the log when they came back, which, he seemed to imply, they always did.[45]

When confronted by the commissioners with the many charges made against his establishment, Drouet defended his management strategy and wriggled off the hook with a letter in which he sought to discredit Jemima Jennings. She was an unreliable witness, a 'giddy girl' who had been unable to cope with the demands made of her, and a fabricator of plausible untruths. He, on the other hand, was a good man, a kind and humane man. In the course of defending himself, however, Drouet also revealed a profound dislike of London pauper children, most of whom were 'shockingly depraved and abandoned characters'.[46] In one sweepingly dismissive phrase, he had lifted a corner of the curtain. Beneath the carapace of compassion, he was that nightmare figure, the man invested with power over the poor but possessed of a callous nature. Well might he trumpet his kindness and humanity in a letter of 1837 sent from Grove House, when the horrors of 1849 had yet to unfold in Lower Tooting.

Chapter Three

Surrey Hall

The great Victorian explorer Henry Morton Stanley, who was born John Rowlands, may be a household name, and his search for David Livingstone may be the stuff of legend, but he had a wretched childhood in Denbigh in Wales. His father died when he was a few weeks old, and his mother, who was only eighteen at the time of his birth, abandoned him. For several years he was left in the care of relatives and foster parents, until, shortly after his sixth birthday, he was taken to the St Asaph Union workhouse. In later life he was still able to call to mind what he went through there, and he set down his recollections as a chapter in his autobiography, in which episodes of reckless defiance, many of them exaggerated in the retelling, are woven into an entirely believable tapestry of indignities and humiliations. The building itself seemed to him to be immense. The iron gates, through which he had to pass in something like an act of submission, were forbiddingly tall, while the first official he encountered, who set the tone for what was to follow, had a memorably sombre expression on his face. Even the first noises John heard at the gate, such as the clanging of a distant bell and the echoing thud of the door as it closed behind him, filled him with feelings of loneliness and desolation.[1]

No doubt these feelings were shared by Elizabeth Frost when she was brought down to Surrey Hall in a workhouse van. She was much the same age as John and came from a world that was similar to his. As the van turned off the main road, she would have peered anxiously at the strange and unfamiliar scene opening up in front of her. When she and her companions from the Islington workhouse were being led up to the house by the gatekeeper, they would have been aware of the faces of children at the windows high above, staring down at them inquisitively. They would also have heard raucous shouts floating towards them from somewhere behind the house, and these they would have taken to be the sounds of children playing outside, but playing in a wild and uncontrolled way.

By the time Elizabeth arrived in the summer of 1848, Surrey Hall had been under Drouet's management for about twelve years. He had taken the lease on the house from William Isaac Bicknell, who had run it as a boys' boarding school before moving up to an address in Waterloo.[2] Drouet would have found it appealing for a number of reasons. First and foremost, by locating his 'asylum' in Lower Tooting, at some distance from the centre of London, he was abiding by both the three-mile and the five-mile stipulations of Hanway's Act. But Lower Tooting was still within reach of the metropolitan workhouses. Children being brought down in vans, and parish officials travelling down by coach or carriage, would complete the journey in a reasonable time. Then again, the house had been used by Bicknell for purposes broadly similar to those Drouet had in mind. The proportions were such as to accommodate a population of children. There were school beds in the house already, and school desks, and benches to go with the desks.

The Surrey Hall estate befitted a man of substance. The buildings and grounds covered roughly seven acres, but the total acreage was in fact fifty-two as Drouet also owned meadows and pastures.[3] Water was supplied from two artesian wells and was sufficient for the washhouses and baths as well as for the table. Outside there was a carriage drive, while inside there was mahogany furniture, Brussels carpets, and a Longman pianoforte. In such a house it was possible to be respectable. Sideboards and card tables added tone to the dining and drawing rooms, dressing glasses and cheval glasses were a similar enhancement to the bedrooms, and goose feather mattresses made the master and mistress's four-poster bed a thing of splendour. On a more practical note, the building boasted a certain amount of gas lighting, and the family had access to a rudimentary water closet.[4]

Elsewhere, in those parts of the asylum where Elizabeth passed her days and nights, the arrangements were rather less refined. There were no water closets for the children, only outside privies consisting of loose boards thrown over filthy cesspools. The boys' urinal was nothing more than a rank little yard without water and without a roof: those who went into it would relieve themselves wherever there was space. The schoolrooms behind the house were shoddy constructions that had been thrown together hastily as the number of inmates grew.[5] They were also excessively crowded, a fact that did not escape Richard Dugard Grainger when he visited Surrey Hall early in 1849. Grainger, a General Board of Health inspector in his late forties, discovered that anything between 500 and 600 children, together with teachers and furniture, would be squeezed into a room with an area of 250 square yards. The air was always stale because the builders had put windows in only one wall.[6]

The curriculum included the three Rs, but the emphasis was on moral instruction in the form of regular readings of passages from the Bible and the singing of hymns. Whatever impression this education made on Elizabeth, it was of less moment than the so-called industrial training, the preparation for employment in the outside world, which entailed hours and hours of needlework under the supervision of the schoolmistress, Sarah Shambler, or her colleague, Sarah Goat. From Monday to Friday the girls would toil for half the morning and all afternoon. On Saturdays they spent the morning mending their own clothes, and they might be visited by the chaplain, to whom they recited the catechism and mathematical tables. A good many were also employed making shirts, and although they were paid according to their level of skill, none earned more than 4d. a week. Drouet sold the shirts wholesale to shops in London and pocketed the proceeds. His cynicism did not go unnoticed, but the views of his critics were water off a duck's back, and they did not deter him from forcing the children to carry out domestic tasks, such as laundering or scrubbing floors. If payment was made, more often than not it took the form of extra food. The children derived no lasting benefit from their involuntary labours other than what Drouet would consider training for a life in service.[7]

Drouet was able to use food as barter for the simple reason that it was generally in very short supply. This was not exactly a secret shared only by the children. It was common knowledge among the parents too, and Catherine Williams, a mother in the Holborn workhouse who wrote long and angry letters to the guardians, no doubt represented the fears of many. She would rather be chargeable to a parish that had no association with Drouet, such as St Luke's Old Street, where 'I shall have a Board of Christians that will see my children justified' – treated justly – 'not send them to Tooting to be starved to death.'[8] Probably the guardians who read Catherine's letters were inclined to dismiss her complaints as exaggerated. They might even have noted that, according to Drouet's printed dietary, three meals were provided every day consisting of bread and milk, legs and shins of beef, suet pudding, potatoes, cabbage and peas, and treacle and cheese, in one or other combination and in quantities befitting a child's age.[9] But the unofficial view was that no such generous diet ever materialised. When an old fellow in one of the workhouses saw that boys who had been sent to Surrey Hall had come back looking like so many bags of bones, he could not contain his distress. 'It brought tears to the eyes of all who looked on them,' he was heard to say. In his opinion, other boys who had stayed in the workhouse were in far better shape.[10]

Hunger would therefore have been a permanent feature of Elizabeth's existence, but as the weeks went by, and autumn gave way to winter, she would also have been tormented by the cold. The schoolroom where she sat for much of the day had only a single small stove and was therefore inadequately heated. Matters were made worse by the deteriorating floorboards. In some dormitories these were so rotten with age that they had turned into a sort of honeycomb. When they were scrubbed, they absorbed the water, which was then released into the atmosphere. As a result these rooms were clammy and damp, but it took an unusually objective inspector, with the clear-sightedness of a George Bermingham, to judge these conditions unacceptable. Bermingham, a medical officer from the St Pancras workhouse, visited the asylum on a cold day and found himself chilled to the bone, even though he was dressed for the weather. He would have wondered how much worse it must have been for scantily clad and undernourished children.

If, as seems likely, Bermingham was despondent at his discovery, he would have found no comfort in the yard behind the house. Quite the opposite. A brutal northeasterly wind had been blowing for days, yet the children, who had been sent out from the schoolrooms to play, had their heads and shoulders uncovered. He would report that Drouet allowed them to go out 'in the coldest day in winter in the same dress they would wear in the hottest day in summer'. Meanwhile, he called about twenty of the children over to him, some of whom were girls: 'Their little flannel petticoats were so gauzy and thin that you could literally read through them from age.'[11]

*   *   *

Elizabeth's experience of Surrey Hall, defined by her fear of new surroundings and unfamiliar faces, and by the absence of everything she had previously known, would have been common to all children placed in pauper establishments. One such child, William Hew Ross, who in later life rose to a respectable position as a schoolmaster, remembered and wrote about the first days he spent in the workhouse in Greenwich. He entered in about 1850, at the age of eight, around the same time and the same age as when Elizabeth went to Surrey Hall. His father had sailed off to the West Indies, never to be seen again, and his sickly mother and a little brother had died. For a while he and his younger sister were cared for by their grandmother, but she was starving herself in order to keep them fed, and in the end she just could not cope.

On his own in the dormitory for the first time, William quietly cried with his head under the bedclothes while the other boys larked about. The feeling of shame stayed with him throughout his adult life. 'Night after night I did the same,' he wrote, 'and used to long for the night to come so that I might cry without being noticed.' He wondered what had become of his sister, who had been taken to a separate part of the workhouse. He saw her for the first time about a month later, when their grandmother hobbled the three miles from Woolwich to Greenwich with the aid of a walking stick to visit them. They all sat together in the porter's lodge, and from that point on, if William ever spoke to his sister, it was on visiting day. 'We used to talk a great deal about old times,' he recalled, 'and both of us used to wish we were away.'[12]

Elizabeth's nights in the crowded dormitory in Surrey Hall would not have been any happier. She slept with girls from other workhouses, and although at best this would have had no effect on her, at worst it would have intensified her sense of abandonment, the more so if she had been the only Islington inmate, or one of very few. A nurse, Eliza Raymond, was attached to the dormitory, which was referred to as Raymond's Ward.[13] She was a Holborn woman, aged about forty-three, and probably an inmate of the workhouse who had been sent down to Lower Tooting with the children she was nominally in charge of. In line with what is known about the employment of pauper inmates, it is likely that she would have been given remuneration in the form of board and lodging and pocket money. She had a daughter, Louisa, in the asylum, who was eleven or twelve years old. Louisa suffered from a deformity in one leg which required her to wear an orthopaedic shoe attached to an iron brace. In an age unsympathetic to disability, she would have been as likely to meet with mockery from adults and children as with understanding and compassion. Some time ago she had been operated on by John Rowland Gibson, a surgeon who served as medical officer at the Holborn Union workhouse, but she was still lame. Her shoe was worn out, and the iron brace was broken, but for a child who was dependent on the parish there was no guarantee that the cost of replacements would be met. It was for the workhouse guardians to decide.[14]

It would be a fine thing if the mother of the unfortunate Louisa, schooled in her own daughter's unhappy experiences, treated Elizabeth Frost and the other children in her dormitory with conspicuous kindness. Sadly, though, there is no evidence that she did, and good reason to think that she did not, as the reputation of nurses in mid-century pauper establishments was far from flattering. The common assumption was that workhouse nurses were unreliable because they drank, and no doubt they often did since in most cases they were themselves inmates of the workhouse who were given extra rations of food and also of beer, or even gin, as payment for services that might be dangerous or repulsive, such as helping in a fever ward, or laying out a dead body.[15] The unpleasant nature of their occupation must have been incentive enough to take advantage of the beer and gin. Additionally, there was nothing in the way of a social convention, let alone a law, that made it unacceptable for a person to drink while at work.

In fact, medical professionalism was not expected or required of nurses until later in the century, when the efforts of reformers, most famously Florence Nightingale, swept aside the assumptions that had formerly held sway. One of these was that nurses required little or no training, and the guidelines for the administration of workhouses, published in 1847 by the Poor Law Commissioners as the *General Consolidated Order*, stipulated only that 'no person shall hold the office of Nurse who is not able to read written directions on medicines'. In practice, though, illiterate nurses would have been able to identify the most common medicines by their appearance, and administer them in standard dosages, typically one or two tablespoonfuls to be taken three times a day. If workhouse nurses had any real responsibility, when not carrying out the orders of medical officers, it went no further than looking out for 'any defects which may be observed in the arrangements of the sick or lying-in ward', and ensuring that there was a light at all times during the night. To all intents and purposes, they were menials lumbered with the tasks of any domestic servant, namely cleaning, laundering, and cooking meals.[16]

Another assumption was that nurses in workhouses, given half a chance, might steal food and medicines. The nurses at Surrey Hall had just such a reputation, at least among the children, who benefited from a black market in 'sweet stuff' to supplement the meagre diet allowed by the thrifty Mr and Mrs Drouet. A Holborn boy, Henry Hartshorn, admitted to the guardians that because he was always hungry, he bought sweets and fruit from the nurses in exchange for the money he earned in the shoemaker's workshop, where he fashioned 'five pair of uppers for a penny'. He was fourteen, old enough to have learnt some tricks to make his life more comfortable, even if it meant being exploited by adults. He also told the guardians that he sometimes bought cakes to make up for the lack of bread, though he found that the sweets were better than the cakes, a difference in quality that must have weighed with a half-starved teenage boy. Another fourteen-year-old, Fanny Bailey from the Kensington workhouse, also did well by the nurses, but only if she had been sent to the sick ward, where she found that they bent the rules on food.[17]

Some of Drouet's nurses were more than capable of dealing cruelly with the children. There were reports of ritual humiliations, as when boys who wet their beds were made to sleep in foursomes on a cold oilcloth thrown over straw, and of casual abuses of the sort suffered by five-year-old John Wilkins, who was struck on the nose with sufficient force to make it bleed and to give him nightmares.[18] At the other end of the scale was the cruel treatment of Mary Cassidy, a sad little four-year old who suffered from a bowel complaint, as well as catarrhal ophthalmia and ringworm. Her mother, Jane Cassidy, believed that she had been dropped into a bath of cold water in freezing winter weather as punishment for dirtying herself. It would appear that a nurse by the name of Sarah Dolly had ordered one of the older boys, Henry Brocking, to carry out the punishment. When Henry refused, she took it upon herself to dunk the little girl in the icy water, smelling of excrement.[19]

Jane Cassidy was an inmate of the Chelsea workhouse and she complained to the guardians, as did another mother, Mary Ann McKee, whose daughter had been subjected to the same cold-water treatment. Jane McKee's case was especially distressing because she was sickly as well as incontinent, and ten days before her mother attended the meeting of the board to air her grievances, she died. The guardians seemed completely indifferent to these tragic circumstances and let the matter drop. They had been swayed by Nurse Dolly's denials of the charges made against her, and by her insistence that Mary Ann McKee had spoken to her abusively. They also listened to two statements, one made by Henry Brocking and the other by Eliza Jones, another nurse accused of punishing Jane McKee. Nurse Jones claimed that she had not beaten the girl but had made her stand with her face to the wall. Her defence was accepted, but in a way it hardly mattered what the guardians believed. It was easy to deflect the complaints of poor parents who were illiterate and inarticulate, beholden to the parish, and browbeaten by officialdom.[20]

Whether Nurse Raymond was callously vindictive, like Sarah Dolly and Eliza Jones, or sensitive to the suffering of children, is a question that will never be answered. Two versions of the truth can be constructed with equal plausibility: one is that she treated Elizabeth Frost and the other children in her dormitory shamefully; while in the other she responded to their predicament with tenderness and compassion, as she did to her own child Louisa in her hour of need.

It is, however, beyond dispute that her dormitory, and indeed all the dormitories, would have been barely habitable. Of the many witnesses to this appalling state of affairs, the most outspoken was the government inspector, Richard Dugard Grainger. Having visited Surrey Hall in person, he was in a position to assert that the cramming together of the beds, which were separated one from another by six inches at most and occupied by more than one child, posed serious health risks. The girls were worse off than the boys. The windows in their dormitories were few in number and small in size and the fireplaces were boarded up. In these conditions it would be difficult for the stale atmosphere, which in nineteenth-century medical theory was a major vector of disease, to be sanitised by a flow of fresh air.[21]

Added to these physical hardships, and to the generally unpleasant animal smells that would inevitably have developed in such conditions, the arrangements for urinating and defecating were entirely primitive and consisted of tubs sitting in the middle of the dormitories at all times of day and night. These were unlined and hopelessly unhygienic. One eight-year-old boy by the name of Joseph Andrews articulated, very graphically, how he and others were under orders to carry the tubs downstairs every morning.

Once they had hauled them down into the yard, they emptied their revolting contents into a cesspool. Then, having rinsed the empty tubs, they filled them with the water they would use upstairs to wash the floors. While all this was going on, the nurse in charge of the dormitory, who slept in another room, would have had the good sense to keep well out of the way.[22] If any of the girls ever had the opportunity to describe equivalent 'facilities' in their dormitories, their words have not been preserved. But it is nowhere suggested that the girls were accorded special treatment in this respect, and so the inescapable conclusion is that they, like their male counterparts, were given no other means of relieving themselves in the middle of the night than the crude expedient of tubs.

*   *   *

The question that is inevitably raised here is just how Drouet got away with it. At least part of the answer is that he controlled with considerable skill what he made public and what he kept hidden. An example is a meeting he agreed to in 1841 with the guardians of the Manchester Union. They were investigating best practices in London pauper establishments, and they had applied to Drouet, on Mott's recommendation, to have access to Surrey Hall.[23] A visit of this kind would now be called a school open day, and, as is always the case on such occasions, the establishment in question was shown to the visitors in a relentlessly positive light.

The Manchester guardians were invited to observe a method of teaching that had been brought down from Scotland by the schoolmaster, a man by the name of Andrew Liddle. His approach to education was firmly based on the idea that effective learning required discipline, and this, together with the emphasis he placed on knowledge of the Bible, impressed the visitors, although they were not to know that a year later he would be forced to resign following allegations that he had punished a boy brutally.[24] They were invited to listen to the singing of a hymn and a 'moral song' by 120 of the children, many of whom, they thought, could not have been more than five years old. They were invited to watch boys gardening, tailoring, shoemaking, basket making and tinplate working, and girls washing, laundering, cooking, and making and repairing clothes. They noted that all the supervisors were adults, and paid, and therefore unlikely to lead their pupils into the ways of pauperism. They were shown testimonials from employers of Surrey Hall graduates who were satisfied with the results of the training they had received. They were told that most of the children came into the asylum destitute and orphaned, that many were infected with the values of beggar parents, and that all left cured of their dishonest and criminal habits.[25]

It was a stage-managed performance, and Drouet would repeat it later in the year when a member of the royal family, the Duke of Cambridge, came down to Surrey Hall to inspect children who had been sent there by the Richmond Union. The *Morning Post* noted that Drouet was told by his visitor that he was 'much pleased with the general healthy and cleanly appearance of the children'. It would be all too easy to dismiss this as a publicity stunt, but the fact is that the Duke had a benevolent interest in charitable causes. He was president of at least six hospitals, and for several years he had given his patronage to the London Society for the Protection of Young Females, the aim of which was to deal with the problem of juvenile prostitution. Furthermore, he had close ties with the Richmond Union since Kew Palace, where he was residing at the time, was in one of its five constituent parishes. In the same week in which he went to Surrey Hall, he attended a meeting of the guardians, as he frequently did, in order to observe how the board carried out its business and how it sought to ensure the comfort of the poor. So it may fairly be supposed that the Duke's concern for the welfare of the Richmond children was sincere, and that it was for this reason that he extended his visit to nearly three hours. But he would not have seen the beatings in the schoolrooms, nor the crowded dormitories, nor the rancid cesspools in the yard.[26]

All problems arising from the management of the asylum were exacerbated by the ceaseless expansion of its population. At the time of the Manchester visit, there were some 600 children in residence: by 1846 the number had risen to nearly 800.[27] Drouet had no intention of stopping at 800, though, and it was in that year that he acquired the lease on the White House as an adjunct to Surrey Hall. Formerly the White House had been a private lunatic asylum belonging to a William Moyses, and it had fallen into such disrepair that when the Strand Union sent inspectors in 1849, with a view to buying the premises, they were covered with swarms of fleas. Their experience 'spoke strongly of the misery & wretchedness' Drouet's children had been compelled to endure.[28]

However dire the accommodation had been in the months and years before, a large intake of girls from the workhouse in St Pancras in November and December 1848 pushed the asylum to its breaking point.[29] Drouet could not have been unaware that he was courting danger because he had already been advised not to take in too many children both by his resident surgeon, William James Kite, and by his former medical attendant, Walter Chapman. Furthermore, at the beginning of November, he had been given a written order by two Poor Law Board inspectors, Edward Carleton Tufnell and Richard Hall, to hire more teachers with the help of a government grant and to limit numbers to 400 in the 'large' schoolroom, where all the boys were taught together, 160 and 120 in the senior and junior girls' schoolrooms, and 250 in the infant school.[30] He also received complaints from the more conscientious of the visiting guardians, one of whom, a medical officer from the Kensington Union, hauled him over the coals for the unacceptable crowding in the rooms.[31] He chose not to act. Overwhelmingly, it was agreed by independent observers that he made disastrous decisions as a consequence of incompetence, or a desire to maximise profits, or both.

Elizabeth Frost, quartered in the squalor of Raymond's Ward, fell ill in the early hours of 30 December. It had been a bitter night, foggy and damp, and the morning air was cold in the extreme. The alarm was raised by the nurse when the girl sat bolt upright in her bed and began to vomit. The violence of the retching must have woken her companions, and they would have watched helplessly, and in terror, as she repeatedly ejected the contents of her stomach over the bedding and the floor.

It is not hard to imagine how the commotion spread. Eliza Raymond would have hurried along passages and corridors in search of help. She would have roused the Drouet household and called for William James Kite. Any suspicion that Kite might have had that this was an emergency would have been confirmed the moment he reached the dormitory, where Elizabeth's condition soon took a turn for the worse. The vomiting was now accompanied by diarrhoea of an abnormal intensity, a watery, stinking flow over which the little girl had not the slightest control. No nine-year-old could go through what she went through and not feel ashamed and afraid. Her body went into a kind of free fall as wave after wave of agonising spasms took hold of her stomach and bowels.

Elizabeth was removed to a sick ward. There she was attended by Kite, and also by Walter Chapman, who, as medical officer of Lower Tooting, had good reason to be concerned. Although he was aware that a number of children in the asylum had recently come down with dysentery, the symptoms Elizabeth had displayed were in his view those of cholera. He fully recognised that the crowded schoolrooms and dormitories of the asylum provided just the environment in which the disease would take root and then spread rapidly. He also had Kite's word for it that, by his refusal to cap numbers, Drouet had overseen a dangerous explosion in the size of the population. Too many children were occupying too few beds, breathing too little fresh air, and having the use of too few sanitary arrangements.[32]

*   *   *

The century's second cholera epidemic had broken out three months previously in late September, and fear of the disease was felt as strongly in Lower Tooting as anywhere else. Philip William Flower, a local businessman, had already raised concerns with the Wandsworth and Clapham Union in March 1848 over the 'unwholesome and dangerous state of a sewer and cesspools in and near Christ Church Grove', a cluster of buildings comprising not only labourers' dwellings but also a national school and two alehouses.[33] Flower's was not a lone voice, though, and in October, in line with the recommendations of the newly formed General Board of Health, a local committee was set up to deal with the hazards defined by the Nuisances Removal and Diseases Prevention Acts, which included damp, filth, rotting organic matter, and other sources of unclean air. Effective prevention necessarily started with 'the perfect cleansing' of premises and 'the removal of dung heaps and solid and liquid filth of every description'.[34]

The Committee of Health, which numbered nineteen in all, was made up of men with businesses, like Flower, but also men with trades. From the list of names recorded in the minutes of a meeting of the Wandsworth and Clapham guardians, it is possible to identify, among others, a wealthy farmer, the owners of two boarding schools, a baker and a metal worker, as well as the rector of the parish church and the district medical officer, Walter Chapman.[35] These local health officers, who all gave their services free of charge, were authorised to enter and inspect houses and other premises, and they would have done so in response to warnings of risks to public health of the sort communicated to them in November by William Bainbridge, a surgeon of Upper Tooting. Bainbridge realised that among the many instances of low-level illness there were also some more serious cases. He knew of a farm labourer's child with scarlet fever, which was a killer in the nineteenth century, a woman suffering from a bowel complaint, and another woman just getting over a severe attack of gastroenteritis. The last of these had for several days been vomiting large quantities of faecal matter. 'She inhabits one low dirty room,' Bainbridge wrote, 'the window half-covered with an out-building, and close to a filthy cesspool, and a great deal of filth.'[36]

Bainbridge wanted areas like Christ Church Grove to be properly cleansed. Drains needed to be fitted with water barriers to seal in noxious gases. Walls, ceilings and floors needed to be disinfected with limewash. But the problems of public health were inseparable from those of poverty, and Bainbridge also highlighted the case of cottages that were being flooded by two overflowing privies standing on nearby higher ground, a problem the landlord was ignoring in the hope of driving out one of his tenants.[37]

Quite possibly Chapman and Kite were not that surprised to find cholera in the asylum, even if they were alarmed. All the nuisances the committee was targeting in Upper and Lower Tooting were also to be found in and around Surrey Hall. The asylum was potentially as dangerous to human health as any labourer's cottage in Christ Church Grove, although given the number of children occupying its schoolrooms and dormitories, a better comparison might be with the dilapidated lodging houses crammed with impoverished tenants in the capital's slums. As subscribers to the miasma theory of disease, the two doctors would have been concerned about the lack of adequate ventilation in rooms. A further worry was that a child who was already afflicted with cholera would, by the action of human effluvia, poison the air. Indeed, it was suggested that Elizabeth had been infected as a result of living and sleeping in the same rooms as girls from different metropolitan workhouses. Possible culprits were girls from the Wandsworth and Clapham workhouse, where cases of cholera had occurred in recent weeks.[38]

Kite attempted to treat cholera in a number of ways. He relied initially on the classic combination of opium and calomel. Opium was recommended as a means of controlling the evacuations as it fortified the intestines against irritants. Calomel had a powerful purgative effect that cleared the stomach and bowels of infected matter. He also administered chloroform by inhalation to dull the pain in a body subjected to cramps, and he routinely resorted to a range of stimulants that included domestic standbys such as wine and brandy but extended to ether, ammonia, carbonic acid and camphor. At all times it was vital to stem the flow of warmth from the limbs, and to this end Kite made use of mustard plasters and brisk rubs with turpentine or ointment of cayenne pepper.[39]

But none of these worked for Elizabeth, and as the shadows of evening gathered, the ailing child began to slip away. Eighteen hours had passed since she had first fallen ill, and now her pulse was fading, her circulation was slowing, and her eyes were sinking into deep, dark-rimmed sockets. She cried out plaintively for water. Then, after drinking the water, she was calm, and she fell asleep and died.[40]

She was buried on 5 January in the parish churchyard of St Mary the Virgin in Upper Street in Islington. That day there was snow in London and it fell on the sad little ceremony, and lay cold and white on the ground. The burial was conducted by the Reverend James Rose Sutherland. He was approaching forty, and one of his two daughters, Sophia, was aged eight, not much younger than Elizabeth. Elizabeth's send-off would most likely have been a hurried and unremarkable affair. There would have been few mourners, if any. It is possible, of course, that her mother was in the workhouse at the time and had been told, but her whereabouts on that Friday are a mystery, and it is just as likely that she had not the faintest idea that her nine-year-old daughter was dead.

In all, ten parishioners were buried that day. Nine were children, and of these, two were infants and one was a two-year-old, and all three lived in the streets around St Mary's. But the other six were inmates of the workhouse and their coffins would have been deposited in the same grave. There are no headstones for these unfortunates, but their names and ages have been entered in the burial register, and it can be inferred that nine-year-old Emma Freeman, seven-year-old Maragaret Dyson, six-year-old Sarah Parker, and four-year-old Mary Ann Nicholls had been at Drouet's with Elizabeth. Three died of cholera after Elizabeth: first Margaret, then Sarah and then Emma. Margaret and Sarah were both gone in twelve hours, but Emma battled for three days.[41]

Elizabeth had a sister, Eliza. She was two years younger and was also sent to Drouet's asylum. And so it is natural to wonder if the two girls slept in the same dormitory, if the younger saw and heard the older struggling with cholera, and if anyone, when the time came, thought to tell Eliza that her sister had died. It is impossible to know. Curiously, it was Eliza's name and not Elizabeth's that was entered in the burial register. Possibly the muddle began with Drouet, and if not with Drouet then with Kite or Chapman. But the source of the error is not really the point. The real point, and the real sadness, is that somebody's carelessness or indifference denied Elizabeth what might have been a memorial of sorts. To have her proper name entered in a burial register would at least have been an acknowledgement that she had once been alive.

Eliza's early years were hardly different from those of her sister. She too was a dependant of Islington and was shunted from one establishment to another. She too was removed from the workhouse in Liverpool Road to Mrs Hartley's poor house at Ford's Green, and from the poor house back to the workhouse. She too spent brief spells at home with her mother and her brothers, Henry, John and Thomas, her older sister, Elizabeth, and younger sister, Emma. But when Elizabeth died, she was sent off yet again, this time to Park House in Church Street in Hackney. She was still there in 1851 when the census recorded the names of nearly a hundred children, their ages ranging from two to fourteen, and a dozen adults, who included two general nurses, a convalescent nurse, a schoolmaster, and a schoolmaster's assistant who was designated a pauper and was fifty years old.[42]

The proprietor of Park House was Janet Liddle, who was thirty-one years old. Previously she had been employed by Drouet as a school governess at Surrey Hall.[43] In August 1848 she was observed at work in the infant school by a visiting committee from the Strand workhouse, and was praised for her 'kind and conciliating manner' in her dealings with the children.[44] She had been an apprentice of sorts, learning from the master how to run a pauper asylum of her own. She was probably the sister of Andrew Liddle, who resigned in 1842. The allegations that clouded his career centred on a boy from the Strand workhouse, George Wink, who was about twelve years of age. Towards the end of April, a man by the name of James Edwards, who claimed to be George's brother, sent a letter to the guardians in reference to an incident involving the schoolmaster. In his letter he included a statement he had received from George:

> On this day when I was in the workshop, I happened to be off my seat and the master he up with his strap which had got a buckle at the end and he laid it into me as hard as he could and he as [*sic*] made large bumps on my head and then he kicked me as hard as he could.[45]

James was incensed: 'I do not dispute the right of those who have the government of the poor to use the necessary means of correcting them, but this to me if true is a most unjustifiable mode of correction'. The guardians acted promptly by summoning George to the workhouse, where a medical officer examined him and reported that he found him to be 'in good condition and in perfect health'. The guardians, having dismissed the allegation of brutality, ordered the boy to be 'properly punished' by Drouet for his 'gross misconduct'.[46]

One shudders to think what form this retribution took, but it did not exactly draw a line under the matter, for a few weeks later Liddle left Surrey Hall. Although he gave as his reason the offer of a more advantageous situation at a school in Islington, it is hard to dismiss the thought that his exoneration had been a whitewash, and that he had become a liability and had been told by the guardians or by Drouet to leave.[47]

Chapter Four

Drouet's Children

Many of the children who were sent to Drouet's asylum are known by name. The 1841 census lists nearly 600, and names are scattered throughout the copious records kept by the workhouse guardians, in letters and reports, and in the correspondence of Poor Law officials. The fragmentary evidence of these young lives makes for unhappy reading. Time and again one encounters a boy or a girl who was left alone in the world when their parents died or ran off and deserted them. One ten-year-old girl, Sarah, had no surname and nothing was known about her parents. No one knew who they were or where they were from, or even if they were dead or alive. Sarah had been abandoned as an infant and left in Dover Road, where, by some miracle, she was found. She was taken as a little bundle of wriggling rags to the workhouse in Newington, and they named her Sarah Dover after the place where she was discovered. Another little girl, Margaret Sullivan from Ireland, thought she might have been thirteen years old. She was an orphan, and it was noted in the records that she had no friends, which was a way of saying that she had no connections with adults who might take her in.[1]

Surrey Hall seems to have been a place to send children who were beyond any normal sort of help. Joseph Beck is an example. He was chargeable to the parish of St Paul, Covent Garden, in the Strand Union, although, as in the case of Sarah Dover, his place of birth was never fully identified. The guardians seem not to have been especially concerned about Joseph until, in the course of a visit to the asylum in 1847, they were informed that he had been there for many years and was much older than all the other boys. He was in fact twenty-one, so not a boy at all, but because he was physically small and of 'weak' intellect, and had not developed in any obvious sense, he had been allowed to languish and to all intents and purposes remain a child. Now the guardians took him away. He was in the workhouse in Cleveland Street for a time, but in due course he was sent to Millfield House, an infant poor establishment at Tanner's End in Edmonton. It is not entirely clear how long he stayed, but he was certainly there in 1851 when the census recorded him as one of a hundred inmates, a mix of girls and boys, whose ages ranged from three to seventeen. Joseph, who by then was a man in his mid-twenties, had seemingly been abandoned, in perpetuity, to the company of children.[2]

Another 'inconvenient' child who had been shuffled off to Surrey Hall by the Strand guardians was Sarah Ann Scott. She was an orphan and had formerly been a pupil at the St Clement Danes Charity School in Milford Lane, but she suffered from epilepsy, and the school authorities did not know what to do with her. They laid the problem before the board, explaining that her seizures rendered Sarah incapable either of sitting in a classroom or of carrying out household tasks, and the board arranged to have her taken down to Surrey Hall. But Surrey Hall could not manage her either. When a fit came on and she fell to the floor, writhing uncontrollably, she frightened the other children. At Drouet's request she was taken up to the workhouse in Cleveland Street, where she would have been placed in a ward for the female insane.[3]

Not all the children had been abandoned or orphaned, though, and there were a few whose parents were moved to speak up on their behalf. One such parent was Mary Rachel Bewick, a Stepney woman who had fallen into destitution following the death of her husband. Her two daughters were at Surrey Hall, and she was concerned for their welfare, having learnt that the children in their dormitory were sleeping as many as five in a bed. On one occasion, when visiting the asylum, she complained to the dormitory nurse, who gave her short shrift. 'There are so many children coming in,' the nurse said, 'that we are obliged to put so many together.' But Mary refused to keep quiet and repeated these claims in a meeting with the local Committee of Health, swearing blind that every word of them was true.[4]

The chairman of the committee, Erasmus Gilbert Livesay, who ran a boarding school in the village and had a dim view of Drouet's operation, was inclined to believe her. On the other hand, Samuel Harding, one of the Surrey Hall schoolmasters, took exception to her allegations. 'I do not mean to say that such a thing has never happened,' he said in reference to children sleeping five in a bed, 'but as a general rule of the establishment, and as a general thing, such a statement is false.' Harding added that when he had been a boy, and his cousins visited, he and they would sleep three in a bed. Drouet had not done anything different, and he pointed out in his employer's defence that if children were suddenly delivered from a workhouse, they had to sleep somewhere, and so they might well have slept in crowded beds for a night or two.[5] Harding was a resolute apologist for Drouet, but even he might have wondered what to say in answer to Thomas Beech, a twelve-year-old from the Kensington workhouse, when he claimed that he had slept in rooms with five beds in each and in each bed six boys, three at the top and three at the bottom. In these rooms a 'bed' was a straw mattress placed on the stone floor of the room and covered by a sheet.[6]

All the evidence indicates that any contact the children were allowed with their families was always limited and strictly controlled. Relatives outside the workhouse might apply for permission to have a nephew or a niece, a grandson or a granddaughter, a younger brother or sister at home for a time, as a short holiday of sorts, but only for a week, and in some cases only for a couple of days. This is not to say that all applications to the guardians were approved, though. For example, Chelsea would not allow James Giles to remove his little sister, Agnes, for a fortnight because he was 'totally unknown' to the members of the board. Elsewhere, if permission was refused but a reason not given, it may well be that far from being unknown to the guardians, the applicant was only too well known to them. In these cases, clearly, a judgement against a man's or a woman's character had been made.[7]

Again, although there are records of children being visited at Surrey Hall, restrictions invariably applied and permission had to be sought. Hannah Wilkins, for example, who clearly remembered being allowed out of the Kensington workhouse 'several times' in the seven months her two children were in the asylum, could also recall, only too well, the strict procedure she had to abide by once she arrived. Having given Drouet's porter the names of her children, she would sit, perforce, in the lodge by the front gate until they were brought out to her. From that point on, the porter would remain in the lodge, watching and listening. This limited access to her children, and the lack of privacy while she was with them, caused Hannah great distress, the more so because she could see that they were underfed but could help only by bringing with her little treats of bread and butter, which they did not so much eat as devour. At each visit their health had visibly declined, but Hannah was powerless to intervene.[8]

Even guardians had to submit to supervision in order to talk to 'their' children. Interviews would take place in the parlour in the presence of Mr and Mrs Drouet, the governess and schoolmasters, and the nurses. Such close control of the flow of information contradicted the official line that Surrey Hall was more accessible than other pauper establishments. These set aside fixed days for inspections, whereas Surrey Hall, as Samuel Harding was once heard to say, was 'open to the public' from seven in the morning until nine at night. According to Harding, the asylum was also 'public' in that he would take groups of children out into the village to exercise. The local residents could see with their own eyes the fine condition they were in, and in the eight years he had been working for Drouet he had only ever heard compliments along the lines of 'God bless the dear little children, how well they look; how tidy they are; how clean they are; what a nice man Mr Drouet must be.'[9]

There can be no better example of a child who experienced Drouet's mania for control than Patrick Sheen. He was ten years old, and once every three weeks, when his mother came down from the Holborn workhouse, he would be allowed to sit with her in the lodge. But it was forbidden to go out walking with her for fear that he would run away.[10] It was a real enough fear because children who loathed the asylum often tried to escape when the chance arose. They must have been a forlorn sight as they wandered across the fields, through the lanes behind the houses, and along the roads they hoped would lead them to freedom. These were not the clean and tidy creatures mythologised by Samuel Harding: they were desperate young runaways and most probably they did not get very far. But one did make it all the way home. He was ten-year-old Matthew Ryan, and he showed up on his mother's doorstep in Kensington, quite without warning, and told her and her inquisitive neighbours that he was not getting enough food. She looked at Matthew for tell-tale signs of starvation, convinced herself that none were to be found, and a few days later took him back to Surrey Hall.[11]

Fourteen-year-old Thomas Merritt, who was also from Kensington, absconded after being physically assaulted by the assistant schoolmaster, John 'Johnny' Kerr, and sought shelter with his aunt. He must have believed that he was safe there, but he was not, and before long the guardians caught up with him and ordered him to return.[12] Exactly what happened to him when he was back in Kerr's classroom hardly bears thinking about, but his punishment would almost certainly have been that of the many runaways whose escape from and return to the asylum have been noted in workhouse records. Another escapee, Thomas Mills, who ran away but came back of his own accord, was first beaten with a birch rod and then dressed in girls' clothes. Undeterred, Thomas ran away again. This time, he managed to get all the way back to town, where he was hoping to see his friends, but because he could not find them he walked the streets all night, alone and cold. His jailbreak came to a miserable end the next morning when he was stopped by a constable, who led him off to the police station in Hammersmith, and from there to the Kensington workhouse in Wright's Lane. He was collected a day and a half later by Drouet's shoemaker. Once he was back in the asylum, he had his head shaved and his clothes confiscated. He was only allowed to keep his shirt, and he remained half-naked, in bitter weather, from seven that evening until twelve the following day.[13]

* * *

Although in most cases runaway children were trying to escape from hunger, they had other reasons too. One was loneliness, and it is a sorry fact that a boy from the Chelsea workhouse, Edward Ralph, absconded because he was unhappy at not being able to see his friends from home.[14] Another reason for fleeing Surrey Hall was the fear of adults, and any impression that the punishments handed out to Thomas Merritt and Thomas Mills were in some way exceptional, and were reserved for unusual breaches of discipline, is misleading. Physical abuse was inflicted on the children almost as a matter of routine. Drouet himself was notorious for his sudden displays of anger, and although these might take the relatively mild form of a verbal assault, as when he 'blew up' girls who complained to him about the food, other interventions might be a good deal harder to ignore. There were reports of a boy being flogged for running through the yard reserved for the use of the girls.[15]

On occasions the punishment was delivered by a female member of staff, and the assistant matron, Sarah Jane Day, was happy to box a girl's ears if she spoke out of turn. However, the worst of the assaults on the children were without question the work of the male staff, and the most determined offenders in this respect were the two schoolmasters, Samuel Harding and

Joshua Brown. A particularly disturbing instance occurred in the late summer of 1848 when evidence emerged that two St Pancras brothers, Joseph and Henry Sherreard, who were eleven and nine years old, had been kicked and punched in the classroom. Because they were severely undernourished, they had both been removed from Surrey Hall to the home of an uncle and aunt in a little street off Hampstead Road near Regent's Park, where they were receiving visits from Joseph White Johnson, a district medical officer. Johnson found that Joseph had a nasty and unexplained bruise on his leg, and that Henry, who was dying of tuberculosis, had a similar wound on his head, supposedly inflicted by one of the schoolmasters. Unsettled by these discoveries, he went down to Surrey Hall to investigate, and with him went a second medical officer, Henry Charles Robinson, who, in the report he submitted to the guardians, gave it as his opinion that 'a great deal of severity – not to use a harsh term – has been exercised by the masters and others in authority, as well as some out of authority, towards the boys.' Drouet was promptly summoned to the workhouse to explain what had happened, and when the report was read to him, he assured the guardians that he would 'institute a most rigid inquiry' into the matter. Thereafter, the Sherreard case was never mentioned again, and there can be little doubt that the guardians were happy to draw a line under this tangle of allegations from one side and scarcely credible promises of cooperation from the other.[16]

Children who survived the Drouet regime and were questioned about their experiences gave harrowing accounts of Harding and Brown. Their behaviour was characterised by a complete lack of a sense of proportion, so that even the slightest overstepping of the mark might meet with retribution of a fearful severity. One surefire way for a boy to attract trouble was to protest to the schoolmasters that he wanted to use the tap in the girls' yard but could not get past the two loutish teenagers standing guard at the gate. Another was to ask for permission to visit the latrine during school hours, which was regarded as insolent and led to the same painful repercussions as failing to learn the prescribed material, or being caught surreptitiously reading a book beneath the desk. There were first-hand accounts of children being winded by a schoolmaster's knuckles, or flogged with a birch rod so ferociously that red weals were raised on the victim's back. Henry Morrell from Holborn, who was fifteen but could neither read nor write, was once knocked to the floor by Harding and kicked in the head and the ribs as he lay there. He did not or could not say what crime he had committed, but he remembered having 'a bad head' for a long time after the incident. John Welch, who was also from the Holborn workhouse, had an equally brutal encounter with one of the schoolmasters, though in his case his assailant was not Harding but Brown. He had complained to visiting guardians that he never had enough food, which was patently true, as a single glance at his pallid features and spindly legs and arms revealed, but his act of betrayal had not gone unnoticed. 'When the guardians had gone,' he recalled, 'Mr Brown, the schoolmaster, whacked me. He said, "I'll let you know to tell the guardians. I'll give you a little more to eat".' Brown held John down against a desk and beat him with his fist.[17]

In the light of the lengthy catalogue of his abuses, it is little short of remarkable that Harding was a qualified professional schoolmaster. He had been trained at the British and Foreign School Society in Southwark, and a handbook to the Borough Road schools shows how far, during his career at Surrey Hall, he departed from the humane values of the Society's founder, Joseph Lancaster, a Quaker who was concerned to improve the education of the poor. A question trainees were urged to ask themselves, which makes his failure uncomfortably clear, was: 'Are you *strict*, without being *severe*?'[18] A second establishment at which Harding had been trained was the Home and Colonial School Society, which promoted the theories of the Swiss reformer Johann Heinrich Pestalozzi. By respecting the personal dignity of the individual child, Pestalozzi aimed to bring about changes in underprivileged lives. An image of the Society's school in Gray's Inn Lane, which was published in the *Illustrated London News* in 1843, shows pupils in the playground disporting themselves on seesaws and climbing ropes under the benign gaze of a teacher, who stands to one side to preside over the activities, quite without menace. These joyful children could not be less like the terrorised creatures in the schoolrooms of Surrey Hall.[19]

The principles that guided Harding were not those of Joseph Lancaster or Johann Heinrich Pestalozzi but those of Bartholomew Peter Drouet. He is on record as having backed his employer on a number of points. He argued that Drouet, in running the asylum, was exercising his right to make a living in a manner he thought proper, and it was a right all men had. He also maintained that Drouet's business had attracted none of the public expressions of resentment customarily aimed at successful enterprises.

Indeed, if anyone were to criticise his operation, it would be the Poor Law Commissioners, and they had not done so. They had visited Surrey Hall regularly and inspected the premises 'from the coal-hole to Mr Drouet's private apartments' without finding anything to be dissatisfied with. Not that this surprised him, because the children played in playgrounds that perfectly met their needs, their clothing passed muster, and they were adequately fed. That Drouet profited by their labour, hiring them out to tradesmen and others for 5s. a week, was a lie put about by the guardians of the Chelsea workhouse, and Drouet denied it. Where they earned money, it was for their use alone. He would be the first to admit that some children had earned as much as 3s. or 4s. a week, but Drouet neither touched nor saw the money, and Harding could vouch for Drouet in regard to this because it was he who took the money from the children and kept it safe for them.[20]

*   *   *

At all times, though, Harding's resorting to harsh discipline has to be measured against the difficulties he was obliged to put up with. One point is that the schoolrooms at Surrey Hall were populated by the children of the poorest of the poor, whose experience of education, if indeed they had received any, would mainly have been limited to workhouse schools. So it is no surprise that their attainments were varied. On the one hand, Frederick Deadman from Kensington and Sarah Skittlethorp from Holborn, who were aged thirteen and fourteen, had been taught in the workhouse to read and write and to recite the catechism. On the other hand, Thomas Mills had learnt nothing either in the Kensington workhouse or at Surrey Hall, and at the age of twelve was still illiterate and had no knowledge of religious material.[21] William Derbyshire, who was eight, not only could not read or write but had received no benefit from his time in Harding's classroom. 'I would not like to go back to school,' was all he said.[22] Harding's classroom practice must have had less to do with encouragement than control. In a later appointment at a children's establishment in Mitcham belonging to the parish of St George in the East, he was judged by the government inspectorate to be only moderately competent as a teacher, to have gaps in his knowledge, and to fall short in such essential skills as grammar and arithmetic. He had not been long in the post before the guardians got wind of possible problems: he was complaining of the unruly conduct of the boys.[23]

We can gain a fair idea of what Harding may have meant by 'unruly conduct' from contemporary reports of conditions in ragged schools. The boys were universally depicted as feral: 'Accustomed to the freedom of their wild existence, they look at first with scorn upon the restraints which the ragged schools impose. They come as for a *lark*; shout, sing, and blaspheme, and are still in a state of frantic fun at the idea of any one schooling them.'[24]

But noise was only one of the teacher's problems, and a common theme of these reports is the trashing of a schoolroom, with the boys jumping on or overturning and breaking desks and benches. Given that the ragged schools disapproved of corporal punishment, on the grounds that the teacher 'who cannot govern his school without the frequent use of the rod' must be deemed incompetent, it might reasonably be asked how order was restored.[25] The most disruptive boys might be ordered to leave, but one teacher found to his cost that he had merely moved the trouble outside, where 'they commenced throwing stones through the windows, and brickbats at the door', with the result that 'glass to a considerable amount was broken, the staircase often covered with brickbats, and the door nearly knocked in pieces'.[26] A ragged school in Holborn was attacked by youths in the streets hurling 'stones, dirt, and every description of filth'. The risk to the teacher of physical injury was real. When four boys in the same Holborn school began rioting in the classroom, the teacher ordered one of the ringleaders out, whereupon the boy tried to throw a large blackboard at him and was only prevented from doing so by the intervention of the other three. Another teacher was confronted by a boy with a large knife who was set on 'sticking' him.[27]

If the ragged school teacher was expected to meet these difficulties with a Christian forbearance, Harding would seem to have been unencumbered by any such restraint. There were no ameliorating influences on his behaviour. Drouet reportedly protested about the beatings, but he was prepared to beat children himself, and there is not the slightest suggestion that he actively interfered with his schoolmasters' practices.[28] Harding was answerable only to his own conscience, although it is possible that his habit of dispensing arbitrary punishments was encouraged by his lack of age and experience. When he started working at Surrey Hall in 1842, he was only twenty-six and arguably unable to make reasoned, mature use of the absolute power he wielded in the classroom.

It should be added, not so much by way of mitigation as of explanation, that Harding must have been an unhappy man, since three of his four children had died by the time he was thirty-two. But when all is said and done, he was a cruel man, and his reputation went beyond the doors of Surrey Hall. When he took up the post in Mitcham, the ratepayers of St George in the East, having learnt about him, were horrified. In a strongly worded letter to the Poor Law Board, a number of damning charges were made against the man who had once been 'the principal subordinate in the Tooting establishment', and who therefore had a share of the responsibility for all that had gone on there. Going by his track record, the new appointee was evidently unresponsive to 'the peculiar demands of childhood' and 'the general claims of humanity'. Nor was 'the innate cruelty of his disposition' merely a matter of hearsay: it had been witnessed by workhouse guardians and reported by children towards whom it had been directed.[29] Such concerns as these were all the more serious when it was remembered that Harding had previously been accused of using extreme violence against two particular boys. The first of these boys merely had his arm broken. The second died.

The boy who died, William Baker, was eleven years old at the time of the incident in November 1844 and had come to Surrey Hall from the Richmond workhouse. The exact nature of any rough handling he might have been subjected to is not known, but his death certificate states that he suffered convulsions with concomitant cyanosis, indicating that he died of an epileptic fit.[30] It was rumoured that he had been struck on the head, though it was open to question whether such a blow might have brought on the fatal seizure. With so much uncertainty surrounding the true cause of death, the Surrey coroner held an inquest, at which the jury decided that there was not enough evidence to ascribe William's convulsions and 'cyan affection of the brain' to human agency. On a generous view, the presumption of innocence prevented a public shaming even Harding did not deserve, though, equally, it may have allowed a guilty man to get off scot-free.

Joshua Brown also made himself a target for wagging tongues. It would seem that he left Surrey Hall in disgrace for some unspecified misdemeanour. Word even went round that Drouet had sacked him because he had killed a boy, a rumour reported by Patrick Sheen, the ten-year-old from the Holborn workhouse.[31] There can be little doubt that he was as cruel as Harding, and possibly even crueller. The coroner for the Western Division of Middlesex, Thomas Wakley, when investigating the deaths of Holborn children at Surrey Hall in January 1849, made up his mind that the schoolmaster's behaviour bordered on the pathological. 'Brown seemed to be considered by the boys as a sort of flagellating instrument,' Wakley stated, 'to be applied to them whether they did right or wrong.'[32]

Young John Welch told the story of the Kensington boy who fell foul of Brown while playing with other children in the garden behind the Hall. Brown was on playground duty when the boy asked him if he might go out to the latrine in the yard. Flying into a rage, the schoolmaster pushed him against a wall, and did so with such force that he opened up a gash in his head. A stonemason working up at the house witnessed the assault. He marched up to Brown and knocked him out with his fist.[33]

Although it is not clear how, the story got into the newspapers, where it infuriated the letter writer Sidney Godolphin Osborne. The violence of the schoolmaster was nothing less than despicable: it was a classic case of bullying and fully deserving of the reprisal he had met with. Osborne wrote a rather quirky but properly indignant letter to the editor of *The Times*:

If any gentleman, on the spot, will ascertain the truth of this story, and the name of the stonemason, I will cheerfully forward one sovereign to him as a mark of my respect for his true English feeling. It is said that, of all sensations of touch, there is not one which equals in pleasure that felt by the fly-fisher as a large fish takes and is struck by his fly. It certainly is a sensation exquisite in its way; but, when I think of that mason, and try to dream myself into his then position, I feel that I would consent never to throw a fly again, to have felt, for its brief moment, what he must have felt when he struck that coward to the earth.[34]

* * *

Even the violent schoolmasters, however, did not present as great a menace to the children in the asylum as Richard Drouet. He had at one time been a butcher in Kennington, and in due course, after the collapse of the Surrey Hall operation, he would manage public houses in Walworth and Blackheath.[35] Although he was more than twenty years younger than Bartholomew, his membership of the community of London provisioners must have made him an important asset. His role in the Lower Tooting establishment was assistant to his half-brother, although at times henchman would have been closer to the truth. When the asylum, and those who worked in it, became the subject of intense public scrutiny, he was given a very bad press. The *Era* condemned him out of hand as being 'precisely the man that we should suppose Drouet's brother to be'. Between them, the paper claimed, the two Drouets had seen to it that the children were not only starved but brutalised and degraded as well.[36]

Richard Drouet was reputedly pugnacious and rude. When the Kensington guardians announced their decision to remove their children from Surrey Hall, for reasons that will become all too clear, he flew into a rage. It was as much as the older Drouet could do to prevent Richard from going up to Kensington to give the guardians a piece of his mind: he was bent on 'thrashing them all'. The children would have seen him as a sinister figure, and John Welch would have been positively afraid of him on account of a distressing incident caused by no worse a sin than having been caught straying into the part of the yard set aside for the girls. 'He took me up by the neck and trousers,' John recalled, 'and dropped me on a stone.' How the little boy survived is hard to comprehend. He was certainly hurt, and he remembered being 'very ill' afterwards, a comparatively mild description of what was in all likelihood a serious concussion and its attendant complications, which might have been anything from headaches and nausea to problems with his balance and vision. He was reluctant to accuse his assailant before Bartholomew Peter Drouet: he would only be told that he had got what he deserved. Nor did he tell the guardians when he was taken home to Holborn to recuperate, fearing that they might further complicate matters by making a fuss. And so, predictably, following his recovery he was sent back to Surrey Hall.[37]

However, Richard Drouet's worst excesses were sexual, and this grim fact came to light in November 1848 when he was accused of a series of assaults on girls from the Kensington workhouse. The guardians, acting on information received from parents with daughters in the asylum, conducted urgent inquiries, and five girls reported that Drouet had taken 'indecent liberties' with them. One girl, Margaret Dawley, reported that she had been raped. Margaret's statement was concerning enough for the guardians to order a medical examination, and once the medical officer had satisfied himself that she was telling the truth, they laid her evidence and that of the other girls before the sitting magistrate at the Hammersmith Police Court.

Margaret, who had just turned fourteen at the time, was waylaid by Drouet on a Saturday evening in May. He dragged her into a storeroom behind the house and throughout the criminal act he had one hand clamped over her mouth to stifle her screams. For a time Margaret kept it to herself that she had been raped, not knowing who in the asylum would listen to her. Only later, when she had been readmitted to the workhouse, and was well away from Drouet and safe from the danger of repercussions, did she describe the full extent of his 'indecent liberties', and then only to a fellow inmate, a woman with two daughters at Surrey Hall. She had been slow to come forward, but it is easy to understand why. She must have been humiliated, deeply shocked, and afraid.[38]

Having interviewed some of the girls, the magistrate decided that the charges against Richard Drouet warranted investigation and ordered the case to be brought before him, not in Hammersmith but in Surrey, where the assault had taken place. Accordingly, on 13 November, a constable escorted Drouet from Lower Tooting to the Wandsworth Police Court. The hearing was a disgrace. Although Margaret was able to give a blow-by-blow account of the rape and its aftermath, she was contradicted on several points by the assistant matron, Sarah Jane Day, and the schoolmistresses, Sarah Shambler and Sarah Goat, who had been called as witnesses for the defence. Perhaps not surprisingly, the magistrate was persuaded that Margaret had perjured herself, and the case against Drouet was dismissed.[39]

He must have counted himself very fortunate indeed, seeing as in the course of the proceedings, in addition to the charge of rape, he had been accused of a number of sexual improprieties. Esther Birley, who was thirteen, told the court how he had once put his hand up her clothes when she was on the stairs. Rosina Seckerson, who was about the same age as Esther, had been 'bought' with a pair of gold earrings, a looking glass and some money. Other girls Drouet had assaulted at one time or another were named, but their experiences, and those of Esther and Rosina, were readily ignored by the court in line with the seemingly inviolable principle that a man who had the trappings of respectability, even if his character was questionable, was intrinsically more credible than members of the pauper classes. Esther, like Margaret, was easily disposed of as a perjurer on the say-so of Sarah Jane

Day. Rosina had been described as 'a girl of very loose morals' by the older Drouet when the guardians informed him of the charges made against his half-brother. Margaret was 'a bold and forward girl'.[40]

The case may have been officially closed, but the Kensington guardians still had their concerns. They had taken their girls back into the workhouse in the week before the trial and now decided not to send them back to Lower Tooting. Although the board collectively expressed no opinion on the outcome of the magistrate's hearing, some were saying individually that Richard Drouet was not to be trusted. There was no smoke without fire, but because Surrey Hall had closed ranks to deny the allegations, the verdict had failed Drouet's victims. Their view was probably shared by those newspapers that reported the case, and the editor of one, the *Weekly Dispatch*, went as far as to assert that Charles Buller, the president of the newly formed Poor Law Board, 'will not be satisfied with this investigation'. Sadly, Buller's thoughts on the matter have not been preserved.[41]

There is a clear sense in all this of the vulnerability of the young female inmates of Surrey Hall. Since the age of consent in 1849 was twelve, they were not properly protected by the law, and they were certainly not protected by those adult members of staff who ought to have been aware of the threat presented by the unchecked behaviour of a predatory male. Margaret Dawley made precisely this point. Although she took no one fully into her confidence while she was still in the asylum, she did at least complain of the 'indecent liberties' to Sarah Shambler and Sarah Goat. The two women, patently reluctant to get involved, offered the unhelpful observation that Margaret would have done well to avoid Richard Drouet, who was in their opinion 'a very impudent' man. At the trial, when called as witnesses, they refused to acknowledge even this futile interview, but by then the magistrate had already made up his mind that Margaret had perjured herself. He did not consider the possibility that Shambler and Goat were telling lies. The truth of the matter may well have been that they had heard Margaret's story, but had thought it in their interest as paid employees of the Drouet family not to stir up a hornets' nest.[42]

When the census was taken in 1851, Rosina Seckerson was an inmate in the Lock Asylum at Westbourne Green in Paddington, having first spent time in the Lock Hospital, which occupied the same site. The hospital was a charitable institution, funded by subscriptions, for the treatment of venereal disease. Rosina would have been referred by the Kensington guardians on the advice of the medical officer, and there are grounds for believing that she had been infected by Richard Drouet. Her fellow patients were mostly poor, like her, and they suffered from syphilis, chancroid, gonorrhoea or venereal warts. There were men as well as women in the hospital, but the women were especially woebegone. Most were aged about twenty, and many had entered prostitution as an alternative to domestic service or to escape an abusive relationship. A course of treatment lasted between six and eight weeks, and about a quarter of the female patients then entered the asylum, where they would be on probation for two months before being accommodated for up to two years. A few left after only a few weeks, considering themselves unsuited to the aims and discipline of an institution that had as its full title the Lock Asylum for the Reception of Penitent Female Patients.[43]

Rosina was one of fifty-two penitents. At seventeen she was young, but not the youngest: Anne Bennet was sixteen and Mary Anne Martin and Betsey Long were both fourteen. But whatever their age, the inmates of the asylum answered to the nineteenth-century definition of female deviancy typified by the working-class prostitute or, in its middle-class manifestation, the fallen woman. An *Account* of the asylum did not pull its punches:

> Young women, having been seduced, deserted, and banished from their friends, are frequently left without any other resource than that of entering the recesses of debauchery; the general consequences of which are increasing wickedness, a ruined constitution, a premature death, and as far as we can see, everlasting destruction.[44]

The inmates of the asylum received no formal education. Instead, they were taught the 'decent' working-class skills of laundry work, needlework and embroidery. They were supervised by a matron and her assistants and given moral guidance by the chaplain. They could only receive a visit from a family member or friend if it had been approved, and since they were not allowed to discharge themselves from the asylum, they could only leave by being expelled. To all intents and purposes they were prisoners. But they were in many cases helped to lead happier lives, and Rosina must be counted as one such success, for in 1855 she married, and in 1861 she gave birth to a son.

We know something of the later history of Margaret too. At about the time of Richard Drouet's trial, she was ready to enter paid employment as a servant to a dairyman living in Earl's Court, with clothing supplied by the workhouse. It is not entirely clear if she took up the position, though, and in any case, in May of the following year, she was in the workhouse again. She was in trouble, having been caught fighting with another inmate.[45]

She finally left the workhouse when she found a situation in the home of William and Amelia Cole, who lived in Kensington. They had seven children, and being their only servant, Margaret must have been run off her feet. However, her employment with the Coles did not last long, not because she was dismissed but because she died. In the late spring of 1852, when she was still only eighteen, she contracted tuberculosis. She languished for three months and finally gave up the ghost towards the end of the summer. In her final moments an older sister, Ann, was at her side.[46]

Chapter Five

An Awful Visitation

By the end of 1848 it had become apparent that Drouet had been accepting more children from the workhouses than Surrey Hall could reasonably hold. It was an absurd situation, and the critical moment came in November when the St Pancras workhouse added 110 girls to the 1,370 children who were already in the asylum. Drouet had assured St Pancras that he had received the approval of the Poor Law Board inspectors and could safely accommodate the girls. The first of these claims was somewhat at odds with the same inspectors' recent advice over limiting numbers. As for the second, future events would demonstrate in tragic fashion that the St Pancras girls, and indeed the general mass of Drouet's children, were anything but safe.[1]

Destined to have fatal consequences, the problem of this swelling population of children was entirely one of Drouet's own making, though it has to be said that St Pancras's timing was especially unfortunate because he was already under great strain following the recent loss of his wife. According to contemporary sources, Maria's death in October had not only affected Drouet's own health but had precipitated a general crisis. As a result, the management of Surrey Hall had begun to come apart at the seams, with Drouet finding himself obliged to delegate more responsibility to his paid employees or 'hired servants' than was strictly prudent. Exactly who these 'hired servants' were was not spelled out, but they probably would have included Maria's replacement as matron, Sarah Jane Day, and the asylum's resident surgeon, William James Kite.[2]

Kite had been engaged by Drouet from 31 October 1848. The post of resident surgeon had not previously existed at Surrey Hall, and it is tempting to think that one was needed now to fill the void left by Maria, who had supervised the nurses and had probably been the first port of call for many of the children with routine ailments. However, since Maria's work would have been handed over to Sarah Jane Day, it makes more sense to see Kite's appointment as a response to General Board of Health guidelines on 'an instant recourse to medical aid', a measure deemed necessary because of the cholera that was now epidemic in London.[3] And if the threat of cholera was not on Drouet's mind, economics almost certainly were, for the steady increase in the number of children in the asylum would have made it costly to retain the services of a local doctor. Walter Chapman had previously been medical attendant to the asylum, a position that may also have been held at some point by his father, Charles Chapman, who lived next door to the White House. Kite, on a modest fixed salary, would have been a cheaper and therefore a more attractive option.

As it turned out, though, the appointment was far from straightforward. To begin with, Kite was young. He had been born in Ramsbury in Wiltshire in December 1823, and so he was still only twenty-four when he entered Drouet's employment. This is not to say that he was not suitably qualified: he had been a licentiate of the Society of Apothecaries and a member of the Royal College of Surgeons since 1846.[4] Nor was he notably lacking in practical experience, as he had been apprenticed to his father, who was himself a surgeon, and had subsequently held a number of appointments, in one of which he had learnt at first hand enough about the use of chloroform in childbirth to publish an article on the subject in the *Lancet*.[5] However, by his own admission, he had never worked in an establishment devoted to the care of children, and he had never borne the level of responsibility that came with his appointment as Drouet's resident surgeon. The most he could claim in this respect was that 'he had in two previous situations had the charge of pauper patients', which presumably meant either having been employed in a workhouse or simply having come across poor people in the course of his general medical duties. Probably what served him best in his brief time with Drouet was a visit to the prison ships or 'hulks' moored at Woolwich, where medical practitioners and their apprentices were able to observe a range of debilitating diseases, and speculate on their relationship to cramped and insanitary conditions. It must have been a sobering experience, and Kite came face to face with cases of cholera, which he later claimed had adequately prepared him for what lay ahead at Surrey Hall.[6]

Valuable though this early encounter with cholera must have been, Kite was even then not sufficiently conversant with the nature of the disease to detect the warning signs in the asylum. He was criticised after the event for failing to recognise the significance of three cases of vomiting and diarrhoea occurring a fortnight before Elizabeth Frost fell ill and died. Since he attributed the symptoms to the dampness and cold prevailing throughout the premises, he had seen no need to look for exceptional causes. For this reason, his critics concluded, he missed the opportunity to adopt such measures as would have mitigated and might even have prevented the disaster that immediately followed the girl's death. Even when there could no longer be any doubt that cholera had broken out, which was in the first week of 1849, Kite apparently failed to take preventative steps. One effective precaution would have been to ask the schoolmasters and schoolmistresses to check the state of the children. No such request was made.[7]

It is hard not to feel sorry for Kite. Through no fault of his own, he was faced with an acute emergency few doctors would have been equipped to deal with. If in the event he did not really know what it was best to do, he was typical of the mid-nineteenth-century medical profession, which was still in thrall to the theory that cholera was brought on by bad air. What he did know, of course, was the danger to health posed by crowded premises with poor sanitation. However, he was all too aware that the terms on which he had been engaged put him at a disadvantage in any dealings he might have had with Drouet. Even as resident surgeon, he would not have had a particularly exalted status at Surrey Hall. He had only been qualified for two years, his experience was of arguable significance, he was new to the establishment, and he could not easily have gone against Drouet's wishes.[8] Drouet was more than twice his age, and for better or for worse, he had long been involved in the management of pauper establishments; he had worked alongside Charles Mott; he had appeared as an expert witness in the inquiry conducted by the Royal Commission; he was held in high regard in Poor Law circles; and he enjoyed a position of respect in Lower Tooting society.

In short, as he recognised, Kite was being paid for his medical services to the asylum, not for his views on how it was being run. He simply had to make do with the arrangements he found on his arrival. These were far from adequate. With the exception of the lists of children's names and illnesses Drouet entered in his weekly reports to the parishes, no systematic medical records were being kept, and if Kite was able to keep track of the name and age of his patients, the date and hour of diagnoses, and the outcome of cases, it was only because he had taken it upon himself to keep a register.[9]

Equipment was limited to a spatula, a pair of scales, and an assortment of medicine bottles, some of them labelled, others not. The wards of the 'infirmary' were not wards in the accepted sense. They were merely rooms with fire grates at the far end of one of the dormitories, with no supply of water, no warm bath, and no privy. They had not been in any way adapted for the treatment of the sick, and they actually placed healthy and unhealthy children close together in the same space.[10]

Later, Kite would describe Surrey Hall as a generally healthy establishment, but he only meant by this that the incidence of sickness was small in comparison with the size of the population. The statistics were in any case the norm for children who had been brought in from workhouses. They were suffering from typical workhouse complaints: unsightly scrofulous swellings on the neck, sores on the feet, ophthalmia and the inevitable itch. Indeed, until cholera broke out, Kite seemed chiefly occupied with the battle against itch. Many of the children sent by the parishes were already infected and yet they were all admitted. He never protested, either because he felt it was not his place to do so, or because he, like Drouet, recognised that itch would always be present to a greater or lesser extent in an establishment as crowded as Surrey Hall. He was under orders to examine all children on arrival, but it made no difference as they were instructed to keep their clothes on, and by the time he carried out these examinations, they had already been handed over to Drouet, with their names already entered in the register. Apart from treating the symptoms of itch with a yellow sulphur ointment, the best he could do was to keep children known to be infected separate from the rest. But he was only ever able to separate some of the children with itch, never all, and even then they were separated only during the day. Furthermore, the ward he confined them to was not specifically an itch ward, and there were children in it who had not yet been infected, though of course they would be infected soon enough.[11]

Drouet apparently offered no opposition when it came to treating sickness, although the only specific example Kite was able to give, which was to order supplies of porter for the little boys in the sick ward, would hardly have involved significant expense. Of course, it would have helped him considerably if Drouet had admitted fewer children into the asylum, but this was a measure Drouet would never have agreed to as it would have affected his business's profitability. So overcrowding became an acute problem, and especially in the four dormitories in the attic of the main house, where the older children were forced to sleep in such numbers that they were an easy target for disease. But because revenue was not to be sacrificed to medical policy, Kite had little power to turn new arrivals away, even when they might be importing disease from the workhouses into Surrey Hall. 'Entered all who came in,' the *Morning Chronicle* quoted him as saying, bitterly, 'whether ill or well'. Only if children were suffering from a life-threatening illness, such as typhus, would he have been able to persuade Drouet not to open the doors of the asylum.[12]

Therefore, it should not come as a surprise that Kite discovered four or five cases of dysentery, a fearful affliction that sent temperatures rocketing, stoked fever, and emptied stomachs and bowels. Here, however, he recorded what must be regarded as his greatest success, and he claimed that by the middle of December he had all but eradicated the disease. Diarrhoea was another matter, and there were upwards of sixty cases in the period from Kite's arrival at the end of October to the end of December. At the time he had not been unduly alarmed, in part because its victims were mostly clear of the condition in a day or two, but also because it was another endemic problem of the institutionalised poor.[13] Only later, after cholera had ripped its way through the asylum, was it recognised that the prevalence of diarrhoea had not been taken seriously enough. The schoolmasters and schoolmistresses, who had daily contact with the children and knew of many suffering with pain in their bowels and looseness in their stools, were quick to blame Kite for his failure to introduce effective procedures. With whatever justification, they felt he was either complacent or incompetent. In truth, even if he had organised the schoolmasters and schoolmistresses to keep him informed of the prevalence of diarrhoea, he still would not have been able to deal with it because there were always too many demands on his time.[14]

*   *   *

Surrey Hall may have been located in a tranquil rural spot, many miles from the horrors of the London slums, but the conditions rivalled those that prevailed in any of the metropolitan workhouses. Without a doubt, what Kite encountered when he entered the asylum for the first time would have made a deep impression on him. As he toured the premises, he would have seen children beyond counting, unkempt and unwashed. He would have noticed with alarm that the windows were few and small, that the air was fetid and oppressive, and that the asylum was filled with unappetising smells at all times and the more so when cabbage and cheap meat were being boiled in the kitchens. When he went outside into the long yard behind the main building, he would have found it hard to look past the foul privies, the clutter of rabbit hutches and ferret pens, the stalls for horses and cows, the hen houses, the pigsties, and the poultry and the pigs roaming freely among the children as they played.[15]

To a miasmatist, these would have been obvious sources of atmospheric poison, but a more serious offender was what was known locally as the Streatham Drain, a watercourse carrying the sewage of Upper and Lower Tooting and the neighbouring villages two miles down to the River Wandle. At various points along its course, and along the lower boundary of Drouet's premises, the Drain was bricked over. On the other hand, where it ran alongside the upper boundary, at no great distance from the dormitory allocated to the older boys, it was more or less an open ditch varying in width from six to twelve feet. It was fed by a network of foul channels running behind the houses, and just before reaching Drouet's it collected the liquid waste of Brown & Parsons, a brewery with dirty piggeries in its yard. A nearby garden was fertilised with 'water' drawn from the Drain by means of a pump, and the disease-ridden vapours were carried over Surrey Hall by the winds that blew from the north.[16]

The Drain served not only the population of Tooting but also that of the Surrey County Lunatic Asylum, which stood on high ground above the village and housed between 400 and 500 patients. The efflux from this establishment first flowed into a large cesspool in the grounds, where it sat in a reservoir while the surface of the slimy water bubbled ceaselessly from the formation of mephitic gases. From there the asylum's sewage was carried through a barrel drain a quarter of a mile downhill into an even larger reservoir, where it mixed with the discharge from the Drain. The reservoir was an impressive construction. It boasted a capacity of more than 32,000 cubic feet, and it was fitted with a system of dams that allowed the local farmers to flood their fields and meadows with a rich top dressing of faecal sludge. At the same time, and from the same source, the nurserymen George and William Rollisson, who ran their operation behind the High Street, were able to avail themselves of an inexhaustible supply of potent fertiliser with which to improve their soil. Meanwhile, the miasmata floated back up to the lunatic asylum, or over Surrey Hall, or along Garratt Lane to the site of the almshouses the parish of St Clement Danes was building for the accommodation of forty deserving souls. Whose health was threatened was a decision taken by the wind.[17]

The Streatham Drain had a reputation verging on the legendary. Two medical men sent by the Poor Law Board to examine Drouet's premises commented on the stench, which was noticeable in all parts of the property, but was particularly offensive, indeed almost overpowering, when they walked near the open ditch. They described its contents as an 'inky black mud' that 'poisons the surrounding atmosphere to a considerable distance with most pestilential effluvia'.[18] If they were outraged, so too were the reporters from the London newspapers who descended on Surrey Hall when news of the cholera outbreak got out. They asked residents of Lower Tooting what their experience of the Drain was, and were left in no doubt that in summer the smell of human waste warmed by the sun was unendurable. It was so utterly vile, the residents insisted, that it made them retch.[19]

The school proprietor Erasmus Gilbert Livesay, who was a local health officer, was especially critical of a stretch of the Drain close to Garratt Lane, about 130 to 140 feet from the asylum, where a ninety-degree turn hindered its flow and in doing so created an accumulation of filth. He called it the Tooting Cesspool. At forty to fifty feet in length, and six to seven feet in breadth, the cesspool was too noxious and too much of an eyesore to be ignored. But Livesay was inclined to downplay the danger to public health in order to protect the reputation of the village. In Pigot & Co.'s directory it was stated that 'the air of this district has been long acknowledged to be salubrious and invigorating to the invalid', and this was a recommendation he believed everyone would want to safeguard.[20] Accordingly, he would assert that he personally had suffered no ill effects from his inspections of the ditches, and he could not convince himself that they had been the cause of fever or disease. Furthermore, he had visited a huddle of three or four houses behind the High Street where the children were as healthy as one could wish them to be, or so he was told. They had never been adversely affected by the proximity of the Drain, even in summer when it stank. Also, the health of his fifty pupils and fourteen staff had never been so good as during the last six months. Although the school was a mere half mile from the cesspool, he had had no deaths. 'I previously kept a boarding school at Guildford,' he said, 'but have never had so low medical expenses, in proportion to the number of my pupils, as I have had since I came to Tooting.'[21]

Efforts were made to deal with the Streatham Drain. In the early weeks of December, Livesay had seen workmen clearing out the stretch that skirted the upper boundary of Surrey Hall, and he had been told that boys from the asylum would also be set to work dredging the ditch, shovels in hand.[22] He thought the job had been done well, but not everyone agreed. In the expert view of Thomas Lovick, a government inspector of drains, the excavated muck had simply been dumped on the banks and repurposed as manure, on one side in Drouet's garden, and on the other side in a neighbouring field. Such sloppy work could not by any stretch of the imagination be considered an adequate response to the General Board of Health's warning that 'much mischief has sometimes been occasioned, when the operation has been so ignorantly and unskilfully conducted as to increase the extent of the evaporating surface'. Avoiding the mischief required the supervision of a person who had a thorough knowledge of malarial gases and was familiar with the measures that needed to be implemented in order to diminish their harmful effects. There were also many places where the digging had been carried out poorly enough to leave deposits up to fourteen inches in depth in the bed of the Drain. These emitted dangerous smells, which might be wafted on the wind towards Drouet's buildings, where they would surely enter the dormitories. To crown it all, the work had been done along only the upper part of the Drain's route, while an open stretch along the lower boundary of the yard had not been touched.[23]

*　*　*

On the Saturday of Elizabeth Frost's death, 30 December, the temperature only just rose above freezing. The morning saw six new cases of vomiting and diarrhoea across more than one of the wards. By the end of the day, a dozen cases of cholera had been recorded, but more were to come and on the Sunday there was a sharp increase in the number of children falling ill. At dawn twelve were discovered to be showing symptoms for the first time. Another twelve developed symptoms during the course of the day.[24] Drouet, though, was reluctant to acknowledge the gravity of the situation, certainly publicly, and possibly even to himself, and when the local surgeon William Bainbridge called at Surrey Hall to offer his services and a team of nurses, free of charge, he declined the offer. He insisted that he had no cholera in his house.[25]

As it turned out, it took an outside witness to the confusion to see that a crisis was developing in the asylum that could not and should not be concealed. He was a man by the name of David Kelly, a poor resident of Richbell Court in Holborn who scraped a living cleaning windows, running errands, and generally fetching and carrying. He had two grandsons at Surrey Hall, Jeremiah and James Doyle, aged eight and four, whose father had at one time been with them in the workhouse but had later disappeared, it was said to America. There was a third child but he or she was still in the workhouse with their mother. Kelly went down to Tooting to visit Jeremiah and James every three weeks, always walking because he could not afford to pay for transport, and as a rule going only on a Sunday so as not to lose the shilling he might earn on any other day when he went out to work.[26]

When Kelly visited on 31 December, he started out from Holborn at five in the morning and arrived three and a half hours later. He was told by the porter at the gate that James, whom he referred to affectionately as his 'little Jemmy', was in a dormitory occupied by the younger boys at the top of the house. The dormitory was a small room crowded with beds: Kelly thought that there might have been eight and he discovered his grandson sharing one with another boy. He did not remember seeing a doctor in the room, but he saw a nurse, and she told him that Jemmy had fallen sick the day before during the midday meal. He must have come away with a sense of foreboding because the next day, instead of going out to start his week's work, he went down to Surrey Hall again. This time he was met by Kite, who was waiting for him at the lodge, ready to assure him that Jemmy was out of danger. However, when Kelly went up to the dormitory, he realised that Jemmy was, on the contrary, very sick indeed. On seeing his grandfather peering anxiously at him, the little boy asked for water. A nurse brought water, but she allowed him to drink it in gulps and he immediately brought it up again. Kelly knew that he had been given too much and should have been sipping it. He could also see that Jemmy was suffering from chronic neglect, as indicated by a festering boil, a tumorous swelling, and sores on one of his legs. When Kelly went to find his other grandson, Jeremiah, he noticed similar skin eruptions on his ears, his navel, and his shins.[27]

What Kelly had witnessed was the dehydration that would work alongside the diarrhoea and vomiting to kill Jemmy. He must have been afraid for his grandson, and he would have received little in the way of reassurance when Richard Drouet came up to him in the yard with a written note for the Holborn guardians, the substance of which was that 'the children are dying very fast these three or four days'. All turned out as expected, and on his third visit, two days later, Kelly was warned by the porter that Jemmy was in decline. The four-year-old had been moved to another ward, which was so crowded with sick children that the nurse needed Kelly to point him out, and even then Kelly could not get to his bed. The children were vomiting over one another, over the sheets and blankets, and in some cases on the floor. They were now lying three in a bed, and when Kelly protested, the nurse ordered some to be carried to another ward. But the person she gave the order to was just a child herself, one of the many inmates who had been co-opted to work in the wards cleaning the mess and clearing the slops, removing the stinking bedclothes, and swabbing the slippery floors.[28]

Indeed, the adult nurses were too thin on the ground to manage the wards. They could not minister to one child without leaving others unattended while they suffered their final agonies alone, crying out for water or trying to climb out of their beds. They were too few and they were too poorly equipped. They had only two or three hot water bottles between them, enough to keep only two or three children warm. They were working in dangerous conditions, breathing unhealthy air because a cold wind blowing from the north east had kept the windows closed for several days. Also, the level of light was low: one of the wards for boys was lit by a single candle.[29]

The workhouse medical officers who went down to Surrey Hall in response to Drouet's urgent summons were horrified at the scenes in the wards. Cholera had produced in the children its characteristic symptoms of watery diarrhoea, agonising cramps, sunken eyes and fading voice, a bluish hue over parts of the body, and a coldness of breath and tongue and skin. If a child's body was 'opened' post mortem, it presented the distressing spectacle of a distended gall bladder, lungs filled with blood, and intestines passing a substance resembling gruel. In some cases the flow of urine had been shut off completely by the bladder shrinking to the size of a ball.[30]

Since it was widely held that cholera was the 'final stage' of diarrhoea, the medical officers naturally quizzed Drouet about the eating habits of the children. A certain amount of the information they were searching for was almost routine, such as the state of the equipment in the kitchen and the quality of the water the children drank and washed with. But they also asked about any recent seasonal excesses, which might have been either the glut of rich food paid for by the parishes and served up by Drouet on Christmas Day, or what the *Morning Chronicle* referred to as the 'trash' brought down to Surrey Hall in Christmas week by parents and friends.[31]

Kite was quick to dismiss the concerns over the water. In his opinion, since a constant supply was drawn from the asylum's two artesian wells, it was perfectly safe to drink. It was slightly chalybeate and had a taste of sulphur, and he had once noticed a peculiar smell while washing his face in some that had been standing in his room all night in a jug. He drank the water every day, though, as did Drouet, and neither of them had ever experienced ill effects.[32]

Similarly, he had little time for the hypothesis that the cause of so many deaths was essentially food poisoning, although disproving it called for chemical analysis of the yellowish clear 'water' the children were vomiting. He sent a sample in a sealed container to Alfred Swayne Taylor, an eminent toxicologist at Guy's Hospital. He was able to send with it a good account of the symptoms because he had been in constant attendance on the dying children. Having analysed the sample and studied Kite's accompanying notes, Taylor came to the conclusion that the asylum was in the grip of 'a malignant form' of epidemic cholera. He had some recommendations. First, the children must be given meat every day. Then there must be less gruel and 'liquid food' in their diet. Finally, the sick must be kept in isolation.[33]

On Thursday, 4 January the story broke in the national newspapers. The accounts they gave were broadly similar and included the number of workhouse children sent to Drouet by the metropolitan unions, the cost of these arrangements to the parishes, the early course the disease had taken, and the collective opinion of the various medical professionals that the cause of the outbreak was not bad food but bad air. At time of printing, the casualties stood at fifty-seven ill and twelve dead, but it did not take long for these figures to show a dramatic increase, and Kite was obliged to issue a statement later in the day in which he gave a corrected tally of well over a hundred diagnosed cases of cholera, with twenty-five deaths. Even that statistic rapidly proved to be short of the mark, and a reporter who had been sent down to Surrey Hall from the *Morning Chronicle* learnt that about fifteen more children 'were in such a condition that death was hourly expected', and that 'new cases were also hourly occurring'.[34] Another reporter, who had been sent by the *Daily News*, caught the real tragedy behind the figures: 'The ward in which the poor children, suffering from cholera, now lay [*sic*] presents a most painful spectacle. Here and there is a poor little boy or girl in the last agonies of death, others plaintively gasping and crying out for water.'[35]

He had also been in the carpenter's workshop behind the main building. It had become a dead-house where the bodies of children, some of them lying three in a coffin, were being held 'in awful array' until such a time as they were taken away by the parishes to which they belonged.

*　*　*

Richard Dugard Grainger was affected in much the same way. He had been authorised by the General Board of Health to manage the crisis at Surrey Hall, and had twice travelled down to Lower Tooting, first on Friday, 5 January, and again on the following day, Saturday, 6 January. However, the official nature of his two visits did not preclude a simple human response to the sight of so many dead and dying children, and he was badly shaken. The foulness of the air in the children's rooms was far more repulsive than anything he had ever encountered in any hospital or any lodging house where sick people lay. The cause of the abomination was hardly a mystery and was found in a room measuring sixteen by twelve feet, where five beds were occupied by eleven ailing girls. In another room of the same size, with four beds in it, there were four girls in one bed and three in each of the other three. In a third room, eighteen by sixteen feet, there were sixteen girls, all with cholera, in nine beds. These examples were repeated elsewhere. In a room on the male side of the asylum there were eighteen beds with barely any space between them. Twenty-five boys were in bed with symptoms of cholera. A further ten, who were convalescing, were huddled around a fire. To Grainger's deep distress, only a short while before he entered the room, a boy in one of the beds had died.[36]

The boy's sudden and startling death was a sign of both the rapacity and the indifference of the disease. Indeed, in the interval from Grainger's departure on the Friday evening to his arrival the next day, another forty children had fallen ill, twelve of whom had died. On the day before his first visit, a few children had died after only three hours: ten days later another would die after only two.[37] Some commentators in the press could not square the disaster with a previously optimistic impression of Surrey Hall. As *Bell's Life in London* put it:

> Heretofore the most gratifying reports have been made of the health of these children, often – out of the large number congregated – not more than three or four being in the infirmary at a time, and those afflicted only with the diseases incidental to children, the mortality being far below that even in private families. This is the more remarkable when the localities and classes from which the children came, often the lowest and most depraved in the metropolis, are considered.

According to this line of thinking, the outbreak of cholera was an awful but arbitrary visitation, an assault not only on the hapless pauper children but also on Drouet himself. 'A more kind-hearted or considerate man could not have been selected,' *Bell's* proposed, 'for the charge entrusted to him.'[38]

Grainger was no stranger to cholera, having witnessed at first hand how the 1831–2 epidemic had ravaged the London population. More recently he had been commissioned by the government to travel to the Continent, where in September 1848 he was able to study the progress of the disease in Hamburg and Berlin. He claimed that he had observed 'hundreds of cases' in 'every stage of the disease' in the course of his fact-finding tour, as well as reading the most recent publications and attending post mortem examinations of cholera victims conducted by 'the most celebrated pathologists of Europe'. Now, in the early weeks of 1849, grappling with the outbreak in Surrey Hall, he had an impressive fund of knowledge to draw on. He took as his starting point his unshakeable conviction that cholera was not a contagion. It was akin to fever, and fever thrived on noxious air, as the medical staff of hospitals learnt to their cost when they breathed in impurities emanating from their patients and fell ill themselves.[39]

As Grainger saw it, with its teeming rooms and its inadequate ventilation, Drouet's asylum had all the unhealthy features of an urban slum. Only a short time ago, while working in Scotland for the Metropolitan Sanitary Commission, he had come across a perfect illustration of the problem in a town near Glasgow, where the most deprived dwellings were encircled by a ditch filled with rotting rubbish.[40] It must have occurred to him that those who lived there, constantly breathing in the methane and hydrogen sulphide from the ditch, were in much the same plight as the children in Drouet's asylum, who played on a daily basis alongside the Streatham Drain.

On his return from Scotland, Grainger was reported as saying that 'the hearse was moving through the streets of Glasgow as through the city of the plague'.[41] However, even the man who was capable of this haunting imagery was ill-prepared for what he would find at Surrey Hall. The sight of the little corpses in the carpenter's workshop upset him more than the worst of the scenes he had encountered north of the border. He was reminded, painfully, of all he had seen and read in his travels abroad. The Berlin neurologist Moritz Heinrich Romberg had written in an 1832 treatise that a characteristic of so-called 'dry' cholera was the absence of tears, citing the example of a dying mother who had been unable to weep over the child she was about to abandon. Now, Grainger realised, the children dying in the asylum, tortured by cramp, were the counterparts of the German mother, crying out in agony but unable to shed tears. Long after his visits to Surrey Hall he was troubled by those cries.[42]

In the battle against cholera, Grainger insisted that prevention was better than cure. Preventative measures must include improving drainage, removing cesspools, and ensuring people had room enough to live in and clean air to breathe. But where the disease had taken hold, drastic treatments were called for. The official advice of the General Board of Health, as disseminated in the press, was to treat cholera with opium. One of the formulations the Board recommended required taking 'opiate confection' either with peppermint water or with a little weak brandy and water. Another proposed laudanum as the principal drug. Until the passing of the Pharmacy Act in 1868, laudanum could be bought over the counter in a chemist's shop. It was administered to cholera patients mixed with medicinal chalk and aromatic confection, and in severe cases with the addition of tincture of catechu, an astringent based on tannin. Chloroform was also able to alleviate the symptoms of cholera, and in June 1849 its use was described in a letter sent to *The Times* by John Fairfax Franklin, the rector of West Newton in Norfolk. In the absence of a medical practitioner, the clergyman had treated two of his parishioners with ten drops of chloroform in a glass of brandy, repeating the dose every ten minutes and rubbing the body and spine with spirits of turpentine to keep his patients warm.[43]

William James Kite had done much the same at Surrey Hall. On 10 January, in one of the regular updates he published in the major London dailies, he reported that he had administered chloroform 'with very good effect in more than one case'.[44] Although the use of chloroform in the treatment of cholera had its advocates, it had its critics too, and Kite was attacked by the British College of Health as 'the medical attendant' who was killing the very children he was trying to cure. The attack must have had some science behind it as the mortality rate at Surrey Hall was one that 'no doubt would occur with equal certainty in any large establishment if the same poisons were used for the cure of any supposed disease'. However, there was a personal element as well, and the College wondered 'what experience the medical attendant has in chloroform (which has sent so many to premature graves) and opium, thus to give them to children'. Kite might have responded that he was familiar with both the benefits and the dangers of chloroform, which would have been a waste of effort as the article was essentially an exercise in product promotion, the British College of Health being a cover for the manufacturers of Morison's Pills. A week later, in another advertisement, the College advised that 'the only safe remedy for cholera is Morison's Vegetable Universal Medicine, which, by cleansing the stomach and bowels, strikes at the root of the disease and eradicates it'. The medicine was, in reality, little more than a strong purgative made with aloes and gamboge.[45]

Whatever arguments raged over the efficacy of chloroform, it was universally agreed that a patient showing the symptoms of cholera had to be kept warm. There were many methods by which this could be achieved, and these were variously external, such as the application of heat packs and poultices, or internal, typically draughts of sal volatile, brandy in hot water, and sherry in hot milk. Another means of warming an ailing patient was the hot-air bath, a device for introducing heated air between the body and the bedclothes, the latter being held clear on a supporting framework. The hot-air bath had so powerful an effect that the patient's sweat might soak through the sheets and drip on to the floor. However, it was a treatment with wide support. When cholera broke out in Anchor and Hope Alley, at the south-east corner of the London docks, the Stepney guardians called for four hot-air baths, one to be placed with each of the three medical officers and one at the workhouse.[46]

An even more remarkable use of technology to treat cholera involved electricity. A girl from Surrey Hall aged about eight had been removed to the Royal Free Hospital in Gray's Inn Road. Because she had fallen into a state of complete collapse, she could not swallow, and it was impossible to treat her with medicine. When her case seemed all but hopeless, a hospital doctor by the name of Thomas Bevill Peacock suggested using a generator to bring her back from the brink. The details of Peacock's experiment were described in a letter a fellow doctor sent to *The Times*:

> Dr Peacock applied one pole of the galvanic machine over the heart, the other over the region of the stomach, or rather of the solar plexus (a sort of grand central terminus of the nerves, supplying all the viscera). In half a minute the child began to rally, some strong beef tea was got into her stomach in less than ten minutes, and ultimately the resurrection was complete.[47]

The use of the word 'resurrection' by a writer of a scientific turn of mind told its own story.

Chapter Six

The Parishes Act

In one of his angry letters to *The Times*, Sidney Godolphin Osborne recounted two cases of medical detective work. In the first, the royal staghounds at Windsor Home Park had succumbed, unaccountably, to an outbreak of kennel lameness. In the second, following the French Revolution of 1848, the exiled Louis Philippe had fallen victim to a mysterious illness at Claremont House that turned his teeth black and killed three members of his entourage. In both cases it was discovered that the devastation had been caused by drinking water contaminated by old lead pipes, and in both cases it was the high social standing of the victims, whether animal or human, that had given the investigations the necessary impetus. Having related these anecdotes, Osborne made an ironic comparison with the children who died in Surrey Hall: 'They were neither Royal hounds or Royal guests; they were merely pauper children, little living weights on the parochial rates of certain metropolitan parishes, farmed out to a man in whom of course all confidence was felt.'[1]

Osborne was not alone in his criticism of Drouet, and there would come a time when the outbreak of cholera, with all the publicity surrounding it, would lay bare the awful truth about Surrey Hall. However, in the early days of the crisis, Drouet attracted sympathy as the victim of an undeserved calamity. Remarkably, the workhouse guardians, who week after week were allowed on to the premises, often blithely ignored any possibility that conditions in the asylum might have been to blame. The Newington guardians, for example, who had seen for themselves the chaos in the wards, were still prepared to write a note in the visitors' book expressing their 'sincere commiseration for the painful and anxious situation' Drouet found himself in.[2] The Strand guardians were more than satisfied with the arrangements he was making, and one of the union medical officers, Benjamin Brookes, went as far as to praise him for the kindness he had shown the stricken children and the urgency with which he was attending to their needs. When Brookes spelled out what action had actually been taken, it amounted to no more than each bed being provided with three blankets and the bedclothes being cleaned, which cannot have cost Drouet much effort. In fairness, he had also drafted in three additional medical men, although even this measure might have underestimated the scale of the emergency.[3]

Another person with first-hand experience of Drouet was Keziah Dimond, who was a nurse and deputy matron at the Holborn workhouse. As she was the mother of two boys and a girl who had been inmates of Surrey Hall for over a year, and who narrowly escaped dying of cholera, it might be thought that she would be ill-disposed towards Drouet. Yet this appears not to have been the case. She had gone down to Lower Tooting on four occasions, and having actually witnessed her daughter eating a supper of bread and treacle, which was washed down with milk and water, she concluded that the diet was good in both quantity and quality. 'If I had seen any insufficiency in the food,' she said in her witness statement at Drouet's trial, 'or that it was improper in any respect, of course, as a mother, I should have complained.' She believed that he had been 'kind' to her children and had even thanked him for it, even though she had nursed many of those who had returned from Surrey Hall in frightful shape, emaciated and ravaged by diseases of the skin. She did not think that her position in the Holborn workhouse had any influence on how her daughter was treated. However, she never saw how her two boys or the boys in general fared.[4]

Others who were prepared to give Drouet a good character reference at the trial, or who at least were reluctant to be critical of him on the record, were his resident surgeon, William James Kite, and one of the Holborn guardians, Stephen Pearson. Kite, of course, heartily disapproved of nearly everything about the asylum, but he presented Drouet almost as a benign figure, a kindly man who basked in the respect and affection of all those around him. He denied ever having heard a child complain of being cold or underfed, which may well have been the case but only because the children were generally too afraid to complain. Nor had Kite heard the nurses complain on the children's behalf. Indeed, Kite had not heard anyone either inside or outside Surrey Hall complain about his employer, and neither for that matter had Pearson, who had in fact heard very good things said about Drouet's character, and said by many people, not only in Lower Tooting but also in Holborn.[5]

Pearson may well have been right about Drouet's reputation in Lower Tooting. A prominent local individual by the name of Samuel Curlewis Lord, a clergyman in his late fifties who ran a small boarding school at Fairfield House, also seemed to believe that the residents thought highly of him. At any rate, he said as much, very publicly, to a group of distinguished gentlemen who visited on 6 January to inspect the asylum with Richard Dugard Grainger. Of course, his generosity towards Drouet may well have represented his true feelings, but it is equally possible that in the presence of outsiders, and outsiders with a professional interest in the circumstances surrounding the outbreak of cholera, he simply wanted to be tactful.[6]

It is not clear if Drouet himself took the visitors round, but his half-brother Richard was certainly on hand and answered at least one of Grainger's questions about the state of the asylum. There were also two Surrey Hall insiders, Charles and Walter Chapman, who had both been helping Kite in the sick wards and must have had as good a knowledge as anyone of the nature and progress of the disease. The concerns of the medical profession were represented by two doctors from the St Pancras workhouse, Henry Charles Robinson and Thomas Eld Baker, who had visited the asylum earlier that week and seen the conditions for themselves. A third visitor from the same workhouse was Henry Hetherington. He was a 'director of the poor', as the St Pancras guardians were called. But he was also, significantly, a radical publisher and journalist who tirelessly championed working-class causes.[7]

While it was of immediate importance to see how the asylum was dealing with the impact of the outbreak, questions about its causes also needed to be addressed. To this end, the General Board of Health had instructed the drains and sewers expert Thomas Lovick to accompany Grainger on his inspection of Surrey Hall. It was Lovick who would raise awareness of the horrors of the Streatham Drain in the report he submitted to the Board soon after his return, and his highly critical observations on the flooding of the fields with raw sewage, which were published a week later by all the London newspapers, must have been carefully noted by the health officers from the neighbouring parish of Streatham.[8] In fact, the Streatham authorities had sent their own representatives to join Grainger's inspection. They must have walked round the premises in a state of disbelief.

Along with Lord, the interests of the residents of Lower Tooting were represented by Erasmus Gilbert Livesay, who was quite a connoisseur on the subject of the Streatham Drain and the general problem of sewage.[9] Well might Lord have styled himself and his colleague as 'a deputation from the principal inhabitants'. Not only were they local health officers whose responsibility it was to identify and deal with sources of unacceptable filth in and around the village, but, as proprietors of private boarding schools, they had personal reasons for wanting to keep Lower Tooting clean. Clearly their concerns were as driven by commercial factors as they were by the recommendations of the General Board of Health. In happier times, Livesay would place an advertisement for his school at Eldon House in the *Daily News* in which he made a great deal of its attractions, principally the liberal values it upheld, the modest fees it charged parents, the generous diet it offered its pupils, and its airy and extensive premises. But by way of enhancing the appeal of the school, he then added that 'the village is perfectly free from disease, and fully maintains its established character for healthy situation'. The following week he placed a similar advertisement in the *News* in which he tried to limit the inevitable damage done by reports of cholera in the local pauper establishment, insisting that 'late events have rather increased than diminished' the village's healthy character, 'as it is, and has been, totally free from any disease of an infectious nature'.[10]

For all that the asylum was riddled with serious defects, Lord was at pains to speak on behalf of Drouet, who, as a man of business, would have been regarded by 'respectable' residents of Lower Tooting as one of their own. He was prepared to say that they considered him 'kind in the extreme' in his dealings with the children, although he did not explain on what evidence this judgement was based. His point was that although the residents resented Drouet's establishment, which, to no one's surprise, had been incapacitated by the arrival from outside of a lethal epidemic disease, they did not for one moment resent Drouet himself. They only hoped that steps would be taken to remove his unhappy asylum from the place it occupied at the centre of their crowded village, and they would cheerfully put their hands in their pockets to see it relocated. Lord, who was sensitive to proprieties, stopped just short of saying that no one wanted in excess of 1,400 pauper children in their backyard.[11]

Lord was being extraordinarily diplomatic, and it is perfectly possible that, as a man of the cloth, he was reluctant on principle to damn Drouet openly. However, some very different attitudes were on display a week later

Newgate Prison seen from outside the Old Bailey. Walter Thornbury, *Old and New London*, 1878.

The 1861 census enumerator visiting a poverty-stricken family in a Gray's Inn Lane tenement in Holborn. *Illustrated Times*, 13 April 1861.

Sieving and shovelling in a dust yard, not unlike the residents of Charlotte's Buildings 'working at the carrion heaps'. Henry Mayhew, *London Labour and the London Poor*, 1861.

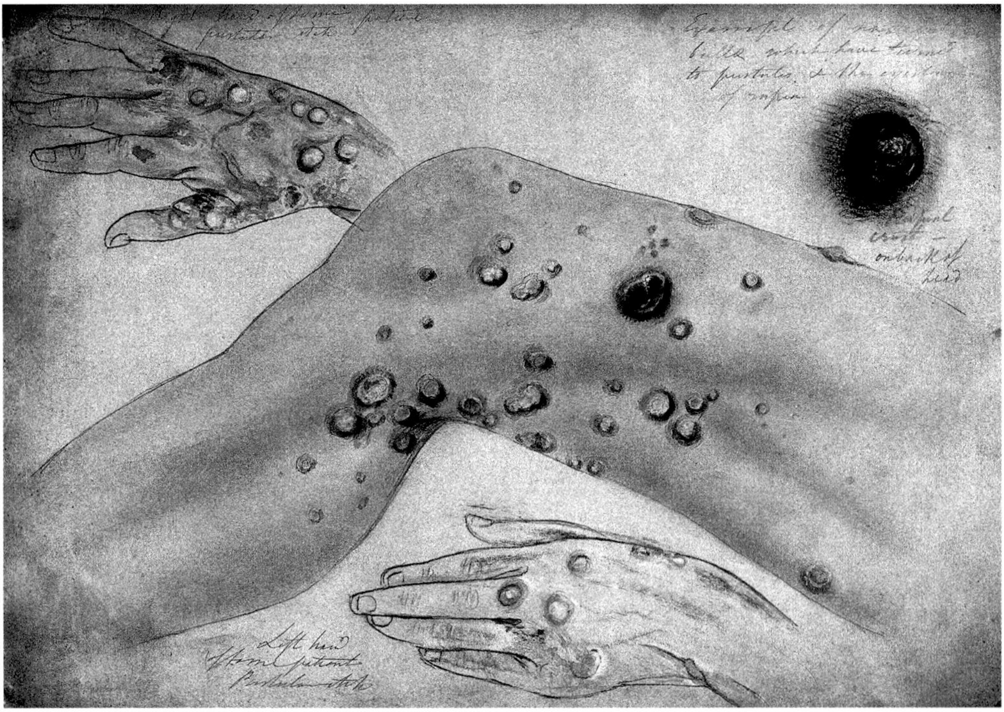

Diseased skin and boils on the hands, head and leg of a woman, showing symptoms of 'pustular itch'. Watercolour by Christopher D'Alton dated 1866. Wellcome Collection.

South west view of St Nicholas Church in Tooting, dated 1832, by Thomas Witlam Atkinson. London Picture Archive.

The Angel Inn in Tooting. W. E. Morden, *The History of Tooting-Graveney, Surrey*, 1897.

Lightermen at work on the River Thames. Henry Mayhew, *London Labour and the London Poor*, 1861.

The only surviving image of Surrey Hall and the White House as they were at the time of the cholera outbreak. *The Illustrated London News*, 20 January 1849.

Mezzotint of a young Richard Dugard Grainger by Thomas Goff Lupton, dated 1827, after Thomas Charles Wageman. Wellcome Collection.

A meeting of the General Board of Health in Gwydyr House in Whitehall. *The Illustrated London News*, 6 October 1849.

Children being carefully supervised in the playground and exercise area of the Home and Colonial Infant School Society in Gray's Inn Lane in Holborn. *The Illustrated London News*, 13 May 1843.

Page from a book of prescriptions dated c. 1850 belonging to Mary Susan Selby-Laundes with a remedy for cholera. Wellcome Collection.

Sidney Godolphin Osborne, who attacked Drouet in letters published in *The Times* in January and February 1849. *The Illustrated London News*, 25 May 1889.

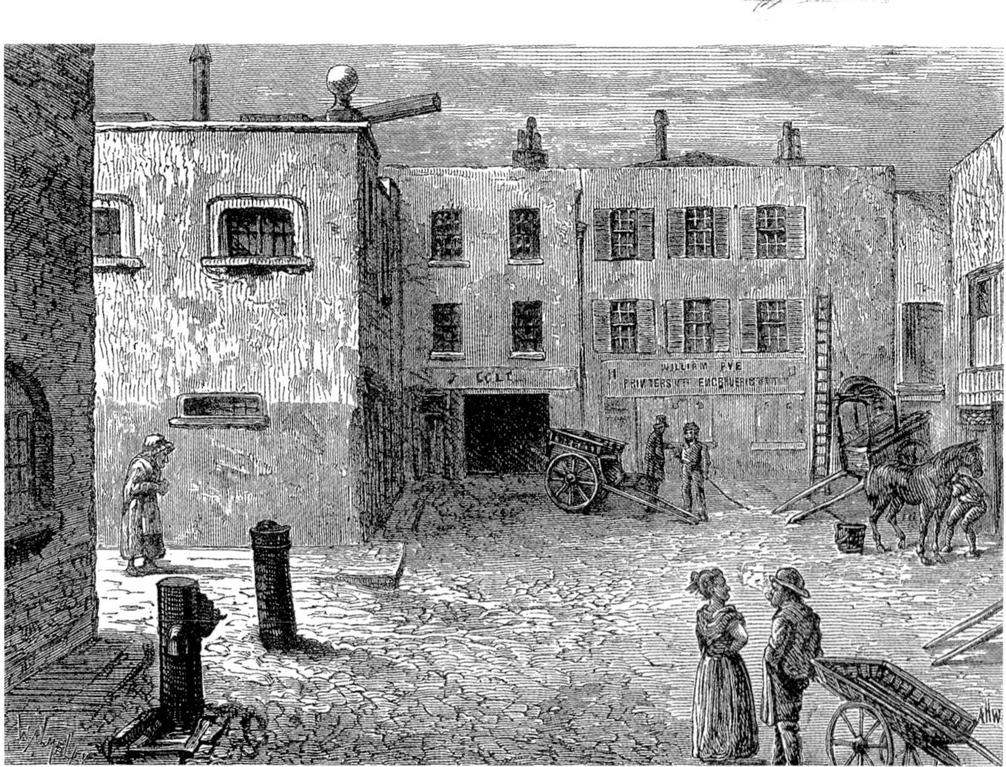

Bleeding Heart Yard in Holborn. Walter Thornbury, *Old and New London*, 1878.

A boy mudlarking down by the River Thames. Henry Mayhew, *London Labour and the London Poor*, 1861.

The Royal Free Hospital in Gray's Inn Road, where the children from the Holborn workhouse were treated after being removed from Surrey Hall. *The Pictorial Times*, 29 July 1843.

Curious spectators watching a coffin being carried into the crowded parish burial ground in Paradise Street in Lambeth. *The Illustrated London News*, 15 September 1849.

Double page from the Tooting Graveney burial register showing entries for children from the Juvenile Pauper Establishment, or Surrey Hall, with 'C' for cholera in the margins. The London Archives.

St Mary's burial ground surrounded by the Russell Court tenements off Drury Lane. *Tait's Edinburgh Magazine*, December 1848.

Stipple engraving of Thomas Wakley
by William Henry Egleton after
Joseph Kenny Meadows. Wellcome
Collection.

Portrait of Charles Dickens, dated ten years
after the Surrey Hall scandal, engraved
by Robert Graves after an oil painting by
William Powell Frith. John Forster, *The Life of
Charles Dickens*, 1873.

Sir Frederic Thesiger, who defended Drouet at his
trial in April 1849. *The Illustrated London News*,
19 October 1878.

Trial in progress at the Central Criminal Court. *The Illustrated London News*, 4 March 1843.

Postcard showing Cliff Terrace, the Drouets' corner of Margate, in the early 20th century. From the author's collection.

View of Margate not long after the time of the Drouets. *The Illustrated London News*, 16 August 1851.

The ivy-covered Old Vestry Hall in Tooting photographed in 1887. London Picture Archive.

Postcard showing Tooting Broadway in the 1920s with the public baths at the left-hand margin. Reproduced with kind permission of Philip Bradley.

The North Surrey District School at Anerley. *The Illustrated London News*, 20 July 1850.

Churchyard of St Nicholas Church in Tooting. Photograph by the author.

Plaque on a wall of St Nicholas Church in Tooting commemorating the children who died of cholera in Surrey Hall and were buried in the churchyard. Photograph by the author.

at a meeting of ratepayers and other residents of Lower Tooting at the Rising Sun, a public house on the north side of the road leading to Mitcham. Drouet had not been invited, and he would in any case have been wise to stay away as the subject under discussion was his asylum, and feelings were running high. Livesay, who was in the chair, catalogued Drouet's failings. Unlike his colleague Lord, he expressed himself vigorously, possibly because he was not a man of the cloth, though more likely because he did not have an audience of government officials and other inquisitive outsiders. He looked on Drouet's establishment as an utter abomination. Drouet owned fifty-two acres of land and yet the premises in which he kept hordes of unfortunate little paupers occupied not much more than seven. The only inmates to be given the full run of all that land were the older boys who were sent out into the fields at haymaking time. Drouet was motivated solely by profit: he had made 'a pretty tolerable income' from the suffering of children 'whose only crime is that they are poor'.[12]

Livesay had judged the mood of the meeting to perfection. His audience voiced their approval of the various criticisms he made of the asylum, and when he declared that the little inmates 'should be taken as much care of as the children of richer persons' because 'they are human beings like ourselves', he was greeted with cheers from the floor. And he had nothing especially flattering to say about Drouet himself. Far from being 'kind in the extreme' to the children, which was the bland assessment Lord had offered on the Saturday tour, Livesay asserted that Drouet was a venal operator who had given into the temptation of making a lot of money under the protective umbrella of the Poor Laws. He wholeheartedly agreed with Lord that the asylum had to be abolished. If there had to be establishments of this sort, then they needed to be suitably located, designed along modern lines to obviate incidents of disease, paid for collectively by the boards of guardians, and run by competent managers. To dissuade these managers from profiteering, they must be paid a decent salary of, say, £500 a year.[13]

*   *   *

When Drouet was interviewed by three Chelsea guardians and asked how he accounted for the outbreak of cholera, he attributed it to a fog that had settled over the village seven days previously. To anyone acquainted with the killer fogs of the mid-nineteenth-century capital, this explanation would not in itself have seemed remotely ridiculous. However, as one of the guardians pointed out, cholera had only broken out in Surrey Hall, whereas a fog carrying the disease would surely have had a wider impact. Drouet was forced to shift his position, but because he was anxious to steer attention away from the filth in his premises, he suggested as an alternative cause of the outbreak the smells from the public sewer on the borders of his property.[14]

Hand in hand with the confusion over how cholera had entered the asylum went the fear that it might escape its confinement. It did not take long for a rumour to surface in the London newspapers that the disease had spread to the village.[15] No evidence for this was ever found, but the anxiety persisted, and Livesay was critical of Drouet for not immediately calling on the parishes to take their children away. The first case of cholera was detected on a Saturday but no official announcement was made until the following Wednesday, and the boarding school proprietor was at a loss to justify a delay that must have cost some children their lives. If cholera ever broke out in Eldon House, he would use all means at his disposal to get his young charges home as quickly as possible, assuming, of course, that they were not already ill. He would not wait for parents to come down, and he most definitely would not keep pupils on the premises in isolation, which was the accepted practice in cases of routine childhood illnesses such as scarlet fever and measles. The Middlesex coroner, Thomas Wakley, commenting later on a collective failure to respond rapidly to the crisis, saw it in terms of social equality. All children, whether their parents were affluent or impoverished, ought to be given the same care and attention.[16]

The coroner regarded the guardians as the 'natural protectors' of the children in Surrey Hall, which, ironically, was the reason given in some quarters for the many criticisms levelled at these workhouse officials during and after the cholera crisis. As there was an expectation that they would save their children by immediately removing them from Surrey Hall, newspaper editorials did not hesitate to subject them to intense scrutiny. They were also seen now as being in part responsible for the tragedy because week in and week out they had observed the state of the asylum without taking effective action. 'The guardians of the various unions,' the *Northern Star* fulminated, 'and their medical officers, hurried down to Tooting, on the heels of each other, and found out – what they ought to have known before – that the poor imprisoned creatures, in that abominable cesspool of infantile wretchedness, were under-fed and over-crowded. They died like rotten sheep.' The *Star*, while denouncing the asylum as a 'great mint' where 'shivering and helpless orphanhood and poverty were to be coined into gold', also poured scorn on the 'honourable and respectable' guardians, who seemed to think that all was in order. They connived with Drouet, selfishly and cruelly, until cholera found them out.[17]

While it is obvious that the guardians had been complacent, looking round the asylum with their eyes closed, questioning children in the presence of intimidating Surrey Hall adults, and filing approving reports, it is a matter for speculation why this was so. Possibly their interest in the children was compromised by distance. The children had been sent away from the parishes to a small village beyond the limits of the city, and, as a result, they had faded from view. They had freed up space both in the workhouse and in the consciousness of the guardians. Because they were the offspring of pauper parents, they were easy to forget and easy to ignore, the more so now that they had been removed to Lower Tooting. They were visited, but in the view of *The Times* the visits were a mockery because the guardians had failed both to draw self-evident conclusions from 'the pallid look, the shrunken limb, the bloated stomach' of the children and to act on the dismal sight of 'the filthy ill-ventilated holes, in which the poor little wretches were thrust at night'.[18] Some even ridiculed these visits to the home of starving children as a ghastly sort of 'jolly' financed by the ratepayers. 'The guardians often came to Tooting,' reported a medical officer of the St Pancras workhouse, 'but Mr Drouet's larder was well stocked, and after a long ride, with sharpened appetites, the good things were laid before them, and it was not surprising that, under such circumstances, their eyes were not very sharp.'[19]

At first, Drouet had hesitated to send word to the parishes, and even when he did, beginning on the Tuesday, it was under pressure from Chapman and Kite. From that point on the messages simply flew out from Surrey Hall. Drouet also notified the Poor Law Board, and because he had come to realise that the help he needed would only be found in a large London hospital, he sent an urgent message to Thomas Addison, the senior physician at Guy's.[20] Meanwhile, the number of deaths had already reached double figures, and Kite had the unpleasant task of forwarding death certificates to William Carter, the Surrey coroner. Only later would he learn of Carter's decision not to hold an inquest on the grounds that the children had died from known causes and under medical supervision.[21]

St Pancras was the first of the parishes to act, and a committee of four guardians went with all possible speed down to Surrey Hall. What ensued was an odd comedy of manners played out against a background of disease and death. To begin with, Tuesday was not a scheduled St Pancras visiting day, and even though Drouet had informed the parishes of events in Surrey Hall, he probably did not expect guardians to turn up on his door without prior arrangement. Nonetheless, as a matter of common courtesy, he invited the visiting committee to eat with him, but he was dealt a second blow to his dignity when his guests refused to touch the food he offered them. They feared that it might be contaminated. However, they drank wine and brandy from the bottles on the table, not so much as an indulgence as a precaution before going into the cholera wards. These alcoholic drinks were widely and erroneously believed to be preventatives against the disease.[22]

The scenes the committee witnessed in the cholera wards must have affected them deeply. Once they had submitted their report on their return to London, the board resolved that two or three of their members, one of them a doctor, visit Surrey Hall every day, or every other day.[23] Some other parishes were equally swift to make emergency arrangements, but there were also instances of almost inexplicable delay. The guardians of Wandsworth and Clapham, for example, heard about the outbreak of cholera for the first time when the master of the workhouse, Henry Knapp, read out Drouet's messages at the regular Thursday meeting of the board, which was a whole two days after they had been received.[24] In an equally striking display of dithering, the Chelsea guardians pushed back an emergency visit that might have taken place on the Wednesday, which was the day they received a message from Drouet, to the Friday. In the course of the two days' delay, Charlotte and James Morgan, aged ten and seven, and Elizabeth Only, aged nine, came down with cholera and died. They were buried in the village churchyard at ten o'clock on the Friday night.[25]

The Fulham guardians also failed to cover themselves in glory. Drouet sent no fewer than three letters on the Thursday and Friday, but it was only on the Saturday that the board met to discuss them. They are terrible documents. 'I am sorry to state cholera has seized upon many of the children,' Drouet wrote in the first, which was sent on the Thursday, 'and I find Emma Lucas

& Jessey Cole' – Jesse Finecole – 'are very ill from it.' 'Very late this evening,' he wrote in the second, which was also sent on the Thursday, 'in going over the names of the children suffering from cholera I find the child Garlick' – Maria Garlick – 'is amongst them and cannot live.' Perhaps inevitably, when he sent the third on the Friday, he was obliged to report that Jesse and Maria had died. They had been buried in the village churchyard at ten o'clock that night. Both were seven years old. Emma would be buried three days later. She was ten.[26]

The guardians of the Strand workhouse were slow movers too, acting only on the Saturday. Six days previously, at two o'clock in the afternoon, the master of the workhouse, Daniel Haybittle, had received a letter from Drouet with the names of children suffering from a bowel complaint. Haybittle had done nothing. In his eyes a bowel complaint was a minor ailment, and the mother of a child who had been brought back from Surrey Hall, with whom he discussed the matter, agreed. As a result the guardians were left in the dark: the first they heard of the crisis was an alert from the clerk, James Kilner, who chanced upon a brief report in the Thursday edition of *The Times*. Even then it was a minor miracle that Kilner read the report at all, as it was short and had to vie for attention with such competing items as the price of raw materials and foodstuffs and the firing of six farms in County Down.[27] An evening meeting of the board was convened, and it was resolved that a committee of four, accompanied by Dr Brookes, visit the asylum the next morning. The guardians must have assumed that their children were dying, seeing as they passed a further resolution that parents were to be informed of fatalities immediately and given the opportunity of attending funerals. The bodies of the dead were only to be brought back with the board's permission, though, in order to prevent the spread of the disease.[28]

* * *

Benjamin Brookes was only one of many medical officers sent down to Surrey Hall from the workhouses. They were remarkable for their collective expertise, several having had military careers in the course of which they had become acquainted with the problems of poor hygiene, inadequate diet and overcrowded wards. Thomas Eld Baker from St Pancras, for example, who was in his late fifties, claimed that in his twenty-four years as a surgeon in the Bengal Army he had treated 'hundreds upon hundreds' of cases of cholera. His colleague Henry Charles Robinson was the son of a military man, although he was qualified in a different way to treat Drouet's children, in being the father of six daughters.[29]

The outstanding example of a doctor with ideal credentials must surely be Robert Semple, the Islington workhouse medical officer. He had been a surgeon in the Royal Navy and was a seasoned professional, one of three doctors appointed to the Islington Cholera Hospital in River Lane at the time of the 1831–2 cholera epidemic. He and his two colleagues had worked to scrupulous standards, each taking 'his regular turn of duty as on board a ship' in order to assess accurately the condition of the patients and ensure that the returns were sent to government health officials. He adopted a similar routine at Surrey Hall, visiting frequently and going through the wards repeatedly. Since the conditions were chaotic, he had difficulty examining the children as thoroughly as he would have wished, but in almost all of them he recognised the symptoms of cholera. He was horrified at the awfulness of it all. Because he treated poor patients in Islington every day, he was familiar with the realities of serious disease, but the suffering of the children in Drouet's asylum was in a class of its own.[30]

Robert Banks Penny, a doctor who was summoned by Drouet from his home in Walworth, must be considered something of a maverick. Although he had no association with any of the London workhouses, he had an impressive *curriculum vitae*. Having completed his medical studies, he worked at Guy's Hospital for a year before establishing a practice in Lambeth. In time he moved to Woolwich, where, in 1844, and in his late twenties, he not only married but also enlisted as a naval surgeon. In 1846 he was on board the *Java*, a troop ship that had put in at Calcutta, when a virulent strain of cholera broke among the 400 labourers working on the upper deck. The sick were taken to the Calcutta General Hospital. About two dozen died, and at first Penny assumed that they had been laid low by fetid air floating up from the hold, though he dismissed the theory on the grounds that there had been nothing in the hold but water. He had stumbled upon the true cause of cholera, which is contaminated water, only he could not see it for what it was. But it struck him as odd that all the men who fell ill had been working on the same side of the ship. Likewise, in one the boys' wards in Surrey Hall, cholera had chosen its victims from one side of the room but not from the other, or so he was told by the nurses. The disease had advanced, mysteriously, inexplicably, in a straight line.[31]

Little did Penny know, as he watched over Drouet's children, that death of a more personal sort was waiting in the wings to claim a son who had been born to him in the late summer of 1848. The child died in the spring of 1849, having convulsed for nine days while teething. His parents buried him in the churchyard of St Mary, off Kennington Lane, where children from the Newington workhouse who had been at Drouet's already lay. Sarah James was fourteen years old and had died after two days of cholera and four of typhoid fever. William Grafton, aged ten, had struggled with cholera for a day and a half, while Horatio Fuller, aged nine, was gone in thirteen hours. They were just poor children: names in a register, bodies in a shared grave.[32]

Alongside the doctors were the nurses employed by Drouet or sent down to Surrey Hall by the workhouses. It would be difficult to overstate the hardships they must have endured. The beds were so close together that to get to one a nurse had to clamber over others. Foul-smelling slops covered the floors and made the stairs slippery. At times the responsibility must have been almost too much to bear, especially for the younger nurses like Sarah Sellers and Elizabeth Elliott, who had been sent down from St Pancras to take sole charge of a ward of thirty-three boys, even though they were both still in their twenties. They had arrived at midnight to find the ward in a filthy state, and from that point on they laboured incessantly. Two boys helped with the cleaning, but there was little else these undersized assistants could do, and the two nurses toiled for eight days and nights without ever changing out of their work clothes, and barely sleeping. Their heroic efforts did not go unnoticed, though. Grainger praised them for their selfless conduct, and they were rewarded with gifts of money by some benevolent individuals, whose names, sadly, are not known.[33]

Sarah in particular had shown exceptional dedication. She caught cholera herself, and although she was extremely ill, and suffered greatly with vomiting and diarrhoea, she struggled on.[34] Other nurses who fell ill were not so fortunate, and four who belonged to the asylum, and had therefore been in close contact with sick children from the start of the outbreak, did not recover. Louisa Batterbee, Elizabeth Gardner and Maria Warren died of cholera, Elizabeth Bazzone of typhoid fever. Given that they were all in their fifties and sixties, it is possible that they were enfeebled by age. But the young schoolmistress Sarah Goat, who was twenty-three, also came down with cholera and died.[35] It would seem that no one was safe, and even Drouet, his half-brother Richard, and William James Kite fell ill, vomiting violently, and were probably lucky to survive.[36]

*   *   *

In Grainger's view the shortage of nursing staff was lamentable. By the end of the first week, nearly 200 children had come down with cholera. He wanted four nurses working in any of the eight wards with twelve or more patients, and three nurses in the less populated wards with fewer than twelve patients. He had explained the need for this number of nurses to Drouet on the Friday, and yet, to his astonishment, he discovered on the Sunday that his recommendations had been ignored. Drouet tried to excuse himself on the grounds that both he and Kite had understood him to be asking for four additional nurses across all eight wards, and no more, but Grainger was far from impressed. It must have crossed his mind that Drouet had not so much misunderstood his instructions as balked at the costs involved. But the causes of Drouet's inaction were of far less moment than its consequences, which were, principally, that the children who had already succumbed to the disease were being left lying in bedclothes soaked with their own evacuations, and then, equally worryingly, that those who were still on their feet had been drafted in to help in the wards.[37]

Grainger, who had effectively taken over at Surrey Hall, was nothing if not energetic, and he must have achieved more in the short space of his visits than Drouet over the course of many years. As well as more nurses, he wanted a greater presence of doctors, one of whom should ideally be a cholera specialist. He wanted the bodies of children who died to be disposed of by burying them in the local churchyard within twenty-four hours of death, not by waiting for the parishes to collect them. He also wanted two outstanding problems to be addressed, one of which was to remove a major cause of disease by digging out the Streatham Drain, while the other was to find a way of relieving the overcrowding that had long been, and continued to be, a blight on the asylum.[38]

As the first of these was too urgent a task to be left to Drouet, who had after all already made a botched attempt at dredging 'his' stretch of the

Drain, Grainger referred it to the General Board of Health. That was on his return from Surrey Hall on the Friday, and he must have made a strong case because on the Saturday morning a gang of labourers were spotted in the village, ready to drive their shovels into the accumulated faecal matter clogging the ditches. There were about fifty of these navvies, and when they appeared in the streets of the village, kitted out and equipped for the struggles that lay ahead, they must have caused quite a stir. As it turned out, they were not needed, because Grainger had come to realise that dredging the Drain would be hazardous, especially while children still remained in the asylum. A safer procedure would be to flush out the channels with water from the artesian wells, which, as one admiring newspaper put it, would be equivalent to the cleansing of the Augean Stables. Grainger was a latter-day Hercules, the editorial suggested, proposing 'to turn a stream of water through the pestilential ditch'.[39]

The other problem, that of thinning out the population of the asylum, required the parishes to remove their children. Actually, the process had already begun in response to the messages Drouet had been sending out, but it was not a coordinated effort, and Grainger realised that an evacuation would only be fully effective if he threw his weight behind it. In fact, Grainger was not the first person of authority to call for this drastic measure. Early on, Thomas Addison had said to the medical men at Surrey Hall that it was 'absolutely necessary' to separate the healthy children from the unhealthy, and it was on the strength of his appeals that Walter Chapman was able to persuade the Wandsworth and Clapham guardians to rescue their children without delay. Shortly afterwards other parishes also made their move.[40]

It was estimated that 500 children had been removed by the end of the first week of the crisis. Grainger conceded that the workhouses were under pressure because medical officers had to examine children and make difficult decisions as to who among them were free enough of disease to be removed, and also because alternative accommodation had to be located and made ready.[41] The procedure was made all the more stressful by the need to move rapidly, and it was perhaps inevitable that it met with some resistance. The Strand guardians, for example, were driven to act only when they received letters, both dated 6 January, one from Benjamin Brookes and the other from Henry Austin, the secretary to the General Board of Health. Austin had the greater clout, and the most apathetic clerk of a workhouse board would have been hard pushed to ignore a letter sent on Her Majesty's Service from the Secretary of State's Office at Gwydyr House in Whitehall, in an envelope on which 'immediate and important' had been written and underlined. Both writers emphasised that no time should be lost in taking the children to a place of safety, but it was Brookes who had the figures and was able to assure the guardians that '4 only of our children have died nor have I heard that any out of the 30 sick are likely to die of cholera', and that there was still time to limit the damage and prevent the fatalities from getting out of hand.[42]

Even those parishes that understood how serious the matter was foresaw problems. At a meeting of the St Pancras vestry, one of the union doctors pushed for quarantining the children in a building outside the city. Another argued for returning them to the workhouse, where, with suitable precautions, the girls' schoolhouse would provide adequate accommodation and would be sufficiently isolated to minimise the spread of disease. The only danger of 'contamination' arose from the effect housing the children in this way might have on weak-minded adult paupers, a dark hint that sexual temptation might prove too much for predatory inmates. In the event, though, it was cholera that did the damage; nearly half of the 200 or so children brought back from Surrey Hall were ill, and eleven died.[43] Outside St Pancras other solutions were found. The Strand guardians were given access to the House of Refuge, a building in Little Ogle Street in Marylebone belonging to the Society for the Relief of the Destitute Houseless Poor, while their Fulham colleagues hired part of a farmhouse in Wormholt Scrubs.[44]

In complete contrast, Chelsea made heroic efforts not to take their children back, holding out against two directives, one from the General Board of Health and the other from the Poor Law Board. A third communication was a letter dated 8 January and addressed to the chairman of the board of guardians. It had been written by Drouet himself, and he could not have made it more obvious that the situation he was faced with had got beyond his control, and that he had reached the end of his tether:

Dear Sir, It is impossible for me to describe the misery there is here; fresh cases are being reported every moment; there has [*sic*] been up to last night 20 cases, six have died belonging to Chelsea and I fear more will die. It is strange to see the poor little things go off, in fact, they are gone before we know it, and that accounts for little Jordan being found on the floor. We have day and night doctors, two from the Board of Health, and – Grainger Esq.

from the Board of Health is here daily, he was here all day yesterday; day and night nurses; and visits from all sorts of medical men and others that know anything about cholera. Nearly 700 children have left and today more will leave and it is intended that all the children are to be removed. I expect by this time you have had notice from the Board of Health to that effect. I am sorry to state several of the children that have been taken away have died since. It therefore requires care where to put them that the disorder may not spread.[45]

The little Jordan who was found on the floor was Sarah Jordan. She was seven years old. She had fallen sick on 3 January, and three days later, under pressure to 'sign off' the dead without unnecessary delay, Kite had certified what he assumed was her death. In point of fact, she was not dead, and she rallied. That was on 6 January. But just when it seemed that Sarah had been brought back to life, the miracle proved to be an illusion. For on the next day she collapsed and died.[46]

While Chelsea dug their heels in, other parishes hastened to rescue their children, and the residents of Lower Tooting were dismayed to see workhouse vehicles trundling down the High Street, a sure sign of the chaos in Surrey Hall. Later, the vehicles trundled back up the High Street and away from the village with their cargo of frightened little refugees, who were all escaping Drouet, though some were bringing disease with them and were fated to die. The traffic went on all day, and it was watched closely by the residents, who shook their heads in consternation and asked each other what on earth was going on.[47]

These rescue operations, which so startled the residents of Lower Tooting, were carried out in the glare of unwanted publicity. 'The whole and the sick were crammed into omnibuses pell-mell,' the *Northern Star* declared, 'and driven off with all speed from the pest house.' In doing so, the guardians 'showed as little common sense as they had formerly done of common humanity'.[48] They had given the disease free rein to spread where it wanted, as far as it wanted, unhindered and unchecked. As if to prove the point, deaths were reported in the workhouses. In the case of Kensington, these were a particularly cruel irony in that the removal of its children was in response not to cholera but to the sexual outrages perpetrated in the previous year by Richard Drouet. The girls had already been taken back in early November, and it may have been an unfortunate consequence of the unavoidable souring of relations that when the guardians took the boys back in the first week in January, they had not been warned that they might be bringing cholera with them.[49]

Wandsworth and Clapham also returned some of their evacuated children to the workhouse, where it was noted by the medical officer that they nearly all had loose bowels. Two in fact had succumbed to cholera: eight-year-old Charlotte Cartwright from Wandsworth would live for only another four days and six-year-old Edward Goodchild from Putney had already died. However, the children who were not returned to the workhouse were either sent back to their friends and families or, if they were friendless, placed out 'at nurse' with ratepayers in the parishes in exchange for a weekly allowance. In this way, Drouet's cholera might have done its terrible work in the very heart of the home.[50]

Chapter Seven

James Andrews

James Andrews was born early in the morning of 20 July 1842 in Union Court in Holborn. He had a brother, Joseph, two years his senior. Their father was another Joseph. Their mother was Ann. At the time of James's birth, the Andrews were living at No. 22. Joseph père, who was in his mid-thirties, was a house or sign painter, and whatever money he made from this occupation can only barely have kept the wolf from the door. When he died, in 1849, a sick man with a diseased liver but still a young man, he was living in the Holborn workhouse.[1] Even before he went into the workhouse, when he lived with his wife and two sons in Union Court, he could provide for his family no more than the meanest accommodation at an address they shared with several other people. In the 1841 census, along with the Andrews, No. 22 was occupied by two porters and their wives, a brass turner and his wife and their little daughter, and an elderly woman who scratched a living making boxes for hats and other ladylike accoutrements. Elsewhere in Union Court, over the next few years, there would be tinplate workers, picture frame makers, birdcage manufacturers, a plumber, a French polisher, and a self-styled artist in fireworks.[2]

The children of these slum quarters led a wild and independent existence. Many were 'mudlarks' who roamed the riversides at low tide with their trousers tucked up above their knees, picking up or digging out pieces of coal that had fallen from the barges. They would carry off the coal in bags or baskets to hawk round the streets of their neighbourhood. Near the shipyards they might find iron rivets or washers, strips of copper, bits of rope or canvas, all of which they would sell to marine stores along with the occasional lump of fat thrown overboard by a ship's cook. They would collect and sell the wood chippings and lengths of timber that floated down from where the boatbuilders worked, and they would take any tools they found either to the shops or to the seamen, who would give them scraps of food in exchange. They might work in teams of twenty or thirty, going out early in the morning or late in the afternoon, entirely at the discretion of the tides. Should they tread on nails or splinters of glass sticking up from the bed of the river, they would dash home to wrap a dressing round the wound. But they would be back as soon as they could. They were fighting starvation, and they needed to carry on mudlarking while time was on their side.[3]

To anyone looking down from one of the river's bridges, the mudlarks must indeed have seemed like little birds hopping over the slimy banks and splashing through the shallows. They were not much liked, though, and they were especially disliked by the boatmen. For not all mudlarking was honest scavenging. The boys would lift one another on to the barges as they lay at rest on their moorings, and knock lumps of coal or pieces of iron into the water. Later, when the barges moved off, they would retrieve their spoils from the river. All too often their pilfering matured into regular burglary, and then, if they were bold, they would clamber down into the cabins of the barges. Most were good swimmers, and if they were surprised by the bargemen or the river police, they would jump into the water to evade arrest.[4]

James was admitted to the workhouse on Tuesday, 29 August 1848, aged six. With him were his father and brother, and though his brother Joseph was older, he too was just a boy.[5] No trace of their mother Ann has survived. She might also have been in the workhouse, and her name might have been buried in a list of institutionalised paupers that is now lost. Equally, she might have been abandoned by her husband, or she might have abandoned him. She might have remarried, in which case her name would have turned off on to another route through the censuses and the workhouse returns, probably never to be recovered. Or she might have been dead, as is strongly suggested by the fact that in 1849, when his personal details were entered on his death certificate, Joseph was a widower. Even so, it has not been established that it was Ann and not a later wife who had died, any more than it has been established in what year she had died, whoever she was.

However, it is reasonable to assume that it was the death of his wife that drove Joseph to take himself and the two boys into the workhouse. His life had fallen apart, and given what is known about his physical condition at the time of his own death, it is likely that he was drinking heavily. Above all, it is surely the case that whatever trouble had befallen the family, the decision Joseph took was difficult and its implications profound. He and his two little sons would have been a pitiful sight as they stood at the entrance to the Union House in Gray's Inn Lane. The sky on that late summer Tuesday was overcast, and showers were breaking out every now and then, as if even the weather recognised that this was not a propitious moment for the Andrews family. Joseph would have been interviewed by a relieving officer. His circumstances would have been laid bare and his entitlement to the help of the parish closely scrutinised. He would have been separated from his children, and his children in their turn would have been separated one from the other as they were in different 'classes', with one being above and the other below seven years of age. From that point on, there would have been no possibility of contact between them. They were each on their own.[6]

Before long the two brothers were dispatched to Surrey Hall. This was bound to happen because the workhouse was full, and the guardians were sending the children away in order to free up room for adult paupers, and above all for paupers who were sick or classified as lunatic. They sent some away in August, which was when Joseph went, having been in the workhouse for only two weeks. They then sent more away in September and October, and it was on 28 October that James, like Joseph, went down to Surrey Hall. With him went fourteen little Holborn mates. Before they left they were examined by the medical officer, who passed them as fit to go. It was a blinkered examination, in a way, because it tested mainly for itch. Children might be undernourished, frightened and alone, but as long as they were free of itch, they were deemed fit to go. And so James and his companions were bundled into a horse-drawn van. As the horses heaved, the van jerked into motion. Then, swaying and clattering, it took the fifteen boys away from their home in the workhouse in Gray's Inn Lane.[7]

On 11 September and 7 October the Holborn guardians went down to Surrey Hall, and according to the reports they filed after each of the visits, they had reason to be satisfied with what they saw. In the first place, a wrangle with Drouet over the supply of water to the boys' washrooms had been sorted out. Then the food, which was bread and cheese, appeared to them to be 'very good & wholesome', although as their visit had been arranged in advance, this should have come as no surprise. The children looked clean and for the most part healthy, and the September report noted only seven cases of 'very slight' illness and some routine ophthalmia, which the nurses were treating by isolating the infected children and washing their inflamed eyes. Interestingly, the October report had no reference at all to medical complaints, which may have had something to do with the very recent death of Maria Drouet, who had always been the person best placed to inform the guardians if children were unwell.[8]

James would have been exhausted after the slow journey from Holborn, and possibly disorientated, having exchanged the imposing edifice of the workhouse for the smaller scale of Surrey Hall in the course of a single day. On climbing down from the van, he would have felt the same shock of the unfamiliar that had been Elizabeth Frost's first experience on her arrival four months previously. Like Elizabeth, he would have been confronted by a sea of strange faces, by crowds of strange children in the corridors and on the stairs, and he would have heard the strange voices of adults giving orders and delivering rebukes.

That night James slept in a bed with Joseph, not because the asylum staff had particularly tender feelings towards the two brothers, but because in an establishment overflowing with uprooted children it made good administrative sense to keep those from the same workhouse together. They slept in one of the four attic rooms of the Hall, where about thirty boys were sharing a dozen beds. The eight-year-old Holborn boy William Derbyshire slept with them, and although he was only little, he was nonetheless the third occupant of a bed that had been designed for one. The two brothers were also kept together in the crowded dining hall, and it is possible to describe what they were given to eat because Joseph, who had a young boy's intense interest in food, remembered every detail. Breakfast was half a slice of bread with gruel. The main meal was suet pudding on one day a week, meat on three, and soup on the remaining three. Supper was half a slice of bread with cheese. Joseph also remembered that they had either bread or potatoes with the meat, but the potatoes were often rotten and were left on or under the table. They ate standing up, as did all the children by order of Drouet, and they drank milk and water.[9]

Joseph's memories of meals with his little brother made him unhappy. Looking back, he realised that they were always hungry, and when James asked him if he could have some of his food, he would sometimes have to refuse because he did not have enough for himself. In any case, they only ate together for four or five days because James picked up ophthalmia almost as soon as he set foot in the asylum, and when it was noticed that his eyes were inflamed, he was moved from the attic to Nurse Warren's ward, which was on a lower floor. During this time of isolation, James had to eat his meals in the ward, and so he lost contact with his brother for two weeks. But once the soreness in his eyes had subsided, he was moved back up to the attic, where, in a return to a normality of sorts, he shared a bed with Joseph and William again.[10]

James was sick again in the first week of January. This time, though, his affliction was of a different order. Now he was seriously ill, and certainly too ill for Kite not to go up to the attic to see if there was anything he could do for him. His condition must have alarmed Kite, and before long, and probably on the Wednesday or the Thursday, he was moved to the resident surgeon's own ward. At that moment in time, almost a week had passed since cholera had claimed its first victim, and Elizabeth Frost's death, which had been the earliest warning of things to come, was now just one of many. Cholera was firmly in control and the asylum was fast becoming overwhelmed.[11]

* * *

If Holborn was slow to respond to the catastrophe that had befallen its children, the blame lay partly with Drouet, who failed to send the guardians his weekly report on the children's condition on time. As it was dated Saturday, 30 December, and included news of four Holborn children with bowel complaints, it was serious enough to send a warning signal that something was amiss. In any other week, it would have arrived on the Monday, but with Surrey Hall already under pressure it was sent to London late and did not arrive until the Tuesday.[12]

However, there was a further failure of communication, and an almost incomprehensible delay, in connection with the note from Richard Drouet. The note was brought up from Surrey Hall by the pauper David Kelly on the Monday. Kelly was quizzed about it by William Roberts James, the clerk to the guardians, on the Tuesday. James applied to Surrey Hall for more information and received it on the Wednesday. As a result, a workhouse medical officer was sent down to Surrey Hall, but not until the morning of the Thursday.[13]

Twenty-four hours later, the medical officer, William Benson Whitfield, communicated his findings to the guardians. The scene facing him as he entered the sick ward in the White House had been one of utter chaos.

The disease was spreading so rapidly that children were being brought in and unceremoniously consigned to any bed that happened to be free. In order to compile a list of Holborn casualties, Whitfield had to go from bed to bed, reluctantly interrogating children who were in the grip of the most unpleasant and violent of symptoms. He reckoned that about sixty were suffering from cholera and that twelve of these were from Holborn. He also learnt that Holborn children had died, although their deaths had not yet been reported to the workhouse.[14]

Whitfield's address to that sombre Friday morning meeting in the boardroom of the workhouse finally set the wheels of a rescue operation in motion. The guardians decided that he must immediately return to the asylum, examine the children again, and arrange to remove those who were not too ill to travel. In order to carry out this vital task efficiently, and also to put pressure on Drouet should he prove uncooperative, Whitfield was to be accompanied by William Roberts James.[15] However, the guardians were divided over the question of where the children were to be placed once they had been brought back from the asylum. Some suggested the workhouse, feeling, not unreasonably, that time wasted looking for alternative accommodation might result in lost lives. Others greeted the proposal with astonishment. It could not possibly make sense, they protested, to sow panic among 800 inmates by introducing children afflicted with cholera into the workhouse. The inmates would be the next victims, and any who survived would become deadly vectors of the disease when they went back out into the streets of the parish.[16]

Eventually, when it was pointed out that the Royal Free Hospital in Gray's Inn Road was known to have some vacant wards, the protesters calmed down. This was an opportunity not to be missed, as was made painfully clear by the arrival of a messenger who had come back from Surrey Hall with news that many children had died in the night, that three of them belonged to Holborn, and that a number of parishes were planning to take their children away. James and the guardians left for the hospital, where the house surgeon, Thomas Carr Jackson, invited them to inspect the vacant wards, and the senior surgeon, William Marsden, agreed to make preparations to receive the children that very evening.[17]

Three wards were set aside, one of which would be used to accommodate the children who were already ill. They met the essential requirements for the treatment of victims of cholera, being detached from the main hospital building, with ceilings high enough to ensure a flow of fresh air, and with room enough for the requisite number of beds. It was a strictly temporary arrangement in that it was meant to last only until a permanent home for the children could be found, and it came with the condition, laid down by Marsden, that the Holborn board pay all the costs incurred.[18] Nevertheless, the hospital had risen splendidly to the occasion, and James, on his return to the workhouse, was able to give orders for three vans to go down to Surrey Hall. He and Whitfield also went down.

Once there, the two men found Drouet surrounded by a crowd of guardians and medical officers, all of them from workhouses with children in the asylum. As he was having questions fired at him, and was plainly feeling the strain, they decided not to try to engage him in conversation. Instead, they set about ordering their children down from the sleeping apartments so that Whitfield might examine them, one by one, in the hall of the main building. Whitfield drew up a list of the children who, in his professional opinion, were well enough to make the journey back to Gray's Inn Road. Many were in the early stages of cholera but not yet so ill that they had to stay. However, thirty-seven were too ill to be moved, more than half of whom would die before long.[19]

It had been cold all day, and as the children stood in line on the drive, waiting to be put in the vans according to their size, they would have been frozen stiff. James and Whitfield must have experienced no little difficulty in marshalling the evacuees and giving special attention to those who were ill but had been allowed to make the journey. They matched names carefully against Drouet's lists so that no child who should have been travelling with them was left behind. They also made every effort to ensure that they were taking only children who belonged to the Holborn workhouse. In the general confusion, and with the light beginning to fade, it would have been an easy matter for children from other workhouses to get on board either by mistake or by design, and later James had to confess that 'one little thing' had indeed climbed up into a Holborn van without being noticed.[20]

In due course, when he was questioned about the removals, James also admitted that six of the Holborn children could not be accounted for. They were neither on the list of those who were removed, nor were they among those who remained. He could only suppose that they had been taken away by their parents, who, unbeknownst to him, had come down to Lower Tooting to carry out their own rescues. The first children to go were a group of around seventy girls, and they left with James at four o'clock and reached Gray's Inn Road at six. The vans then returned for the eighty or so boys, who left Surrey Hall soon after eight o'clock and arrived at half past ten. The vans were covered with large tarpaulins that reached down to the wheels on both sides and were folded under. James was happy with this arrangement, and because the workhouse had sent cloaks and rugs as well as caps for the boys and bonnets for the girls, he believed that the children would be warm enough, even in the skimpy clothes Drouet had provided. Whitfield, though, took the opposite view, that a covered vehicle was not as protected as an enclosed one because it was open to the wind. Nor was it a half-hearted objection, and Whitfield is on record as saying that for the workhouse to provide vulnerable children with such unsuitable transport was morally indefensible. Be that as it may, it was essential for the children to be removed forthwith. By far the greater risk was to leave them to their fate in the asylum.[21]

That Friday the sun set at a little past four in the afternoon, which was precisely the time the rescue of the Holborn girls began. Pulling away from Surrey Hall, the vans turned left into the High Street and slowly passed the houses clustered on either side of the road while the horses found their rhythm, exhaling clouds of steamy breath as they heaved against the load. On leaving Lower Tooting, the road to London ran north east past twilit fields and meadows, then on to higher ground and through the villages of Upper Tooting and Balham. Beyond Balham the vans made their way along the Old Brighton Road with Clapham ahead. In Clapham they travelled along the south side of the common, where the lights of the Windmill Inn burned bright and cheerful in the gathering gloom. The trees were looming silhouettes and the surfaces of the ponds were oil-black. The brave little procession passed another workhouse van in which two doctors and four nurses from St Pancras were travelling down to Surrey Hall. Two of the nurses were Sarah Sellers and Elizabeth Elliott. They were heading into the danger zone, where they were destined to perform heroics.[22]

As the vans were passing the common, at around five o'clock, snow began to fall, and it was still falling when they returned to Surrey Hall after delivering the girls to the hospital. The boys were put on board, shivering in their damp clothes, and the vans set off again. All the way James Andrews was looked after by William McDougal, who was one of the older boys. 'He sat on my knee,' William remembered. 'He said he felt very ill and sick, and laid his head on my shoulder.' Another of his companions in the van, Richard Woodison, remembered James telling him that his head ached. Richard also remembered the snow. When he peered out of the van, he noticed that the snow had begun to settle and was lying in thick, white drifts on either side of the road.[23]

As one might expect, and human nature being what it is, some of the boys might have found it hard to control themselves, so excited and relieved were they to be saying goodbye to the dreadful Drouet. The irrepressible Sidney Godolphin Osborne, writing in *The Times*, had the following to say on the subject:

> One incident, which speaks volumes to my mind, has reached me, on good authority. When the vehicle came up to "the farm" to remove the boys of one of the London parishes, the little fellows asked the driver to let them give three cheers on quitting the scene of their late oppression. He only quieted them by promising that when they got to Clapham-common they might cheer their best, which then they did their best to do.[24]

* * *

When it was founded in 1828, the Royal Free Hospital was in Greville Street. It stood at No. 16 under the name of the London General Institution for the Gratuitous Cure of Malignant Diseases and had as its neighbours a tailor and a tea dealer, an ironmonger, and manufacturers of buttons, shoes, repeating watches and lamps. A few doors down at No. 10 was the Central Infirmary and Dispensary. When the hospital moved to Gray's Inn Road in 1842, it occupied what had once been the barracks of the Light Horse Volunteers. The arched gateway led into a courtyard flanked by the wings of the hospital: these housed wards, waiting and consulting rooms, dispensary, boardroom and counting house. Further along the road to the north stood the premises of the building contractors William Cubitt & Co. To the south stood the premises of Thomas Seddon, an eminent cabinetmaker, then the Welsh Schools, Trinity Church and St Andrew's burial ground.

A total of 156 Holborn children were taken away on Friday, 5 January.[25] On the way up from Lower Tooting, the wind had blown snow through the gaps in the tarpaulins, and the snow had covered the children, who sat clutching their cloaks and blankets tight around them. At the hospital one of the four emergency nurses sent from the Holborn workhouse, whose name was Mary Harris, helped the boys out of the vans. As they climbed down, shivering in the cold, she noted that they 'were snowed all over'.[26]

On the journey it had been evident to the adults from the workhouse that the children were hungry, and so the convoy had stopped off at the Three Horse Shoes, a public house on the north side of the river in Milford Lane. There they had given the children bread and milk. The food might have staved off the worst of the hunger, but it was not enough, and so when they arrived at the hospital, the nurses were asked to provide a second supper. The children ate more bread, with cheese this time, and drank more milk, after which their stomachs were no doubt fuller than they had been in a very long time. They would have been tired out by the rigours of the journey, by the penetrating cold in the vans, and by the swirl of emotions stirred by their evacuation from Surrey Hall. So when they had eaten their meal, the deputy matron, Keziah Dimond, took them to the wards, where she and Mary Harris settled them down to sleep.[27]

Although James and Whitfield had exercised extreme caution in evacuating only those children who appeared to be in good health, there had been no guarantees, and seven girls and eight boys fell ill in the course of that first night in the hospital. As a precaution, they were isolated in a third ward, but not one of the hospital doctors visited them until the following day. Whitfield kept well away but only because it had been made a condition of the children's admission that workhouse medical officers defer to Marsden and his staff. He wanted to warn the doctors that the children might be infected with cholera, but he did not do so, thinking it not right to interfere.[28]

The nurses were divided in their assessment of the condition of the children. Some had thought on the Friday night that there was not too much to be concerned about, possibly because the children were given food and drink and rushed off to the wards as soon as they arrived. But this was an early impression, and it was not long before the deputy matron came to realise that the opposite was the case, and that the children were actually in a terrible state. More than anything, she was horrified to discover how many of them had nasty skin diseases. Almost all of them had sore and blistered hands, many had unhealed eruptions that had opened up into large wounds, and in the worst cases, where chilblains had developed on their feet and had been left untreated, their toes were ready to drop off. She found these pitiful sights all the more distressing because she had known the children in the workhouse, and remembered them as being for the most part as healthy as workhouse children ever could be. But that was before they were banished to Surrey Hall. They were back now and they were pale and thin.[29]

Keziah Dimond was not one to exaggerate, and her displeasure at the prevalence of skin diseases was echoed by Marsden, who calculated that as many as nine out of ten of the children coming back from Surrey Hall were afflicted with itch. It was a damning statistic, and thanks to a statement by Marsden that appeared in the London newspapers, it travelled back down to Lower Tooting, where it came to the notice of Erasmus Gilbert Livesay. When Livesay repeated the statistic at the meeting in the Rising Sun, it was greeted by the Tooting ratepayers with hisses and shouts of disapproval. Livesay, doing his best to speak in measured tones, said that the incidence of itch in Surrey Hall 'really did not look like good attendance upon the part of Mr Drouet', not least because the disease was easily treated with sulphur ointment. At this, Livesay was cheered by his audience. His was evidently a popular view.[30]

But itch was just one of the problems confronting the medical staff of the Royal Free Hospital. Another was the influx of a large number of new patients at only a few hours' notice, a state of affairs making intolerable demands on resources that were already stretched. The surgeon Thomas Carr Jackson, looking back on the episode, said that the hospital was 'paralysed' by the sheer number of new cases. He personally examined sixty-six boys, and among these he encountered thirty-four cases of scabies or cachectic eruptions and another six of sores on the feet. And these were just the skin complaints: there were also children with chronic problems related to an inadequate diet. They had the sallow faces and protuberant bellies that were the immediate signs of malnutrition. With a single glance at their wasted limbs and relaxed muscles, Jackson could see that they had been deprived of the 'animal food', or meat, children of their age needed for growth as well as nutrition. He was also scathing about the clothes they were wearing. They were of poor quality and badly worn and would have afforded little protection against the cold weather. If this was how Drouet dressed and fed his children, then it was hardly surprising that an epidemic of cholera had claimed so many victims.[31]

Mary Harris saw James Andrews for the first time when he was being lifted down from the van, and she realised, then and there, that he was very ill. Once he had been helped inside the hospital, she sat him by the fire in the ward and fetched bread and milk. The sight of James struggling with what was for him an unusual amount of food moved her: 'He held out the bread, and said, "Oh, nurse, what a large piece of bread this is." He did not eat it, or very little of it, but he drank the milk.' Then, because he was overcome with fatigue, and wanted to go to bed, Mary undressed him. As she did so, she could not help noticing how thin his arms and legs were, and how frail his chest was. He was 'a mere frame of bones'.[32]

James had fallen asleep quickly, apparently quite composed, and without giving any indication of pain. However, at about six-thirty in the morning, he took a turn for the worse, vomiting curdled milk and releasing watery blackish evacuations from his bowels. The uncontrollable movements gave off a foul smell and were repeated five or six times. Mary Harris did what she could for James, and she was assisted by William Filby, the Holborn parish gravedigger, who had come to the hospital to help with the Surrey Hall children. Filby was so alarmed by the appearance of the six-year-old boy, who by now was completely at the mercy of the disease, that he hurried off to fetch Whitfield. In answer to this summons, and in defiance of the hospital doctors, Whitfield went into the ward and instructed Keziah Dimond to swathe the boy's chest in flannels, which must be soaked in hot turpentine, and then wrap him in heated blankets. She was also to give him sips of brandy. But Whitfield had no illusions about James's chances of survival. The measures he was taking were futile: at best they might afford the little boy a modicum of physical comfort as his life slipped away.[33]

Keziah was at James's side when he died at half past eleven in the morning. She may have been able to offer him a mother's solace. Filby was there in the room too, but Whitfield, having other emergencies to see to, was not. By now two more cases of cholera had come to the doctor's attention. One was Jane Johnson, aged nine, and the other was Bridget Quinn, who was six.[34]

It is worth recording that Jane was at least spared the worst of cholera's many grim symptoms. Although she felt sick and vomited, the sickness did not last long. Likewise, she passed a white gruel-like substance from her bowels, but only once. She was also fortunate in experiencing neither the breathing difficulties nor the agonising cramps other victims of the disease had to endure. But it was not an altogether easy death. She repeatedly complained of a pain in her stomach and she was tormented by an unquenchable thirst that made her cry out constantly for relief. A nurse made her a little toast and gave her water. In this way the flame of life flickered until shortly after two in the afternoon, at which point, in a voice that was barely audible, Jane asked after a sister who had come up with her from Surrey Hall. They were orphans and were alone in the world. Jane asked that her sister might be sent for to be at her side, to hold her hand and help her on her way. Ten minutes later she died.[35]

Bridget hung on until the following morning when she too died. In one respect she was luckier than Jane, because her mother, who was an inmate of the workhouse, might have been on hand and might even have been able to comfort her to a degree. By now a fourth Holborn child, Michael Harper, was ill and just after midnight he also died. The hospital doctor Thomas Bevill Peacock made sure that the little boy, who was only nine, was swaddled in hot blankets. He administered opium and brandy, without success, and abandoned him to the inevitable as his pulse steadily grew fainter and his temperature dropped. Whitfield came by but he was wasting his time, and it was Mary Harris who did more than anyone for the dying boy by sticking with him throughout his ordeal. 'His skin was cold,' she recalled, 'and his breath was cold also, what little he had.'[36]

*　　*　　*

William Filby was saddened by James Andrews's death. He had known the boy well, having seen him in the workhouse in October of the previous year, before he was sent down to Surrey Hall. James had at that time been in very good health, which made it all the more painful to see him on his return, and to realise how cruelly he had been reduced to little more than a living skeleton in a relatively short period of time. But now he was dead and gone, and on 9 January, which was a cloudy and chilly Tuesday, Filby consigned the ravaged body to the anonymity of a pauper's grave in the burial ground adjacent to Trinity Church in Gray's Inn Road.[37]

For any other pauper child, burial in a parish churchyard would have been the moment when the final curtain fell, but fate had not quite finished with James Andrews. For he had been buried in haste, and after another two days had passed, William Filby was obliged to dig his body out of the grave for the purpose of a post mortem examination. The circumstances of his death and of the deaths of the other three Holborn children had been sent by the guardians to the coroner, Thomas Wakley, who was sufficiently concerned to order an inquest. However, what was in essence a routine legal procedure descended into grotesque farce when Filby dug up James's coffin, carried it down to the vaults beneath the church and raised the lid. He would have recognised him even in death and he was sure that it was some other boy lying in the coffin. The error was rectified, but the damage to the dignity death might otherwise have conferred on James had been done.[38]

Alfred Baring Garrod, a physician at University College Hospital, had been called in by Wakley to examine James's body. He was assisted in the dissection by William Benson Whitfield, and the work of the two doctors was witnessed by William Filby and his wife, and also by a porter from the hospital. The Holborn guardian Stephen Pearson was present too but not in an official capacity. He later explained that he had been in the church quite by chance and had simply stumbled upon the sorry business when he went down into the vaults.[39]

Not only had James's body been buried too soon, but, prior to the first interment, it had been examined internally as well, probably by Peacock. Although by now almost six days had passed since the little boy had died, there were only slight signs of decomposition, and no disagreeable smell. Garrod thought that the reason why the body was still comparatively fresh was that it had been refrigerated, as it were, by the cold weather. Accordingly, the livid hue that comes with death was confined to the nails of the fingers and toes and to the abdomen, and whereas the abdomen was by now stained a yellowish green, all other parts of the body were still mottled with patches of red. Rigor mortis had nearly 'gone off' in the extremities and the jaw.[40]

An immediate sign of the effects of cholera was the shrivelled skin on the soles of the little boy's feet and on the palms of his hands. But it was only clear how much harm had been inflicted by the disease and how much by chronic neglect when the body was opened. To begin with, the lungs were congested and the bronchial glands were enlarged. The mesenteric glands were even more obviously enlarged, and had deposits of tuberculous matter, a phenomenon Garrod had frequently encountered in scrofulous and 'ill-conditioned' children. The peritoneal surface of the small intestine had a pinkish vermilion tint, while that of the large intestine was greyish white, and Garrod noted that the difference in colour was frequent in cases of cholera. Another sign of the cause of death was the stodgy white matter, also in James's intestines, which looked not unlike boiled rice or gruel. When it was examined under a microscope, it was seen to have all the characteristics of the hard stuff in choleraic evacuations. It was also telling that James's blood had the consistency of treacle and was almost as dark in the arteries as it was in the veins. Garrod's chemical analysis revealed that it was 'very peculiar in its composition', having a great deal more solid matter than the blood of children who died of causes other than cholera. And finally there was a thick brown fluid in James's stomach and it had the smell of port wine.[41]

Although it was Garrod's professional opinion that James had died of malignant Asiatic cholera, it was hard to ignore the competing evidence of sustained malnutrition. His body was small in relation to his head, and in this and other ways, specifically in the delayed emergence of the secondary teeth, his development was seen to be 'rather behind' what might be expected in a boy of his age. That James's constitution was weak was more than suggested by his unhealthy colour, but the most startling evidence of the hardships he had been exposed to, and the evidence it was impossible to ignore, was the meagreness of bodily fat. In the region of the abdominal walls, there was a layer only about a fifteenth of an inch thick, while in the omentum there was hardly any at all.[42]

Garrod was shocked by these discoveries, but he was careful not to draw definite conclusions where the evidence did not justify them. An obvious example of where there was need for caution was in tackling the question of the emaciated state of James's body. Garrod was prepared to concede that the forty-eight hours of cholera the boy had endured must have taken their toll, and what he called the 'appearance of shrinking' could certainly have been produced in even that short time by the violent actions of the disease. On the other hand, an attack of cholera of two days' duration would not in itself account for the remarkable absence of fat. Taking everything into consideration, including the possibility that James had just been a naturally unhealthy child, the most plausible explanation was quite simply that he had been underfed. But even then Garrod did not think it was for him to be too specific, and the last thing he wanted to be drawn on was if two months in Surrey Hall would have been enough to cause this level of emaciation. He was inclined to think not, but at the same time he 'would not be positive on that point' because he had never seen for himself what life in the asylum was really like.[43]

Once the examination was over, Filby lifted James's remains back into the coffin. Having fixed the lid in place again, he took the coffin back to the graveyard and lowered it into the ground for the second and final time. Then he brought out the bodies of Jane Johnson and Michael Harper. Both bodies had been examined by Peacock, and Michael's had also been examined by Garrod. As for the fourth Holborn child, little Bridget Quinn, her body had been examined by Peacock and had already been lying for two days in the grave.[44]

Chapter Eight

Burying the Dead

In May 1849, in the *London Journal of Medicine*, Garrod published an article on the pathological condition of the blood of victims of cholera. His findings were based on eight post mortem examinations. Two were those of James Andrews and Michael Harper. Two others were those of a nurse who had died in the Royal Free Hospital and an alcoholic sailor who had lodged at an inn near the railway at Euston Square, where it had taken him a week to die.[1] Garrod was a frontline researcher engaged in the fight against cholera, but it is an uncomfortable fact that under the dispensation of the 1832 Anatomy Act he would have considered the bodies of the unloved and unwanted who died in workhouses, hospitals or prisons to be entirely at his disposal if they were still unclaimed after forty-eight hours. Kite also enjoyed this privilege and later claimed that he had 'opened' the bodies of seven of the children who died in Surrey Hall. 'All the symptoms described by writers on cholera were apparent in these cases,' he would say.[2] It was as if honest enthusiasm had encouraged him to treat the dead primarily as material for investigation. It might almost be said that the human aspect of the tragedy had been relegated beneath the demands of science.

Eighty-seven of the Holborn children in the Royal Free Hospital came down with cholera, that is to say more than half of those brought back from Drouet's.[3] Officially, the only deaths were the four in early January, which was a surprisingly low mortality rate. The newspapers heaped praise on the medical staff of the hospital and congratulated them fulsomely on their dedication and professionalism. According to *Lloyd's Weekly Newspaper*, they had been 'indefatigable in their zeal and attendance on the poor little sufferers', many of whom would 'doubtless survive the painful ordeal' they had undergone thanks to the care with which they had been treated.[4] In the same spirit, the *Morning Post* painted a rosy picture in which attentive doctors ministered to the needs of their little charges. 'Wine and other nourishing things are allowed the children,' the *Post* reported, 'and they appear to be rapidly approaching convalescence.'[5] There could have been no more pointed contrast with the recent sufferings of these same children at Surrey Hall, and it would not be overstating it to say that the children Drouet had brutalised were in a way being given back their humanity. They were being revitalised, restored to life with kindness.

However, a fifth child, Thomas Jones, died later in the month, having been taken ill in the night. He was twelve years old and an orphan, and one of a group of nine boys and seven girls who, on Marsden's recommendation, had been removed to the hospital's former premises in Greville Street. The object of the exercise was to relieve pressure on the Gray's Inn Road wards, and, understandably, it met with more than a little opposition from the local residents. They had to be placated by the board of guardians with assurances that the sixteen children who had been deposited in their midst had been chosen by the hospital medical staff precisely because they were free from disease, and that for this reason they represented no particular danger to the health of the neighbourhood.[6] Even so, it is unlikely that the fears of the residents had been entirely allayed. If news of Thomas's death had leaked out, it would have been a public relations disaster, and this may explain why the unhappy boy was hastily removed from the old hospital building in Greville Street and taken back to the workhouse to die, and why his death was never included in the statistics the hospital released to the newspapers.

Twenty or more adults had close contact with the children in the hospital. Most were nurses and a few were male attendants. They all slept in the wards every night and they all suffered from diarrhoea of a greater or lesser severity. In four cases the diarrhoea developed into cholera, and two of the four died.[7] One of these was a nurse, aged thirty-five, who had been caring for the children from the moment of their arrival. She had not set foot in Surrey Hall, so it could be said that she had caught the Surrey Hall cholera at second hand.[8] No one at any point considered it important to make a note of her name, an official silence that aligns uncomfortably with Marsden's dim view of the nurses dispatched to the hospital from the Holborn workhouse. He thought of them as 'a very bad set' and admitted that, on the first night after their arrival, he had been obliged to send one of them back. She was drunk, and Marsden was worried that if she were attacked with diarrhoea in the perilous conditions of the children's cholera wards, her system, already depressed by alcohol, would not be able to fight off the disease.[9]

The other adult victim of cholera was a man from the workhouse whose name was James Cowdery. He was twenty-nine, a good and helpful man who had brought food from the workhouse for the children in the hospital, hoping in this way to lift their spirits in their hour of need. Sadly, it was in carrying out these little acts of kindness that he caught what had become known as the 'Tooting disease'. Through no fault of his own, he had carried the disease back to the workhouse, where he infected two older inmates who had their beds close to his. They were John King and Peter Kelly, both in their fifties, and they also died.[10]

On 20 January it was reported that thirty of Holborn's children had been diagnosed as too ill to be taken safely up to the hospital, and along with many incumbents of the other parishes, they were left to take their chances in Surrey Hall.[11] Nine would die and fifteen would survive. What had become of the remaining six was never recorded, or if it were, the record was lost. In the view of William Roberts James, they were simply unaccounted for, as if they had only ever existed as names on a list. But the lack of interest in the six children did not go unnoticed. 'We hope some news has by this time been obtained of them,' *The Times* commented in an editorial in which the cholera crisis took on the aspect of a military disaster. The Tooting tragedy had become the equivalent of a lost battle, a crushing defeat: 'The affair has cost us too dearly in killed and wounded to allow of any missing.'[12] And the cost of the 'affair' was high indeed. The *Morning Chronicle* reported that between 700 and 800 children were attacked by cholera, either in Surrey Hall or in the parishes to which they had been removed.[13] By the end of January, 158 had died in one place or another, and of these 113 are named in the burial register of St Nicholas, the parish church, where they were deposited in unmarked graves.

*   *   *

The driving force behind this extraordinary mass interment of Drouet's children is no mystery. As public health was a pressing concern, it was imperative that no time should be lost in disposing of the dead. On 6 January, in his capacity as the medical officer for the Tooting district, Walter Chapman had issued a directive to the parishes who had dealings with Drouet in which he ordered them to arrange the immediate interment of the bodies of any of their children who died of cholera. Speed was of the essence, and because Chapman imposed a twenty-four-hour window on these operations, it proved impracticable for parishes to take the dead back to the workhouse for burial. So the bodies were buried in the local churchyard.[14]

Chapman's directive has to be assessed against a wider background than that of a Lower Tooting health crisis. The general fear of cholera in 1849 was real and justified. But the measures he imposed, however necessary they seemed to him to be, showed scant regard for the powerful sentiments accompanying a pauper child's death. Although his stated aim was to prevent the spread of disease, he was making it all but impossible for parents and relatives to grieve over their children, to sit with them until the time of their burial, to say their farewells. To many, the insistence on the immediate interment of the dead would have bordered on the indecent, implying as it did that the feelings of the poor counted for little, even in a time of crisis.

Insensitivity was not the only criticism made of Chapman's directive, though. There was concern in some quarters that criminal activities might be concealed in the rush to get dead bodies safely in the ground. A particular worry was that the diarrhoea, the stomach pains and the cramps in the legs experienced by victims of arsenic poisoning were also common symptoms of cholera. Since the disease was able to provide a cover for the poison, it might prove to be 'an inducement to murder', as the Middlesex coroner, Thomas Wakley, bluntly asserted, 'and a shield to cruelty'.[15] Hasty burials inevitably resulted in ill-informed forensic assessments, and, as a consequence, murderers might escape justice.

Real though these concerns were, they were powerless to prevent the first burials of the Surrey Hall dead. On 5 January, which was the Friday of the first full week of the disaster, the bodies of fourteen boys and ten girls were taken to the churchyard to be laid to rest.[16] There had been a delay of several days after the earliest deaths because Kite had made an application for a Surrey coroner's inquest, and only when it was rejected was it possible for the burials to go ahead.[17] The twenty-four bodies were collected from Surrey Hall by undertakers who held contracts with the workhouses for the disposal of their dead. One such contractor, who was sent by Wandsworth and Clapham, was Samuel Brandon Gardiner[18]. He had once been a carpenter and was, therefore, a man for whom the making and supplying of coffins was a natural occupation. Now, by order of the guardians, it was his responsibility to see that 'the funerals of all children belonging to this Union dying at Mr Drouet's of such disease [in other words of cholera] be performed from Mr Drouet's house.' Familiar as he was with the realities of death, Gardiner cannot have been unmoved by the sight of the little bodies, for he was a young man and the father of three children, all of them aged under ten.

Not wanting to take the dead children through the streets of the village in broad daylight, which would draw attention to events in the asylum and spread fear, the undertakers had waited for nightfall. At a late hour they brought out the coffins from the makeshift morgue in the carpenter's workshop, loaded them on carts and moved off from Surrey Hall in the wintry darkness, safe from prying eyes. The carts crossed the Broadway and hauled the coffins along Mitcham Road. A short distance before Amen Corner, they turned up into Church Lane, passing the Rising Sun public house on their right. The Lane climbed the hill above the village, but at the foot of the hill the carts pulled over and came to a halt in front of St Nicholas Church, which stood behind the Rising Sun. The distance from the scene of death to the place of burial was approximately 700 yards.

The men from the parishes lifted the coffins from the carts and carried them into the churchyard, where space had been found, and at ten o'clock the burials began.[19] The air was frosty, heavy with snow, and they stamped their feet and wrapped their arms tight around their chests to keep themselves warm. There were no mourners, no family members, no friends. The parish gravediggers stood ready to shovel soil over the coffins once the officiating minister, Richard Wilson Greaves, had said the few necessary words. Like Gardiner, he was a married man with a young family, and one can well imagine that performing his duty to the Surrey Hall dead stirred strong emotions. Four little bodies had been placed in each of six coffins, and the coffins, holding twenty-four little bodies in all, were lowered into the ground at the back of the churchyard, arranged in a row.[20] The next day another thirteen little bodies were buried, but none were buried on the following day, which was the day of rest. Then twenty-one were buried on the Monday, twenty-one on the Tuesday, and on the Wednesday a further twelve.[21]

The burial register for Lower Tooting tells its own story. It is as if the normal rule of random mortality had been temporarily suspended, as almost every entry over a period of two weeks identified the Juvenile Pauper Establishment as the place of death, and a 'C' for cholera was written in the margin against every name. Overwhelmingly, the names and ages recorded in these entries are those of children, but scattered amongst them are the details of the four nurses and the schoolmistress Sarah Goat. The oldest of the adults was Louisa Batterbee, who was sixty-two. Five of the children were only three years old.

In one of the coffins lay David Kelly's grandson, four-year-old James 'Jemmy' Doyle. Horrified by the scenes of illness and death in the asylum, Kelly had wanted to get him back to Holborn and had visited the union office on the Thursday to plead with the guardians, but his efforts were in vain, and on the Friday Jemmy had died.[22] It may seem strange to describe Kelly as blessed with the knowledge of his grandson's pitiful demise, but the awful fact is that the haste to bury the children was so great that their families were not always informed. One such case, which is almost too painful to contemplate, was that of Eliza Cutler, a mother in the Chelsea workhouse. Her son, Henry, aged eight, had been at Drouet's for a year, during which time he had complained to her when she visited that he was not getting enough to eat. Then he fell ill in the first week of January, but a week had passed before a message got through to Eliza that he had died and been buried, even though she had been in the workhouse all the time. It is not known who gave her the news, though it may have been the master, Daniel Sutton, or his wife, Charity, the matron. But somebody must have had the sad task of informing Eliza that her son was lying in the cold ground in a churchyard far from his home.[23]

Another parent, William Mortimer, was the victim of an even more callous indifference. Mortimer was one of the nurses sent from the Holborn workhouse to the Royal Free Hospital. He had two children, Elizabeth, aged five, and William, aged three, who were both inmates in Surrey Hall. The last time he had seen them, in the lodge, was in late December. Then they both fell ill, but Mortimer only found this out because Keziah Dimond brought him word, either having seen them when visiting her own children or having heard about them from some other source. However, they were not among the Holborn children brought back up to the hospital, and so Mortimer was denied the chance to be at their side when they needed him most.[24]

That this caused Mortimer acute pain is all too evident. He had applied to the master, Robert Aldred, for permission to go down to Lower Tooting, and when Aldred refused, fearing that he might bring cholera back to the workhouse, he said that he would voluntarily discharge himself. He would also relinquish his position as a nurse if this would guarantee him freedom of movement. Yet again, Aldred stood in his way, refusing to grant him his discharge on the grounds that in his anxiety to get down to Lower Tooting as soon as possible, he had failed to give the necessary three hours' notice. Mortimer protested that he knew nothing about the need to give notice, but his protest fell on deaf ears, and he saw neither of his children again.[25]

It is a sad irony that Elizabeth and William Mortimer died on the same Saturday and Sunday as James Andrews and Bridget Quinn. At the time, their father was where he had to be, at the Royal Free Hospital, but not where he wished to be, at his dying children's side. As if enforced separation was not painful enough, he did not learn about their deaths until the following Friday, and even then the information came not from any official source but from the workhouse beadle, who, in the absence of any communication from Drouet, had been dispatched on the Thursday to investigate the state of the children in the asylum. In fact, the first person in Holborn to hear the news of the two little Mortimers was William Roberts James. Whereas Mortimer would hear on the Friday from the beadle, James had heard the day before from Drouet but had said nothing, thinking it only right and proper to write first in order to have the report of the deaths confirmed. In the event, confirmation was only forthcoming when Drouet came up to Holborn on the Saturday to explain that he had written a report on the children but had forgotten to send it. The report arrived in Holborn on the Sunday, but it was dated Saturday, and James must have been left wondering if Drouet had been economical with the truth.[26]

Mortimer was adamant that he had been treated very badly. He was incensed at not having been notified by Surrey Hall, and he was inclined to express himself forcefully. What he had to endure epitomised the whole disgrace of Drouet's handling of the crisis, and when he spoke out, he spoke for all the parents who were kept at arm's length from their children, who were helpless witnesses when they contracted cholera, and were kept in the dark when they died. He stood before Wakley and told him his sorry tale: he had once been the father of a girl and a boy but 'they are now both dead'.[27]

Wakley was aware that the cruelties inflicted on William Mortimer were not an isolated case. Other similar cases had come before him in his role as coroner, and so, when it came to discussing the rights and wrongs of the matter with William Roberts James, he was able to make an illuminating comparison. Recently, he said, a woman had applied to one of the London workhouses for a visitor's permit. She was in great distress because a child of hers was in the workhouse infirmary. However, far from receiving the permit, she was informed that her child was dead. Understandably, she was devastated, and asked if she might see her child's body, only to be told that the child had already been buried. Presumably, Wakley did not conceal his thoughts on the matter because James found himself saying, somewhat implausibly, that the Holborn guardians were quick to keep families informed about their relatives in the workhouse. He added that in the case Wakely had referred to, it may just have been that no one knew where the woman lived. It was an unsympathetic remark. Certainly, it would not have gone down well with Wakley, whose objection, when reduced to its essentials, was that workhouse officials were all too often guilty of trampling on poor people's feelings.[28]

*   *   *

On 10 January, in a second directive sent to the parishes, and also to Drouet, Walter Chapman ordered that no more children dying of cholera in Surrey Hall were to be buried at St Nicholas Church. A total of seventy-nine had been buried already and the churchyard had reached its full capacity. From this point on, the onus would be on the parishes to remove dead bodies, and not within the twenty-four hours previously allowed for local burials but within twelve.[29] It was a tall order. The undertakers would have been under pressure to get down to the asylum with time enough to find the right bodies, which would be lying with many others in the carpenter's workshop. To add to the difficulties, no one could predict how many more children were going to die.

Chapman's demands were not unrelated to current concerns about the overcrowding of burial grounds. In the capital the problem was exacerbated by the rapid growth of the population, the high mortality rate, especially among the young and the poor, and the impact of epidemics. Too many dead bodies were being crammed into too few and too small spaces, with results that were as dangerous as they were disgusting. Coffins were piled one on top of another with the uppermost barely covered with soil. In a burial ground such as that in Russell Court, which lay between Drury Lane and Covent Garden, hemmed in on all sides by tenements, the stench of decay was inescapable. A reporter for *Tait's Edinburgh Magazine* visited this fetid enclave late in 1848, at the time of the cholera epidemic, and described the atrocious intermingling of the living and the dead with undisguised horror:

> Better far that one's bones bleached above the desert's drifting sands, than be decomposed amongst the putrid mass of Russell's [*sic*] Court, that emits miasma sufficient to impregnate with fever those wet clothes that, from want of a drying-loft, are hung above the graves, to catch and keep the breath of the dead.[30]

Another scandalised voice was that of George Alfred Walker, a doctor committed to burial reform. In 1845 he published an account of conditions in the Spa Fields burial ground on the border of Finsbury and Clerkenwell. It was a truly ghastly place. Walker looked on it as a hellish landscape where tombstones were levered from the earth and graves were routinely desecrated. The old coffins that had been removed to make way for the new were incinerated in the bone house in a fire that burnt all day and all night. The principal gravedigger, Tom Smith, prowled through his desolate kingdom in the hours of darkness, despoiling the corpses of clothes and teeth and cutting off long strands of female hair to sell to hairdressers.[31] The general feelings of revulsion at the state of urban burial grounds also crept into literature, for example, in the scene in *Bleak House* where Jo leads Lady Dedlock through passages 'reeking with offence of many kinds' to the graveyard in the slum district of Tom-All-Alone's. The young crossing sweeper points through the bars of an iron gate to the grave of Captain Hawdon: 'Over yinder. Among them piles of bones, and close to that there kitchin winder! They put him wery nigh the top. They was obliged to stamp upon it to git it in.' The cheerless vision Dickens ascribed to Jo was evidently not altogether a flight of fancy.[32]

There were other objections to the twelve-hour requirement set out in Chapman's directive. One arose from the use of opium in the treatment of cholera. Opium and its tincture, laudanum, both of which were unregulated at the time and readily available in high street pharmacies, gave relief from the pain of cramps and, by inhibiting the action of the bowels, went some way towards controlling the extremes of diarrhoea. Grainger, for example, always insisted that laudanum combined with a stimulant was 'the best remedy' for cholera in its premonitory stage. He also warned newspapers not to publicise the recommended doses lest readers be too informed and attempt to treat symptoms of the disease themselves.[33] Issuing advice about toxicity was undoubtedly a prudent and responsible measure, and a sure indication of the medical profession's respect for these powerful substances, but a more serious concern was that the profound sleep induced by opium and laudanum might be mistaken for death. The mid-century doctor had few reliable means of establishing that a person had died beyond observing the onset of putrefaction. Therefore, simulated death followed by immediate interment raised the terrifying possibility of a patient being buried alive. Nor was this a baseless fear, as there had in any case been instances of apparent death from cholera where the victim had regained consciousness. An example was reported in the *Morning Chronicle* in 1832:

> On Thursday night as the coffin bearers of a person supposed to have expired of cholera in one of the parishes near Bishopsgate were carrying their burthen for interment, they heard a noise within the coffin, which induced them to lay it down and open it; the individual was found not to be quite dead, and his recovery is not at all improbable. We fear this is not the only instance of premature interment during the prevalence of the epidemic.[34]

In later incidents of a similar nature, a young woman from Taunton, who appeared to have died, was revived by bleeding and saved from premature burial, while a milkman from Camden Town was actually put in a coffin, even though he was still alive.[35] The second of these mishaps was the stuff of nightmares, and the *Monmouthshire Beacon*, in reporting the tragedy, noted that the wretched man had been very speedily buried:

> His friends, who lived in the country, did not arrive in time for the funeral, and insisted on seeing the corpse. On being taken up, the body was found turned on its side in the coffin, and the knuckles were cut in a shocking manner, supposed to have been caused by the poor fellow's struggles to get out.[36]

A 'death' of the kind featured in these lurid stories might easily be caused by a powerful opiate. In one hair-raising case, which was widely reported, a woman who had treated the symptoms of cholera with large doses of laudanum was only saved from interment when her distraught husband, asking for the lid of her coffin to be raised so that he might take one last look at her, noticed a slight trembling in one of her arms. This happened on the other side of the Atlantic in Montreal, but distance would hardly have dulled the edge of the message.[37]

In spite of the fear of premature burial, Chapman's new directive was endorsed by Grainger and, by extension, by the General Board of Health, and so it was not easy to ignore. As well as underlining the need for immediate action on the part of the parishes, Grainger made two recommendations: first, he urged that interments take place under the direction of a medical practitioner to ensure that bodies infected with cholera were disposed of in a safe and properly hygienic manner; then he advised the drivers of vehicles carrying bodies back to the parishes to avoid routes through the metropolis. He was aware that hearses trundling through the London streets 'might excite alarm in the public mind' and that this would only lead to trouble.[38]

In the nineteenth century, cholera in its most virulent 'Asiatic' form was viewed as a frightening disorder originating in distant lands. Many contemporary accounts of the great epidemics employed apocalyptic language. In 1849 the *Annual Register* reported that cholera had been 'mowing down the populations of Asia and Eastern Europe' prior to its arrival in England. Once it had reached these shores, it 'would probably again inflict the chastisement of Providence on this nation'. It was rapacious and indiscriminate, reappearing after the previous epidemic

> in all its terrors simultaneously, and in all parts, visiting alike those spots usually considered most healthy and those from which disease is never absent, sparing neither the rich in their mansions nor the poor in their hovels; sweeping away the well-fed and well-clothed, the hungry and the naked, the robust and the weak.[39]

What is more, the fear of cholera, which haunted the minds of the populace, might combine with a distrust of the medical profession to encourage outbreaks of violence. Quite apart from the doctors' proven inability to control the disease, conspiracy theories circulated according to which the poor were allowed to die in order to supply anatomy schools with corpses, or simply to reduce the cost of pauper maintenance, which was shouldered by ratepayers. During the earlier epidemic, there had been riots in several English cities. In Exeter the disposal of the bodies of the victims of cholera was handled with such insensitivity that the city authorities were faced with several episodes of unrest. In one of these, a gravedigger charged with burying a diseased corpse was assaulted by angry parishioners, and even when the burial was moved to a different site, the procession was the target of shouts and insults hurled by a hostile crowd. It may well have been these and similar incidents an anxious Grainger had in mind.[40]

For a day or two, the parishes played along with Chapman's orders by sending vehicles down to Surrey Hall in order to remove their dead. For all Grainger's anxieties, there were no reports of disturbances, but it is a melancholy thought that whereas once workhouse vans would have wound their way through the streets of the city with their burden of children, bound for Lower Tooting, now hearses were heading back up to the city laden with coffins.[41] The Chelsea minutes reveal how dealing with the deaths of children soon became just another administrative matter. The guardians placed an order with Henry Nodes, a local furnishing undertaker, for six children's coffins in a range of sizes, which they would deliver to Surrey Hall. They also wrote to Drouet, asking him from this point on to send bodies back to Chelsea without delay, and it seems that he had reason to do just that, as on 17 January five children were buried in the churchyard of St Luke's along with four inmates from the workhouse and a poor woman who lived in the parish. All ten were buried in unmarked graves.[42]

On 11 January, which was the day after Chapman issued his second directive, no burials took place in St Nicholas churchyard. There were two on the following day but neither contravened the ban. One was of Louisa Batterbee, and the other of William Taylor, who was eleven months old. William was the child of a local family who may well have been able to afford a private grave.[43] If the parishes generally were prepared to comply with the latest directive, as would seem to have been the case, it is also perfectly clear that the Strand guardians resented the ban, and no sooner had the communications from Chapman and Grainger been received by the board than indignant voices were raised. In part the protest was fuelled by a reluctance to bring back bodies when it would be safer and more convenient to dispose of them in Lower Tooting. But it was also objected that the ratepayers would be paying to bury children who, at the time of death, had been residents of another parish. Technically, it was for Drouet to shoulder the costs.[44]

So a resolution was passed, unanimously, that representations be made to the General Board of Health. It was the work of a moment. The Board's offices at Gwydyr House in Whitehall were only about two miles from the Strand Union premises in Cleveland Street, and two guardians, Thomas Fielder and Robert Jaquet, set off straight away. Fielder was a carver and gilder with a workshop in Greek Street, and Jaquet was the proprietor of Johnson's Tavern in Clare Court, and being men who ran their own businesses, they would have spoken with some warmth on the subject of burial fees. As guardians, of course, they had a duty towards the poor of the parish, but it was their task to ensure that the ratepayers were not burdened with unwarranted extra costs. They may also have had a particular animosity towards Chapman, a lowly district medical officer, who, in their eyes, was interfering with the union's affairs.[45]

They made a persuasive case, and the outcome of their petition was that the Board upheld the complaint against Chapman, conceding that he had overstepped the mark. Powers in connection with burials he certainly had, but they were few, and they did not extend as far as he appeared to think. The clarification of the Board's position, which Fielder and Jaquet duly brought back from Gwydyr House, had important consequences because the Strand guardians were now able to advise Drouet that Chapman had issued orders he had no right to issue.[46] In effect, the General Board of Health had given the parishes its assurance that they might legitimately leave their children in Lower Tooting, and it is unlikely to be a coincidence that fourteen more Surrey Hall children were buried shortly after on the thirteenth, and a further eight on the sixteenth. The last of the victims of cholera to be buried, on the eighteenth, was Elizabeth Gardner, another of Drouet's nurses.[47]

*   *   *

The growing sense of a collective indifference in the face of tragedy can only be reinforced by the decision of the Surrey coroner not to hold a single inquest into the many deaths in Drouet's asylum. The coroner in question, William Carter, had all the necessary documentation because Kite had been submitting the children's death certificates to his office from the outset of the crisis.[48] As the designated medical attendant in the asylum, whose signature appeared on the certificates, Kite would understandably have been anxious to have an official investigation not only to satisfy his sense that it was the proper thing to do, but also to safeguard himself against charges of medical incompetence or malpractice. However, even though he was entitled to ask for such a procedure, Carter turned down his application. His intransigence would have surprised and probably angered Kite, but it would also have rankled with Grainger, who, dismayed at the scenes in Surrey Hall, had put it to the General Board of Health that an inquest must be held immediately. The Board agreed and even corresponded on the matter with Sir George Grey, the Home Secretary. But it was not in the Board's power to enforce an inquest, and no pressure was put on Carter to reverse his initial decision.[49]

Carter, who may well have wanted to avoid investigating a rapidly mounting toll of deaths, gave two reasons for his refusal. First, at the moment of death, the children had been attended by Kite, a medical professional. Second, Kite had stated on the death certificates that the children had died of cholera, and had therefore died of causes that were technically natural and did not call for an inquest. As it turned out, though, it was not only Kite who was offended by Carter's decision. It also provoked a hostile response from his fellow coroner, Thomas Wakley.[50]

As a founding editor of the *Lancet* and the member of parliament for Finsbury, Wakley had considerable clout. Significantly, in rules issued to local parish officers in 1839, he had ordered that coroners were to be notified of all cases 'when persons die who appear to have been neglected during sickness, or extreme poverty', and 'when persons die in confinement'. Confinement, naturally, applied to official places of incarceration, such as prisons and police stations. But it also applied to pauper establishments. In Wakley's view, a judicial inquiry into the cause of a death was a fundamental protection, ancient in its origins and of universal validity. If it was accorded to 'criminals of the vilest character' as a safeguard against abuses while in custody, then it must surely be accorded to 'weak and helpless children' afflicted with 'a ravaging contagion' in an infant pauper asylum, which was as much a place of confinement as any gaol. To Wakley's way of thinking, Carter was guilty of a dereliction of his duty as coroner. Carter might well argue that no child's death in Surrey Hall qualified in itself for an inquest, but when a child's death was one of a hundred children's deaths, then a different set of criteria applied. Carter's disgrace was to turn a blind eye to one of the outstanding features of the Tooting tragedy: its terrifying scale.[51]

Wakley's essential humanity does not appear to have been shared by those whose specific task it was to dispose of the Surrey Hall dead. Drouet, whose thoughts on the matter were ruled by the need for haste and convenience, was concerned only that they should be removed from the premises. He was indifferent to conventional sensitivities. He had been too long in the lucrative business of pauper management to see his children as children. They were commodities, and had previously had value, but now, as lifeless bodies cluttering the carpenter's workshop, they were no more than outdated stock. As such, they had to be shifted, but it was not for him to worry where they went. Even Kite admitted that he had no idea where the children he had once cared for were being taken, or where they were being laid to rest.[52]

Richard Wilson Greaves was concerned only that the cost of the interments at St Nicholas Church was fully met. In this he had the support of Daniel Norris, a local builder who served as the village undertaker. Norris was also the parish clerk, whose duties had long ago been defined as ringing the church bell, winding the dial of the clock, giving out notices during services, having charge of the registers, and making himself a general source of information on parish affairs. Now he joined forces with the rector to bill the parishes £2 11s. 6d. for every child they had buried. They must have involved Surrey Hall in the process because both Alfred Charles and Richard Drouet sent Chelsea and Strand letters reminding them of the need to pay.[53]

The Strand guardians, ever anxious not to upset the ratepayers, greeted the bills with utter consternation. They clearly felt that the sums they had been presented with were excessive. What is more, they suspected an element of sharp practice, and they acted on their suspicions by refusing to pay. When they quizzed Greaves and Norris about the exorbitant bill, they were astonished to learn that the regular fee of 10s., which was charged for burying a resident of Tooting, had been doubled to 20s., or £1, which was charged in all other cases. It was explained to them that since the children were not parishioners, they had no legal claim to interment in the churchyard. They had been buried there not by virtue of an entitlement but out of necessity. In addition, each burial had incurred a surplice fee of £1 1s. and an undertaker's fee of 10s. 6d. The first of these fees was payable to Greaves and the second to Norris.[54]

Somehow, the story got out. It made good copy, and the *Hampshire Telegraph* published an article, 'The Tooting Paupers and the Tooting Parson', in which it rounded on Greaves. 'It is an ill wind which blows nobody any good,' the *Telegraph* solemnly declared, 'but it certainly never occurred to us that the frightful mortality among the pauper children at Tooting, would prove so perfect a piece of good luck to the rector of that place.'[55] Meanwhile, the Strand guardians, who were incensed at what they regarded as an unseemly exercise in profiteering, took their grievances to the Poor Law Board. The clerk, James Kilner, argued that the children were 'entitled, as of right, to be buried in the church yard of the parish in which they died'. There were therefore no legal grounds for the doubling of the fees. The Poor Law Board agreed with Kilner that 'the obligation of burying these bodies fell upon the occupier of the house where they died'.[56]

Greaves for his part took legal advice from Dr Jesse Addams of Doctors' Commons, the college of ecclesiastical and admiralty lawyers in Knightrider Street in the City of London. Addams offered as his opinion that the children could not be regarded as being in the acceptable sense parishioners of Lower Tooting.[57] However, he was unable to state the grounds on which he had come to this conclusion, and so the disagreement rumbled on for weeks and months, as correct in its challenge to legal principle as it was squalid in the face of so much suffering, and so many young lives cut short.

In the end, Greaves and Norris backed down and submitted amended bills. These had been calculated at the normal rate for residents of Tooting, and the parishes duly paid. But as late as the summer of that year, Greaves was still nursing his resentment. When he wrote to the Strand guardians to acknowledge payment, he did so with an ill grace, insisting that he still believed himself legally entitled to receive, in full, the payment he had originally demanded. He added that he was accepting the reduced payment of £1 1s. a head, out of which he was obliged to pay the parish clerk's fee, only to draw a line under the matter. Really, though, the squabble had been a sideshow, from beginning to end. The bigger question was not how much should be paid for a child's burial but who was to blame for its death.[58]

Chapter Nine

Investigating Drouet

In most people's minds, reading the lurid accounts of events in Surrey Hall, there can have been no doubt that Drouet was a guilty man. Of course, it was not immediately obvious exactly what he was guilty of. So the question of the attribution of blame became a burning issue, one that dominated the inquests that took place in January, and preoccupied the writers of editorials who were covering this dramatic and scandalous affair.

Five parishes held inquests into the unnatural deaths of specific children. Whereas the inquest in Kensington was completed in a single sitting on 18 January, the remaining four, which were subject to adjournments, called for several sittings spread over a number of days: 8-18 January in St Pancras; 8–23 January in Holborn; 13–30 January in Islington; and 15–31 January in Chelsea. In Islington, in the Eastern Division of Middlesex, the coroner was William Baker. In the other four, in the Western Division, the coroner was either Wakley or his deputy, George Ireland Mills.

In ordinary circumstances it would have fallen to a member of the medical profession to notify the coroner of the need for an inquest, but when the four Holborn children died in the Royal Free Hospital, it was not a doctor but a guardian, William Winch, who called for a judicial inquiry. He sent a letter with the necessary details to the coroner's office a full twenty-four hours before the official report was received from the hospital, and he must have written immediately on hearing about the deaths of James Andrews and Jane Johnson, because the letter reached Wakley the next morning. Winch, who was in his forties, had no medical expertise. He was an ivory dealer with a business in Great James Street. What he had instead was a clear and confident sense of the duties of a workhouse guardian, and he was congratulated by Wakley for acting so properly and so swiftly.[1]

It was at the inquest in Holborn that Wakley made his most trenchant criticisms of the Drouet regime. Indeed, he turned the occasion into something of a show trial, and his summing up of the evidence ran to many thousands of words. He was heavily invested in this particular inquiry for the very good reason that he had a strong connection with the Royal Free Hospital. Not only had he accepted a role in its financial management alongside William Marsden, but his son, Thomas Henry Wakley, worked there as an assistant surgeon.[2]

In his role as coroner, Wakley was of course in a position to articulate his personal feelings about the Surrey Hall scandal, and it was a privilege he took full advantage of. In his opening address to the Holborn jury, his compassion shone forth. Although he had no doubt that the removal of children from the asylum had been the right course of action, he was aware that not all of them had been rescued yet, and the plight of those who remained was a matter of grave concern, obviously in terms of the threat to their physical health, but also in consideration of the mental anguish they were surely experiencing. 'What must be their feelings,' Wakley was reported as saying, 'when they saw van loads and coaches full of other children removed from the abode of disease, while they were still left exposed to its fiercest ravages!' Even the least sentimental among the jurymen would have found it hard not to be affected by protestations such as these.[3]

The inquests in Chelsea and Kensington were held in the boardrooms of the workhouses in Arthur Street and Gloucester Road. But this was not the general procedure, and the inquest in Holborn, having got under way in the Royal Free Hospital, where the jury viewed the bodies, moved after two sessions to the Globe Inn in Derby Street at the top end of Gray's Inn Road. The other two inquests also had public houses for venues, Islington at the Old Mermaid in Church Street, and St Pancras at the Elephant and Castle near the old church in King's Road. For all that it might appear odd to hold an inquest in a public house, it was a common practice. Such an establishment would have room enough for a sizeable gathering, and it might already have been used for not dissimilar purposes: auctions, religious services, and hearings before the magistrates. However, it was widely felt that the uninhibited atmosphere of a public house, and its association with drunkenness, hardly accorded with the serious and solemn business of an inquest. Wakley was one of those who disapproved. In the words of his biographer, the medical journalist Samuel Squire Sprigge, he feared that 'the taint of the tavern-parlour vitiated the evidence, ruined the discretion of the jurors, and detracted from the dignity of the coroner'.[4]

The jurors Wakley so readily dismissed as inebriates would have had to satisfy two conditions: in the first place, they had to be residents of the parish in which the children had died, and in the second, there had to be no known misdemeanours against their name. No expertise in the ways of the law or in medical matters was called for. Jurymen were selected by the coroner from lists of eligible parishioners and generally they were drawn from a pool of substantial householders. Hardly ever were they chosen from the professional and leisured classes, possibly because it was in the interest of coroners, most of whom were solicitors, to have the advantage over the jury of higher social status and greater technical knowledge. Nor were they summoned from the labouring classes, who did not qualify as ratepayers, and were therefore unlikely to be accepted as being respectable.[5]

As well as looking at the suitability of potential jurymen, coroners had to contend with the reluctance of many parishioners to carry out this civic duty. So great was this problem that at times they found themselves having to resort to financial inducements. At the inquest in Chelsea, for example, which ran to four sittings over seventeen days, Wakley bound the members of the jury over in £20 each to go the full course. It is easy to see why he had to assert himself in this way when one look at the newspaper reports reveals the length and complexity of the interchanges between coroner and witnesses. The longer an inquest lasted, and the more adjournments were found to be necessary, the more the jurymen were in danger of succumbing to tedium.[6]

Jurymen could also be actively obstructive. The foreman at the Holborn inquest was unhappy that Wakley had encouraged the jurymen to go down to Surrey Hall. His argument was not with the exercise as such, the purpose of which was to give serious and well-informed answers to questions of undeniable interest to the public at large. No, what irked him was the trouble and inconvenience the exercise had involved. For one thing, he and his colleagues had had no choice but to pay the travelling expenses from their own resources. Then it had taken time to get down to Lower Tooting, prowl about the premises, talk to Drouet, and come back up to London. For men who were engaged in business, and who for the most part were not in a position to hand over the running of the business to a second-in-command for any length of time, the whole operation had been an unnecessary imposition. It had achieved very little at considerable expense. A related concern was that an ill-informed rumour was being bruited about to the effect that the members of the jury were being given generous allowances to go on one fact-gathering journey after another. People suspected them of making a tidy profit from a serious judicial inquiry, whereas in truth they were out of pocket.[7]

Whatever accusations of profiteering were levelled at jurymen, no one would have envied them the task of viewing a body. But it was an absolute requirement in all inquests.[8] Indeed, so important was it as a guarantee of transparency that it had to be carried out as soon as the jury had been sworn in, and before the coroner set out the case and called for statements from the witnesses. Whereas members of the medical profession or the police force were able to look at a dead body with a degree of emotional detachment, a typical juryman would have had no such defence against the cold reality of death. The jury at the Holborn inquest were faced with the most unpleasant prospect of viewing four children's bodies. All were skeletal and two had been anatomised, and on the reasonable assumption that the respectable householders had human feelings, it would have been hard for them not to step back or turn away.

Indeed, these particular jurymen were more than usually put upon. As Gray's Inn Road was in the parish of St Pancras, they were doubly eligible and had to shuttle between two inquests. Having attended at the Royal Free Hospital, they had to reconvene later that day at the Elephant and Castle for the inquest into the deaths of four St Pancras children. Three had been buried already, but rather than having their bodies disinterred, the coroner, George Ireland Mills, ruled that it was only necessary to view the unburied body of the fourth. The cause of death, he assumed, was the same in all cases. That fourth child, Joseph Coster, was a seven-year-old who had been rescued from Surrey Hall, malnourished and with his ribs covered in sores, only to die in the workhouse. He now lay on a table in the public house. But by the time the inquest was adjourned at midnight, his body had served its purpose, and the next day it was lowered into the ground in the graveyard of the parish church.[9]

*   *   *

Whereas the inquiry itself was in principle a series of dialogues between the coroner and individual witnesses, the jury were not entirely passive.[10] They were permitted to have their say, and where they exercised this prerogative, the results could be explosive. At the Islington inquest under William Baker, the vestry clerk representing the board of guardians, who was a solicitor by the name of Robert Oldershaw, made the inflammatory claim that parish officials visiting Drouet's establishment had never been less than satisfied, and he had the written reports to prove it. Really it was a whitewash, an attempt to exculpate Drouet in the hope of covering up their own failures. It was also grossly insensitive given that the ravaged bodies of four Islington children, the youngest of whom was only three years old, were lying in a shed at Park House in Hackney, where they had died. For a jury of Islington ratepayers, this was too much, and when Oldershaw foolishly asserted that Drouet's dormitories were spacious and well ventilated, they broke in with hoots of sardonic laughter. 'You were never there, gentlemen,' Oldershaw retaliated, 'and you are not competent to form an opinion.' The foreman of the jury pointed out that Oldershaw's bland assessment of the asylum had been contradicted by the workhouse medical officer, and no doubt the argument would have long continued had the coroner not called an adjournment.[11]

Two days later, the controversy stirred up by Oldershaw still fuelled the inquiry, though the issue now was whether to call as witnesses children at Park House who had been removed from Surrey Hall. Perhaps predictably, the jury was divided. Some of its members insisted that the evidence of the children was essential. Others disagreed, presumably because they feared that involving child witnesses would complicate, and therefore prolong, the proceedings.[12] As the coroner refused to intervene, the matter went no further, but at all the other inquests children were indeed brought in to make statements, and one can well imagine that the impact they had on the jury was anything but insignificant. After all the adult statements, and the expert views, and the preambles, directions and summings up of the coroners themselves, here were the actual survivors of the Drouet regime. Anyone wanting to picture the sort of children who had been abandoned by the parishes to a terrible fate had only to look at the boys and girls now standing before the coroner. They had only to note their ages and observe the marks of neglect and starvation imprinted on their bodies and in their faces.

The most dramatic of these encounters occurred at the inquest into the death of John Wilkins, the five-year-old from Kensington. He had been farmed out with Drouet for seven months along with his sister, Eliza, who was nine. Now, in the Gloucester Road boardroom, their mother Hannah had many complaints to make about Surrey Hall, one of them being that Eliza had come back with a bad case of itch. At Wakley's behest, Eliza was brought into the room, carried by a nurse like a babe in arms and wrapped in a blanket. The master of the workhouse and two medical men confirmed that she had been very ill for some time:

> On the blanket being opened at the feet, the lower part of the legs were found to be covered with rags, but sufficient of the feet and legs were visible to show that the flesh was covered with brown marks of itch, which were said to extend in the same manner all over the body of the unfortunate girl.[13]

Even the medical professionals found it hard to control their reaction. Wakley himself admitted that it was the worst case of itch he had ever encountered. It was 'really frightful', he said, and Eliza was 'a perfectly sickening sight'.

Eliza was an unusual 'witness' in that she did not have to say a word: the mere sight of her unfortunate condition was impactful enough. But other children did speak at the inquests, and all the evidence indicates that they found it quite an ordeal. When John Welch was escorted into the Globe Inn to make his statement, it was obvious that he would not be clearly visible to all the members of the jury, being small for his age. Wakley ordered the boy to stand on a table, which cannot have helped his composure, and he might even have had the misfortune to notice Drouet, who was sitting in the room with his lawyer.[14]

The response of jurymen to these juvenile witnesses was at times astonishingly condescending. At the inquest in Holborn, they were especially vocal. They laughed at accounts of the cruel punishment meted out to the boys, and at the sadistic language the schoolmaster Joshua Brown employed against John Welch when he was caught complaining about the shortage of food. They laughed at Henry Hartshorn, who claimed that he had always been hungry at Surrey Hall, because boys the world over claim all the time that they are hungry, and then they laughed again when Henry claimed that he had only ever been 'whacked' once, as if he believed that he had been unfairly deprived of his due. They laughed when they were told that the schoolmasters routinely 'whacked' boys before letting them go out to the latrine in the yard. Wakley was dismayed at the schoolmasters' twisted ingenuity and did not laugh. On the contrary, he observed, icily, that 'if a boy bore a thrashing, then there could be no mistake that he really required to go out'. At this, the jurymen laughed again.[15]

Even more disturbing than the mocking of the child witnesses were instances of intimidation. One of the guilty adults was William Roberts James, the clerk to the Holborn guardians, who was himself a witness and was called on to give a detailed breakdown of the workhouse's dealings with Drouet. Later in the proceedings, when ten-year-old Patrick Sheen was giving evidence of conditions in Surrey Hall, and was in the process of revealing the impotence of the visiting guardians, one of the jurymen spotted James trying to 'catch the eye of the boy' in an effort to keep him quiet. Being a man of principle, the juryman tried to persuade Wakley to have James removed from the room. James flew to his own defence, asserting that far from giving Patrick Sheen a threatening look, he had merely 'put his head forward' in order to hear properly what the boy was saying. By now Patrick was crying. 'Did you know that Mr James was present when you entered the room?' Wakley asked. 'No,' Patrick replied through his tears. Wakley understood why the boy was upset. 'Do not cry,' he said, assuring him that he must not fear being punished for speaking the truth.[16]

At the same inquest Henry Hartshorn had testified to a number of the abuses practised at Surrey Hall. When the session ended, Drouet approached the boy. He was incandescent with rage. 'As for you, you lying young scoundrel,' he spluttered, 'you'll be taken notice of before the night's over!' There is nothing to suggest that any actual harm came to Henry as a result of Drouet's empty threat. Nevertheless, at the next session a man from the workhouse, a tailor by the name of Joseph Saunders, was prompted by the foreman of the jury to report the incident to Wakley. Since he was under orders to keep a careful eye on the boys, Saunders had seen what had happened. While ruling that Drouet's behaviour had not actually been in contempt of court, as the boy had already given his evidence, Wakley pointed out that it had been reprehensible. He added that it had also been highly impolitic because it presented Drouet in a less than flattering light. As if to underline Wakley's observation, the foreman of the jury confirmed that news of the incident had indeed become public knowledge, and this being so, he was glad on Drouet's behalf that the truth had finally come out. The version of events currently going round the neighbourhood had been greatly exaggerated, he contended, possibly to the point where, in the retelling, a threat of violence had become an actual assault.[17]

That there was gossip of this sort is far from remarkable. Crowds routinely gathered outside the inquests, at times spilling chaotically into the road. On the whole, they consisted of local men and women who were either concerned about the deaths of so many pauper children, and wanted something to be done, or were drawn to the inquests by a taste for spectacle. When the proceedings opened in Chelsea on 15 January, several hundred spectators gathered at the bone house of the church of St Luke. There, in sombre mood, they watched the jurymen walk over from the workhouse, which stood a street away, to view the bodies of the dead children. Many had come to express pity for young lives lost and horror at the crime, but not all. Violent death had a strange appeal, and in 1849 it was still lawful to assemble in a public place to watch a man or a woman die with a noose around their neck.[18]

Drouet himself must have been an attraction of sorts. From the moment news of the catastrophe broke, he was set to become a household name. As more and more details came out in Kite's statements to the press, and in Grainger's mammoth report on his visit to Surrey Hall, which Wakley was determined should not be 'locked up' at Gwydyr House but made accessible to the public, his notoriety would have grown. He was not perhaps an obvious criminal. He had not killed with poison, nor had he dispatched his victims by brute force. He had not murdered a member of his family. But by the same token he had none of the excuses of the regular criminal: he could plead in his defence neither penury nor the moral blindness engendered by envy or lust. He was fully master of himself in all that he had done. He would have been viewed with fascination as well as with disgust.

The parishes had more than one chance to afford him an ironic welcome as he attended some sessions of the inquests in person. Probably he would not have attended any if he had not felt that he had been put under pressure by Wakley. He had heard that at the first session in Holborn, which he had contrived to miss, the coroner had let it be known that his absence was not appreciated as he was keen to question him on where he had sourced the children's food.[19] Drouet must have seen the direction the matter was going in because he made a point of attending subsequent Holborn sessions with his lawyer in tow. By then he had also attended the first of the Chelsea sessions. There, he fielded Wakley's questions. But no one seems to know if he was among the spectators when the jurymen went to view the bodies in the bone house.[20]

There are no records of Drouet attending any of the other three inquests. Indeed, he wrote twice to William Baker, on 25 and 29 January, to account for his absence from the Islington sessions. He could not really have had a better excuse, as he was able to say, quite truthfully, that a warrant had been issued for his arrest and he was already entangled in the complications surrounding his bail.[21] For many, it was a moment of supreme drama, but for Drouet, the man who had presided over so much misery, it was the beginning of the end. His much vaunted respectability and what he thought of as his good name would soon be in tatters. His world was about to fall apart.

*   *   *

The arrest had been announced at the Globe Inn on 23 January. Whereas the juries at Kensington and St Pancras, who had reached their verdicts five days before, found only that cholera had been the cause of death, the jury at Holborn, having deliberated for nearly three quarters of an hour, had found Drouet guilty of manslaughter. The session had started at ten in the morning and it was now eleven at night. Wakley turned to the police constable whose role it was to enforce the decisions of the coroner. 'Is Mr Drouet here?' he asked. 'If he is, take him into custody.' The constable told Wakley that Drouet had absented himself two hours earlier, and it was then that Wakley, with the power invested in him by coronial law, issued the warrant for his arrest.[22]

Wakley's dislike of Drouet was so deep that he wanted to see him behind bars. However, the law that granted him powers of arrest gave him no authority in the matter of bail. That discussion took place not in the Globe Inn but in Westminster Hall, where William Ballantine, Drouet's lawyer, submitted his client's application to Sir William Erle, a puisne judge at the Court of Queen's Bench. Erle at first rejected the application on the grounds that the witnesses' depositions were still with Wakley, and that Drouet had not yet surrendered to the warrant for his arrest. Later the same day, though, Erle agreed to have the depositions brought to him, issuing a writ of *certiorari*.[23]

Ballantine for his part assured Erle that Drouet would come up to Westminster Hall in three days' time to surrender to the warrant. He had in fact advised Drouet to remain in Tooting and not attend other inquests, where he might find himself taken into custody before Erle had seen the Holborn depositions. By the start of the following week, the depositions had finally been retrieved from Wakley, and Drouet surrendered to arrest.[24]

Bail was set by the Court of Queen's Bench at £200 for Drouet and £100 each for two sureties or £50 each for four.[25] For the time being Drouet was free, but he was also in poor health. His chronic cardiac condition had been aggravated by the enormous strain of seeing five inquests simultaneously reduce his reputation to rubble, and Ballantine, in his dealings with the Queen's Bench, put forward 'inflammation both of the heart and lungs' as a reason why his client had gone to ground in Lower Tooting.[26] This sort of appeal would have cut no ice with Wakley, though. He had been thwarted in his efforts to get Drouet behind bars, and although he acknowledged that the Queen's Bench had followed proper procedure, he was disappointed at the outcome and was certainly not afraid to say so. What irked him, apart from his belief that Drouet had absconded from justice, was that bail had been set in a case of such magnitude. Erle was perfectly capable of refusing bail: he had done so only recently in the case of two silversmiths charged with fraudulent practice. To Wakley it seemed as if the crime of manslaughter was being treated as less serious than the crime of fraud.[27]

Ballantine continued to exploit his client's illness. In particular he tried to persuade Erle to have the trial moved from the Central Criminal Court, which included Lower Tooting in its jurisdiction, to the Court of Queen's Bench. When Erle objected, Ballantine pointed out that whilst a defendant was under no obligation to appear in person at the Queen's Bench, except by order of the court, the same dispensation did not apply in the Central Criminal Court. He offered the alarming scenario of an ailing Drouet at the bar, anxious and stressed, and maybe even suffering a fatal collapse. Nor was he exaggerating the dangers, as he had signed affidavits attesting to Drouet's condition from Walter Chapman and William James Kite, as well as from a third medical man, Septimus Wray.[28]

Ballantine was one of the top barristers of the day, and Drouet, who had been well advised by his solicitor in his choice of a representative, could scarcely have retained a more formidable ally. He was determined to keep his client well away from the Old Bailey, and as well as playing on the fragile state of his health, he questioned the basis on which he had been committed to trial. As he put it, there was not 'a scintilla' of evidence against Drouet that actually needed to be tried by a jury. What is more, by summoning children as witnesses, Wakley had resorted to 'the most unfair and scandalous means' to influence the jury at the inquest in Holborn. And because the newspapers had published inflammatory articles in the wake of that inquest, a fair trial was now all but impossible.[29]

The articles Ballantine was referring to listed overcrowding as one of the main criticisms of Surrey Hall. The figures were damning. Drouet had taken twice as many children as he had room for, cramming 1,400 into premises designed for no more than 700.[30] An even starker analysis had been presented by William Marsden at the inquest in Holborn. He had gone down to Surrey Hall to measure the wards, and with the help of a surveyor had calculated that the volume of respirable air available to any one child in the dormitories would be exhausted after eight hours. In the boys' schoolroom the measurements were even bleaker: the room was occupied for up to six hours and each child breathed fresh air for only a little over two. The wind was an additional danger: when it blew from the north east it brought down with it the poisonous London air.[31]

As well as being an evil in itself, the overcrowding had led to other examples of negligence, such as the shortfall in the number of domestic and medical staff and the woefully inadequate education. More than anything, it had exacerbated the problem of malnutrition, by allowing, for example, the tougher children to take advantage of the unregulated distribution of food to steal from the weaker. Marsden was again able to provide figures. He had taken the measurements of comparable sets of twenty-five boys from Surrey Hall and twenty-five from the Welsh Charity School in Gray's Inn Road. The Welsh boys were on average over seven pounds heavier and they measured almost an inch more round the arm. The Surrey Hall boys not only had comparatively wasted limbs but measured over an inch more round the abdomen, and these physical characteristics, in Marsden's judgement, had been produced by a diet with too little solid matter and far too much fluid.[32]

Drouet's diet was universally condemned. Generally, it was the meagre quantities that attracted the criticism, but the quality of the food was also subjected to hostile scrutiny, as exemplified by a comment in the *Era* that drew on Dickens as well as Christian morality:

> Drouet may, with his brother and other underlings, set up a "Do-the-boys Hall", and even obtain boarders; they may appeal to the inhabitants of Tooting, and find sympathy in the butchers and bakers there (not but that we believe they bought wholesale stuff in the cheapest possible market), but they never can "farm" parish children again; their cruel occupation is gone, and the great amount of their iniquity lies between them and One who takes special interest in poor and friendless children.[33]

The *Era* was not making unfounded allegations. Drouet had indeed drawn on his experience of workhouse provisioning to work hand in glove with local suppliers, one of whom, a butcher at Kennington by the name of Jonathan Gain, was married to his half-sister Margaret Elizabeth. The suppliers were duly summoned by Wakley to make statements in Holborn, and it is hard to imagine what the jury made of them as they recited prices per weight of product in the mysterious language of pounds and shillings, and tons and hundredweight, in much the same way as Marsden quoted the measurements in inches of the children in the hospital and the volume in cubic feet of breathable air in the rooms of the asylum. They itemised the Prince Regent potatoes and the York Red potatoes and the Quebec potatoes, the beef on the bone, and the beef without bone, and the whole wether sheep with an earnestness that provoked the laughter of the jury. They expatiated on the quality of their bread and their flour and their split peas. But aside from the unintended comedy, what emerged with absolute clarity was Drouet's concern to spend as little on essential supplies as he could get away with.[34]

*   *   *

The *Era*'s allusion to Dotheboys Hall was more than literary name-dropping. For in all discussions of the plight of the poor, and especially of the children of the poor, no one spoke more persuasively than Charles Dickens. It is almost inconceivable that at a time when his fame was firmly established, and when he had already explored related themes in works such as *Oliver Twist* and *Nicholas Nickleby*, Dickens would choose to remain silent about a tragedy of a peculiarly harrowing kind. True to form, he spoke out in a series of four articles in the *Examiner* in which he chronicled events from the first outbreak of cholera to Drouet's trial at the Old Bailey. The articles were anonymous, but they were fully characteristic of the social commentary in Dickens's journalism and novels, both in style and in theme.[35]

There is no evidence that Dickens went down to Lower Tooting in person. However, he would have had at his disposal the quantity of newspaper reporting that was appearing every day, and he would also have had access to inside information through his close connection with the secretary of the General Board of Health, Henry Austin, who was married to his sister Letitia. Austin and Dickens had helped one another in their respective work on other issues of public importance, one supplying details of official policy, and the other providing a rich source of publicity. In 1849, by virtue of his professional position, Austin was at the centre of the latest storm, and it is perfectly possible that he and his brother-in-law collaborated in some way.

Dickens had begun contributing to the *Examiner* at the prompting of his friend and biographer, John Forster, who had assumed the editorship of the newspaper in 1847 and saw it as his role to maintain its radical traditions. The four Drouet articles were published over a period of three months as a continuous series uninterrupted by other subject matter. Possibly they were commissioned by Forster, but Dickens would in any case have taken a natural interest in what must have seemed to him the realisation of the sort of social injustices he had been treating in his fiction. It is, therefore, a curious fact that the first article appeared as late as the Saturday of the third week of the crisis, on 20 January. But it may have needed the bombshell of the 13 January newspaper reports to persuade Dickens to add his voice to the outcry, and as the *Examiner* was a weekly newspaper, anything he wrote after that date would appear at the earliest on the following Saturday. Besides, he had been lured away from London from 7 to 10 January by the Stanfield Hall murders in Norfolk. Bartholomew Peter Drouet and James Blomfield Rush were competing for his attention.[36]

In that first article, which was published under the title 'The Paradise at Tooting', Dickens went over much the same ground as the editorials in the principal London newspapers. He inveighed against the vicious characters of Drouet and his half-brother Richard, compared the indifference of the Surrey coroner William Carter with the righteous energy of Wakley, and denounced the shortcomings of the Poor Law Commissioners and the many parish officials, and above all those of the Holborn guardians. Nothing he said had not already been said elsewhere. But by the time he concluded the opening paragraph, he had created an extraordinary and unforgettable picture of a 'paradise' in the country, a model establishment run by a benevolent owner, where poor children from the workhouses were sent to die:

> When it first became known that a virulent and fatal epidemic had broken out in Mr Drouet's farming establishment for pauper children at Tooting, the comfortable flourish of trumpets usual on such occasions (Sydney Smith's admirable description of it will be fresh in the minds of many of our readers) was performed as a matter of course. Of all similar establishments on earth, that at Tooting was the most admirable. Of all similar contractors on earth, Mr Drouet was the most disinterested, zealous, and unimpeachable. Of all the wonders ever wondered at, nothing perhaps had ever occurred more wonderful than the outbreak and rapid increase of a disorder so horrible, in a place so perfectly regulated. There was no warning of its approach. Nothing was less to be expected. The farmed children were slumbering in the lap of peace and plenty; Mr Drouet, the farmer, was slumbering with an easy conscience, but with one eye perpetually open, to keep watch upon the blessings he diffused, and upon the happy infants under his paternal charge; when, in a moment, the destroyer was upon them, and Tooting churchyard became too small for the piles of children's coffins that were carried out of this Elysium every day.[37]

The second article, 'The Tooting Farm', which was published a week later on 27 January, added nothing of significance on the subject of the asylum itself. Instead, Dickens concentrated on the implications of the guilty verdict that had been returned against Drouet four days previously at the Globe Inn. He also expressed his fear that the scandal might be exploited for political ends by Chartist agitators.[38] In the third and fourth articles, 'A Recorder's Charge' and 'The Verdict for Drouet', which appeared on 3 March and 21 April, although he revisited the horrors of the asylum, he was principally concerned with the pursuit of Drouet through the Central Criminal Court.[39]

This is not to say that Dickens lost sight of his original subject of the sufferings of the Surrey Hall children after the publication of the first article. On the contrary, there is clear evidence that he was still dwelling on this painful matter long after the event. In *Bleak House*, for example, the Snagsbys' servant, Guster, had been in Surrey Hall as a child, an orphan consigned to the charge of 'the Christian Saint whose shrine was at Tooting'.[40] There were also references in articles in *Household Words* looking back to the events of 1849. For example, Dickens proposed in 1850 that the 'most infamous and atrocious enormity committed at Tooting' had been a more effective spur to public discontent with the treatment of pauper children than the activities of Chartists.[41] Three years later he wrote about an inmate of Urania Cottage, the home for destitute women in Shepherd's Bush, who had been brought up as an orphan in Surrey Hall. Although 'it did not appear that she was naturally stupid', she was intellectually underdeveloped, a problem Dickens attributed to the neglect she had suffered during her formative years. It was thought that she was about eighteen years old, but she herself had no idea when she had been born. She had once been apprenticed to a woman who made artificial flowers. But she was treated badly, and when she ran away, she took with her some of her mistress's old clothes, a crime that landed her in prison for six months. 'This girl had not a friend in the world,' Dickens observed, 'and had never known a natural affection, or formed a natural tie, upon the face of this earth.' She was a classic example of a poor unfortunate who had once been one of Drouet's children.[42]

As well as lambasting the Poor Law authorities for turning a blind eye to the outrages of men like Drouet, Dickens called for the dismantling of the entire system of farming workhouse children. He set out his position forcefully in 'The Tooting Farm':

> If the system of farming pauper children cannot exist without the danger of another Tooting Farm being weeded by the grisly hands of Want, Disease, and Death, let it now be abolished. If the Poor Law, as it stands, be not efficient for the prevention of such inhuman evils, let it be now rendered more efficient. If it has unfortunately happened, though by no man's deliberate intention or malignity – as who can doubt it has? – that the children of sundry poor men and women have been carried to untimely graves, who might have lived and thriven, let there be seen a resolute determination that the like shall never happen any more.[43]

It seems not unlikely that Dickens often raised this question, and there is mention in Forster's biography of a dinner party at the writer's house in Devonshire Terrace at which he apparently waxed eloquent on the subject of Drouet. No doubt the name had come up in conversation because the trial at the Old Bailey had recently ended. But it would also appear that the subject was not treated equally seriously by the assembled company of intellectuals. When two of the guests were suddenly taken ill in the course of the evening, it was jokingly suggested that Dickens was 'no better himself than a second

Drouet' on account of the poor quality of his food and his failure to provide the necessary medical care for his victims. The joke started with Albany Fonblanque, who was Forster's predecessor as editor of the *Examiner*, and 'was well kept up' by the fashionable homeopathic doctor Frederic Quin, the painter and sculptor Edwin Landseer, and Percy Smythe, 6th Viscount Strangford. Forster was happy to note that the 'uproarious mirth' dispelled the gloomy mood that had descended over the occasion. 'For nothing really serious had happened,' he explained, presumably unaware of the sad irony of this remark.[44]

Not that Dickens was above such tasteless humour himself. At Gad's Hill Place he displayed in his library a large collection of sham books with eye-catching titles of his own devising. Some had a connection with his strongly held views, an example being the *History of a Short Chancery Suit* in twenty-one volumes, while others were merely witty, such as *Socrates on Wedlock* and *Jonah's Account of the Whale*. Among these bizarre items was a *Drouett's Farming* in five volumes, and in the light of the wordplay in many of the titles, there can be little doubt that 'farming' was intended to be understood in two ways.[45] One cannot help wondering if Dickens would have done well to express his view of Drouet in a less facetious manner. When all is said and done, though, he was an important witness to the fallout from the Surrey Hall scandal. He was one of those who responded vigorously to the revelations of the inquests and the trial, and in doing so he made himself a publicist for the view, which must have been held widely, that a local outrage had properly become a matter of national shame.

Chapter Ten

On Trial

On Saturday, 13 January, for the first time, Kite was able to report to the General Board of Health that no new cases of cholera had been diagnosed among the children remaining in Surrey Hall. It was a turning point, even though some of those who were still being treated for the disease, or for complications arising from it, would die in the days ahead. Then on the following Saturday, he went a stage further by recording that no deaths had occurred in the previous forty-eight hours. 'From the withdrawal of the healthy children from the establishment,' he added, 'the disease has left us as suddenly as it came upon us.' It was almost as if cholera had a mind of its own.[1]

Soon after the end of the epidemic, Kite bowed out from Surrey Hall. He signed the death certificate of a boy who died of pneumonia in the second week of February, but there is nothing to indicate that he signed any more after this date, and later he would say that he had been employed at the asylum for five weeks before the outbreak of cholera and for two after it had died out. In due course he would establish himself in general practice in West Bromwich. But his situation in the immediate aftermath of the Surrey Hall episode is unclear, beyond the fact that he was one of the six medical men called in at around that time to treat the ailing Drouet. However, his principal employment had run its course. He had been taken on to provide medical care to the children, and all but a handful of those children had now gone. Surrey Hall continued to be a home for Drouet and his family but as an institution it had ceased to exist.[2]

All this while, Surrey Hall's ill fame was gaining currency, and in a bid to outmanoeuvre his detractors, Drouet opened the doors of the establishment to the public. They were open on a daily basis from ten in the morning till midday, free of charge, and a newspaper advertisement issued an invitation to 'all Persons who wish to satisfy themselves as to the Accommodation his Establishment afforded the Children'.[3] Sidney Godolphin Osborne was outraged. In a letter to the editor of *The Times*, dated 5 February, he declared that the 'new exhibition' outrivalled even Madame Tussauds by offering the spectacle of not just one but many chambers of horrors. Moreover, although he was well able to imagine that those chambers had been tidied up for the benefit of the public, they were possessed of a haunting actuality. It was all very well for the beds to have clean linen, and to be neatly arranged in dormitories with fresh wash on the walls, but they were still beds in which real children had once lain and in which real children had suffered and died.[4]

Osborne called out the fakery in no uncertain terms. Although he had not visited the exhibition to see it for himself, he imagined Drouet and his staff taking visitors on a tour of the premises, at pains to present a picture of a well-run operation, which, while totally at odds with accounts of the 'real' asylum, would go some way towards silencing the critics. Everything on this tour would be staged. The Chelsea children, who had still not been removed by the guardians, would be on display with their 'cheeks well flannelled up', as if clean faces were the norm. The schoolrooms, where in earlier times so much unhappiness had been inflicted by the harsh discipline of the masters, would be buzzing with purposeful activity. The older children would be merrily reciting their lessons in a bogus display of knowledge, which had no doubt been learnt under duress. The younger ones would be 'drawing pretty horses' with the help of a kind young schoolmistress, who would be a picture of wholesomeness and radiant goodness of character. But the masterstroke would be the sight awaiting the visitor in the dining hall, where Drouet, all smiles and joviality, would be handing round buns to his grateful little charges.[5]

The visitors to Osborne's imagined Surrey Hall, if they were not entirely taken in by the deception, would at the very least play along with it. They would admire the good order and clean condition of the asylum and express their satisfaction in written testimonials, exactly as the visiting guardians had done. Walking from one pristine room to another, they would chatter about biased coroners and jurymen, posturing government officials, and the busybodies who published letters in *The Times*. Among them would be the provisioners who had done business with Drouet, paying homage to their benefactor.[6]

The letter, almost all the way through, resorted to irony and ridicule, but at the very end the tone changed as Osborne defined the whole tragedy of the child whose life is wasted in futile poverty:

The beadle, echoing the parochial mind, may look at him as a sort of vermin, but the country has a stake in him – nay, God has a soul in him. He is not an animal of that low nature that, like a hound puppy, we may put it out "to walk" – only bargaining that it is fed so that it can grow. If fed as he should be, and tended and taught as he ought to be, the pauper boy has every chance of growing into a man, who may by his industry and honesty contribute to his country's wealth, by his faith and virtue to his Maker's glory; if starved, neglected, foully taught, or not taught at all, he may be the subject of an inquest on the circumstance of his death, or the subject of a trial at the bar of justice, in that, living, he has lived to commit those crimes which entail, for the good of all, the punishment, even to death, of the criminal. I don't think the Tooting Pauperama will pay.[7]

The Tooting Pauperama was Drouet's stage-managed cosmorama. He had turned Surrey Hall into an entertainment, all pasteboard and paint.

At about this time, the simmering discontent over the deaths at Surrey Hall finally boiled over. An angry public flocked to meetings in lecture halls in the heart of the metropolis. Even the weather, which was truly awful, seemed to be responding to the mood of the moment, and on the morning of 12 February a dense fog settled over the city. The sun, which had been seen early in the morning as a ball of fire rising above the horizon, was soon obscured, and when the street lamps were extinguished, a darkness ensued that was as black as night. The link-boys' torches and the lights in the shops were of little avail as pedestrians stumbled and vehicles jammed up against one another. At nine the fog began to lift, but until the sun broke through, the sky was suffused with a deep red colour described by many as the colour of blood. For a while there was chaos. Those with businesses or places of work to go to made desperate efforts to steer a way through the gloom. Several tried to cross roads by threading a route through the traffic, hoping that it would stay stationary, only to be crushed between two vehicles when one juddered forward or the other slipped back. One man was kicked by a horse pulling a butcher's cart, another escaped injury by inches when an omnibus rammed into his carriage, driving its pole through the dashboard. A policeman on duty at Camden Station was killed by a train.[8]

The public meetings were only in part about Drouet, whose crimes by now had been fully exposed by the coroners and painstakingly documented in the press. Since his case was now a matter for the courts, the more pressing concern was to push for the abolition of the New Poor Law, as it was the

New Poor Law and its bureaucracy of commissioners and boards of guardians that gave men like Drouet space in which to operate. For this reason the meetings were highly politicised, rich in eloquence, and emotionally charged. One of the speakers, George Wilson, had spent time in the Croydon Union workhouse. There he had been separated from his wife and prevented from seeing his children, two of whom had fallen ill and died. He spoke from the heart and stirred strong feelings in his audience with his unadorned statement of his experiences. He was a true grassroots campaigner.[9]

Other speakers were seasoned agitators and the most notable of these was Charles Cochrane. He was a social reformer, and in 1842 he had founded the National Philanthropic Association, which numbered amongst its operations a soup kitchen and a refuge for homeless men, women and children. Then in 1846 he had set up a Poor Man's Guardian Society with the aim of alleviating the effects of the 1834 legislation, and had published a weekly penny newspaper to promote the work of the Society and appeal to potential subscribers by means of graphic accounts of the extreme deprivation he saw all around him on the streets of the capital. On his death in 1855, the *Gentleman's Magazine* noted that he had been vilified by the parish authorities, who were convinced that his 'philanthropic exertions had concentrated all the idlers and vagabonds in this huge metropolis' into Leicester Square.[10] The *Magazine* presented him as well meaning but officious, an eccentric and possibly a charlatan, who in his younger years had taken to the road as an itinerant musical beggar, an adventure he celebrated in *Journal of a Tour* under the assumed character of Señor Juan de Vega, a Spanish minstrel. However, his relevance in 1849 was securely founded on such public-spirited interventions as his protests against the infamous mismanagement of Marlborough House, the City of London Union workhouse in Peckham, where violence was a common occurrence and casual paupers were forced to sleep naked and three in a bed. Viscount Ebrington, the Parliamentary Secretary to the Poor Law Board, wriggled out of all responsibility, but he still thought of Cochrane as a very persistent thorn in his side.[11]

By far the most dramatic of these meetings was convened on 27 February in front of St Paul's Church in Covent Garden. The venue was chosen as being conspicuous, and the advertised time of the meeting, which was one o'clock in the afternoon, would have guaranteed a sizeable assembly. In the event it was claimed that a crowd numbering in the thousands, and composed in large part of members of the poorest classes, had gathered in front of the hustings. The atmosphere must have been lively, to say the least, and the moment Cochrane clambered on to the platform to deliver his trademark assault on the New Poor Law and underline its role in the deaths of Drouet's children, it was easy to see that the meeting would get out of hand. Cochrane's oration may have won the raucous approval of the crowd, but it turned out to be little more than a preface to the audacious performance of the next speaker, the radical writer George Reynolds. In Reynolds's view, the legal wrangling over the charges against Drouet amounted to an establishment plot, the aim of which was to protect the interests of a callous entrepreneur who had destroyed the lives of innocent children. It was not good enough that Drouet would face trial for the lesser crime of manslaughter, and he, Reynolds, was now moving an amendment to the effect that the deaths in Surrey Hall were tantamount to murder.[12]

The crowd greeted Reynolds's inflammatory words with resounding applause, but one man who was conspicuously unamused was Francis Smedley, the High Bailiff of Westminster. It was on his authority that the meeting had been allowed to go ahead in the first place, and he had made it a condition that there should be no prejudicial references to Drouet, who must be presumed innocent until a court proved him guilty. Now that Reynolds had failed to abide by his condition, he was bound not to sanction the amendment. This was the spark that was needed to set the meeting alight. The crowd hissed and hurled insults at Smedley as he tried to restrain Reynolds, and then cheered loudly when Reynolds took off his hat and signalled to them to bellow their support for his amendment. There was a scuffle, with two of Reynolds's companions seizing Smedley by the collar, and Smedley pushing Reynolds to the back of the hustings while threatening him with his legitimate powers.[13]

Smedley then further infuriated the crowd by declaring the meeting to be at an end and leaving the hustings. But the drama was not over, for when Reynolds took the chair and tried again to move his amendment, he was astonished to discover that the document had been whisked away by the departing bailiff, who by now was nowhere to be seen. Undeterred, he took aim at the Poor Law Board, and the wild acclaim was still ringing in his ears when four carpenters climbed up with hatchets with orders from Smedley to smash the hustings down. The crowd dispersed, but Reynolds had won the day, and he was escorted from the market by an entourage of costermongers, errand boys and pickpockets from the neighbouring slums.[14]

*   *   *

On 24 January, Wakley had appointed William Carter prosecutor in Drouet's trial.[15] Carter was the beadle of St Pancras, the parish in which the four children in the Royal Free Hospital had died. Wakley had also decided that the case against Drouet should make reference to only one of the children. He had chosen James Andrews, as James had been the first of the four to die. There had also been many witnesses to James's illness in the asylum and decline in the hospital, and one of these, his eight-year-old brother Joseph, might win the sympathy of a jury. The deaths of three Chelsea children, all girls, were added to that of James Andrews. Two of the three, Martha Pollington and Mary Killick, aged thirteen and nine, had been attended in their final hours by a workhouse nurse from Islington. She was Sarah Freeman, and she had children of her own in the asylum, one of whom had recently died. The third girl, Emma Ingar, who was also nine, had died at four in the morning with her mother at her side.[16]

Meanwhile, the trial at the Old Bailey had been set back from the February session to the session starting on 9 April. One reason was that William Clarkson, who was acting as counsel for the prosecution, had applied for and been granted a postponement, which would give him time to prepare a case. Another was that the court had listened to Ballantine's concerns over Drouet's health, which was now so precarious that at one point it had even been rumoured that he had died. The origins of the rumour were obscure, but it caused a sensation in St Pancras, where it was suggested that Drouet had sent the master of the workhouse a dying statement repudiating the charges made against him, which he naturally regarded as baseless. In an operatic touch he asserted that he died a murdered man. The St Pancras vestry professed itself aghast at the news, and with some dexterity succeeded in painting Drouet as a victim, first of circumstances beyond his control, and then of a hostility whipped up by those two adversaries of his, the coroners' juries and the press. One kind soul added the loss of his wife to the list of Drouet's misfortunes.[17]

To scotch the rumour of his death, Drouet's solicitors had a disclaimer printed in the evening editions. Kite also issued three press releases on three successive days to the effect that Drouet was alive and had been visited by a heart and lung consultant, but was in such poor shape that only his medical attendants and his half-brother Richard were permitted to see him, and that all discussion of his recent troubles was forbidden. A fourth release was issued a week later. It had to go out under the name of Richard Drouet because by then Kite had packed his bags and gone.[18]

That the cards were stacked in Drouet's favour first became apparent when the four bills were submitted to the grand jury, and the Recorder of London, Charles Ewan Law, cast doubt on the sufficiency of the evidence. Law argued that it was not possible to identify what exactly the defendant had done to cause the death of the children, and even though the grand jury returned the bills as true, his comments refused to go away. They glided easily from an adherence to judicial principle to protective assumptions about men of money and respectability. Dickens, who had read the details reported in the newspapers, was appalled by what he saw as a blatant case of intellectual dishonesty, and he analysed it incisively in 'A Recorder's Charge'. To argue that the specific and identifiable act was the only basis for a prosecution was, he felt, to fly in the face of common sense, and yet 'again and again the Recorder jingles and juggles with this phrase'.[19]

However, Dickens's reservations about the Recorder of London were eclipsed by his dislike of Thomas Joshua Platt, the judge who had been appointed to the trial. In August 1848 he had published an article in the *Examiner* describing a court case Platt presided over at the crown court in Gloucester. The defendant 'peeping over the dock' was a boy, Richard Hooper, charged with stealing a purse containing two half crowns and a threepenny piece from a woman in the village of Leckhampton. Hooper was only ten. Evidently, though, the boy's age carried little weight with Platt, who sentenced him to seven years' transportation. Actually, Platt was prepared to reduce this swingeing and disproportionate punishment to one month's imprisonment on condition of good behaviour, and the following day he did indeed revoke the sentence of transportation. However, the term of imprisonment he imposed in its place had increased from the original one month to two years.[20]

Dickens was bewildered by these vacillations, which betrayed professional incompetence as well as a lack of sympathy for erring human nature. In his *Examiner* article, 'A Truly British Judge!', he painted a pathetic picture of a senior member of the judiciary dealing clumsily with, and effectively tormenting, a child, albeit one who had committed a crime. Platt would probably have protested that he had been striving to get the sentence right, but Dickens was having none of it:

> Of course one cannot irreverently assume that the learned Judge, in at last making up his mind, so agitated upon the fate of this little wicked boy, deprived him of his liberty – tore him from his rural home at the picturesque village of Leckhampton – separated him, at his tender years, from the sweet face of green and flowery nature, and the sweeter sympathies of kindred – and consigned him for two tedious years to the contamination, the stone cells and passages, the chilling damps, the rugged turnkeys, stolid chaplains, and staring red brick walls of the great Gloucester Penitentiary, out of a *tender regard* for the child's future morals.

Dickens thought of the trial as bad theatre. It was a courtroom melodrama, an entertainment of sorts brought up to the provinces by a second-rate metropolitan company, with a 'serio-comic functionary' in a leading role.[21]

Given his unfortunate earlier impression of Platt's capabilities, Dickens would have been anticipating a similarly dismal performance at Drouet's trial, which ran for two days from 13 to 14 April. But by all accounts his poor opinion of Platt was not shared by the judge's fellow professionals. He was regarded by them as a plain speaker with no flair for eloquence, and more a man of sense than a man of books, but for all that, and possibly because of that, they liked him. At the time of the trial he was sixty years old. His smooth, oval face appeared to one of his associates to be 'made to create laughter', and yet he habitually wore a lugubrious expression.[22] He made no bones about his support for Drouet, and he was helped in this by the comparative weakness of the prosecution, which was led by Montagu Chambers. A former Grenadier Guard who had been educated at Sandhurst, and a future Liberal member of parliament, Chambers was not yet forty. A whiskery portrait of him in middle life expresses not so much passion and flamboyance as geniality.[23] His opponent was Sir Frederic Thesiger, who was in his mid-forties and already a veteran of parliament as a Conservative, with experience as solicitor general and attorney general. Thesiger was known to put witnesses at their ease with his nonchalant manner. He also had a way with juries, winning their confidence with a well-timed smile, disabusing them of their suspicions by making them laugh, and even getting them on his side with a crafty wink.[24]

*　*　*

Almost as soon as Chambers presented the case for the prosecution, its glaring weakness, which was the near impossibility of providing evidence of a criminal act, became apparent. This was exploited repeatedly by the defence. So when Chambers wound the story back to a point in May 1848, citing the moment at which the Holborn guardians first came face to face with the ugly realities of Drouet's regime, Thesiger hauled him up over exactly the issue the Recorder had raised, which was the admissibility of the prosecution's evidence. Thesiger argued that events occurring in May could not conceivably have any relevance to events occurring in October, when James Andrews arrived in Surrey Hall. There was a logical gap. The best Chambers could do was to try to show that Drouet had 'killed' the little boy by imposing a regime of deprivation so severe as to leave him incapable of surviving disease.[25]

The defence used the same tactics to pick holes in the witnesses' statements. At times this verged on the grotesque. The surgeon Alfred Baring Garrod was accused of presenting 'evidence' based on the dissection of a body that was unidentifiable because it had been exhumed, and it needed a statement made under oath by William Filby, the parish gravedigger, to verify that it was indeed James's body he had dug up for the purposes of the post mortem examination. Again, the workhouse deputy matron, Keziah Dimond, had seen for herself the wretched physical condition of the children who came back from Surrey Hall, and yet, the argument went, much of the information she was offering was not demonstrably relevant to James. One witness after another was subjected to this rigorous test of the admissibility of their evidence. The nurse Mary Harris looked after James in the hospital, but as this was the first time she had ever seen him, she was adding nothing of value as to the cause of his emaciated condition.[26]

The charge against the prosecution that its criticisms of Drouet were general, and possibly but not necessarily relevant, was made time and again. After all, rigorous standards of proof applied in a court of law. Furthermore, the stakes were very high, as emphasised by Platt when he warned that a verdict of manslaughter might condemn Drouet to be transported. So the defence was, perhaps, conducting its case correctly. When Whitfield was asked about the sleeping arrangements in Surrey Hall, but could not provide details of a precise place or places where James might actually have slept, it was perhaps reasonable for the defence to question his evidence. Again, when Grainger described his impressions of the asylum, it was perhaps reasonable for the defence to object that he had no direct knowledge of the one thing that mattered, which was what James had actually experienced.[27]

Above and beyond the inability of the prosecution to make a strong case, what emerged from the trial was the willingness of the defence to make clever points at a witness's expense. Platt too was quick to engage in this verbal bullying, and in doing so confirmed the belief of many commentators that he was biased in favour of Drouet. When Grainger said that on one of his visits he had found too many beds too close to each other in the sleeping rooms, Platt retorted that if there were too many beds, then they were inevitably too close to each other. Again, he pounced on Whitfield's description of the effects of malnutrition he had encountered in the children in the hospital. By 'tumid abdomen' he presumed that the witness meant 'swelled belly'. In any other courtroom, the quibble might have been seen as a reminder to an expert witness to use plain language. But in a trial revolving around the deaths of so many young innocents, it might be judged ill-timed and tasteless. None of this escaped the newspapers, and they were only too happy to signal their disapproval of Platt. The *Morning Chronicle* and the *Bengal Catholic Herald* condemned his 'most unbecoming rudeness' and his 'sneering manner', while the *Morning Post* proposed that the trial had proved only that lawyers were incapable of understanding a medical question. 'The affair was converted into a farce,' the *Post* said, 'and, inspired by the fun of the occasion, the presiding judge became a jester.'[28]

These remarks from the bench, though they came across as hostile and uncalled for, were not always devoid of meaning. One example is the reaction to Kite's account of his battle with itch. Platt asked whether Kite had ever heard of cholera being produced by itch. While this seemingly facetious question raised a laugh in the courtroom, a serious point was being made about the relevance of the witness's evidence. Platt might even have been criticising Kite, indirectly, as a young doctor who had been too distracted by his battle with itch to respond appropriately to incipient cholera.[29] A second example is the question Platt put to John Rowland Gibson. He was the workhouse medical officer who had examined James and other Holborn children before they travelled down to Surrey Hall. When he admitted that a child might be thin as long as it was not conspicuously ill, he was asked if many of the boys in James's group were thin.[30] It might appear to have been a needlessly provocative question, but in fact it was a sensible one, because if the boys being sent down to Surrey Hall were already malnourished, then all was not well in the workhouse.

Laughter was not the only way in which the courtroom interacted with the proceedings. Drouet had supporters in the gallery, and at one point they made their presence felt. It happened when the prosecuting counsel William Clarkson alluded to the fact that at the coroner's inquest some of the children summoned as witnesses had been allowed to give unsworn testimony. Although it was not uncommon for young children not to be required to swear an oath, on the grounds that they might not fully understand its significance, Platt retorted that it had been 'a most unjust and irregular proceeding'. Not unnaturally, his comment was received as an implied attack on Wakley. As such, it was also a signal for those in the public gallery who believed that the coroner had persecuted Drouet in three parish inquests to express their feelings. This they did by applauding Platt enthusiastically. Meanwhile, Drouet tapped the front of the dock with his hand, as if applauding the applause. Instantly, the court officers shouted for silence, and the Drouet faction were quiet again.[31]

If nothing else, this wrangling serves to show that these survivors of Surrey Hall had a starring role in the drama. The first to be summoned was Patrick Sheen. For a little ten-year-old, this must have been nothing if not unnerving, and as he walked to the stand, Patrick would have felt all eyes on him. The twelve jurymen to his left would have been watching him closely, assessing him by his size and by his workhouse clothes. The men in their dark gowns and powdered wigs in the cockpit and the two judges in their resplendent robes on the bench would be peering at him. The contrast between the formality of the gentlemen of the court and the drab appearance of the little boy could not have been more revealing. It was an electrifying moment when the first of Drouet's children set foot on the stage and spoke his opening lines. The witness was asked to identify himself. 'I am a poor boy belonging to the Holborn Union,' he said.[32]

Clarkson was a burly man in his mid-fifties, double-chinned and with a bluff manner.[33] In answer to his questions, Patrick explained that he had slept as one of three in a bed and had been placed with boys who were aged eight or over, while James Andrews and the younger boys were placed elsewhere. Thesiger objected that the witness had been in one class and the dead boy in another. By way of countering the objection, Clarkson observed that he had no other means of showing the treatment James was likely to have received. As he said rather pointedly, the prosecution had only the living witnesses at their disposal: they 'could not call the deceased'.[34]

As one child witness made way for another, a picture of life in Surrey Hall began to emerge. But the children supplying the incriminating details had to submit to having their mental faculties publicly tested. When Joseph Andrews said that there had been 'about a dozen' beds in the room where he and his brother had slept, Platt asked: 'How many is a dozen, my little lad?' If Platt intended to show that the witness had limited intellectual capacity, then he failed, because Joseph replied 'Twelve' without the slightest hesitation. There was laughter in court.[35]

Other children were less able to cope under pressure. William Derbyshire was overawed by the occasion and looked frightened. His answers had to be dragged out of him, and even when he plucked up enough courage to speak, he could barely be heard. In the end he was told to stand on a table in the cockpit.[36] One after another, the witnesses had their say, and recalled the meagre rations, the cold, the squalor and degradation. However, they found it hard to say anything definite about James's time in the asylum. Because he was one of the younger boys, they had only occasionally been with him in the same part of the asylum. Much of their evidence was based on hearsay. Also, much of it was based on assumptions that children in all parts of the asylum were treated in the same way.

There cannot have been many in the courtroom who were surprised when Platt directed the jury to acquit Drouet. Nonetheless, he spelled out his reasons for dismissing the charges. To show that Drouet was guilty of manslaughter, the prosecution had to find evidence that James might have survived an attack of cholera had he not been weakened by conditions in the asylum. They needed the one witness they had never been able to produce, namely a medical officer who had examined the boy before *and* after his time in Surrey Hall.[37]

It was six in the evening on 14 April, the second and final day of the trial, when the foreman of the jury stood up and announced a unanimous verdict of not guilty. Drouet's supporters in the public gallery were quick to back the verdict by applauding loudly. The applause must have been very loud indeed, and maybe also laced with colourful language, because Platt was unhappy; so much so, in fact, that he threatened to jail any badly behaved individual his officers laid their hands on. The prosecution informed the bench that in view of the verdict, and because the evidence was not as strong, the cases of the three Chelsea girls would not be pursued. That being so, Platt said, the jury must acquit the defendant in those three cases as well.[38]

Drouet left the court a free man, and as his friends swarmed round him, offering their congratulations, he was seen to shed tears. But a reporter for the *Morning Chronicle* probably spoke for the majority when he wrote in the Monday edition that 'we have not yet learnt whether Mr Baron Platt shook him warmly by the hand or not, but from his demeanour throughout the trial we think it not unlikely that he may have done so.'[39]

* * *

In the final paragraph of 'The Verdict for Drouet', Dickens had something to say about the tears. He accepted as a perfectly natural explanation that Drouet was relieved that the verdict had gone his way. But he also wondered if he was distressed at the imminent collapse of his highly profitable farming operation. It was a savage comment, but behind it lay a fervent desire for radical change.

Dickens subscribed to the popular view that Platt had put his own unfortunate stamp on the proceedings. With the frequent interjections and haughty disdain for the witnesses, the judge had presided over the same 'bad theatre' as the lamentable trial of little Richard Hooper in the Gloucester crown court. He had tried but failed to relieve 'the inexpressible sadness' of the witnesses' statements with his flippant tone. But for Dickens the true moment of drama, which encapsulated the whole sorry business, came when

Mary Harris recalled how James Andrews had struggled to eat a small piece of bread. Platt had merely remarked that the piece of bread was too large, which Dickens felt was to miss the pathos of the boy's plight:

> "*Oh nurse!*" says the poor little fellow, with an eager sense that what he had longed for had come too late, "*What a big bit of bread this is!*" Yes, Mr Baron Platt, it is clear that it was too much for him. His head was lifted up for an instant, but it sank again. He could not but be full of wonder and pleasure that the big bit of bread had come, though he could not eat it.[40]

Dickens immediately added a reference to the Restoration dramatist Thomas Otway, who died in dire poverty. Legend has it that after a prolonged period of near starvation, he wolfed down a bread roll and choked on the first mouthful. 'The difference is hardly worth pointing out,' Dickens observed. 'The pauper child had not even strength for the effort which choked the pauper poet.'

While ready to castigate the judge for his insensitivity, Dickens accepted that the prosecution case had been vitiated by generalities. A lack of cast-iron evidence of the treatment of James Andrews, a 'wretched little figure' who 'could not always be visibly separated from a crowd exactly like himself', had been its fundamental weakness. Platt had been right to urge the jury to return a not guilty verdict, and he, Dickens, had no complaint about the outcome. He had reservations about the performance of Chambers and Clarkson, though, which in his view had been poor. He might perhaps have added by way of mitigation that presenting a case fraught with legal problems had inevitably played into the defence's hands. Similar points were made elsewhere. A *Morning Chronicle* editorial was inclined to think that the prosecution had been ill served by the parish beadle's attorney: he had 'got up the case for the prosecution much as a parish beadle's attorney might be expected to do.' In a way, the fight had been lost before the trial even began.[41]

Some might even have thought that the fight had been lost as early as the decision to charge Drouet with the 'lesser' crime of manslaughter. In order to show just what a mountain Chambers and Clarkson consequently had to climb, the *Daily News* broke the prosecution case down into five distinct stages:

To establish such a charge it was necessary to prove – first, that the boy had been delivered into Mr Drouet's keeping in a sound and healthy state; second, that he had been under-fed, insufficiently clothed, made to sleep in an ill-ventilated and over-crowded room, and so-forth; third, that while he was being thus treated his health gave way; fourth, that the organs affected, and the manner in which they were affected, were first or premonitory symptoms of cholera; lastly, that he died of cholera, nothing having occurred to him beyond his treatment in Mr Drouet's establishment to superinduce or aggravate an attack of cholera.[42]

A better approach, according to some legal analysts, would have been to play a high-stakes game by charging Drouet with murder. Although it might seem far-fetched to anyone other than a prosecuting lawyer to describe him as a murderer, it was felt that there were reasonable grounds for such a charge, in that Drouet had been not only negligent but deliberately and persistently negligent, and had wilfully ignored any number of warnings from medically qualified professionals.[43]

As a counterbalance to the anger over the verdict, there were attempts to show that it was actually a good thing. The *Morning Chronicle* argued that although acquittal might appear to be a perversion of justice, acquittal was still better than conviction. For if Drouet had been convicted, and if he had been punished with what the *Chronicle* envisaged as a life sentence in the penal colony on Norfolk Island, toiling in a chain gang, then a line would have been drawn under the affair. The desire for retribution would have been satisfied. Nothing would have come of it, nothing would have been learnt, and nothing would change. Men higher up in the Poor Law hierarchy who were 'far more guilty' than Drouet would never be called to account.[44]

The other positive reaction was published in the *Lancet*, which might seem remarkable given that the journal was edited by Wakley, who had always made it abundantly clear that he wanted Drouet convicted of manslaughter. However, the *Lancet* declared that 'a great result' had still been achieved in that the iniquitous practice of child farming had been brought into the open, where it had been made the subject of far-reaching investigation. The verdict itself was of little significance because it relied on a technicality. Since no decision had been made on 'the real merits' of the case, that is to say on the moral status of farming, it was not Drouet who had been vindicated but the defenceless child of pauper parents.

Nor was the *Lancet* in any doubt that the way had been paved for change. So confident was it that the tragedy in Tooting would prove to have important consequences that it cited, by way of comparison, the case of Frederick John White, a private of the Seventh Hussars who had died at the Hounslow Cavalry Barracks in 1846.[45] White had been sentenced by a court martial to 150 lashes for an alleged assault on his sergeant, and was brutally flogged by two regimental farriers armed with cat-o'-nine-tails. A month later, having to all appearances recovered from his wounds, he succumbed to 'inflammation of the pleura and of the lining membrane of the heart', and died in the station hospital. The medical details were certified by three army surgeons, who appended a disclaimer, under pressure from the colonel of the regiment, to the effect that the punishment had not contributed in any way to the man's death. However, the vicar of the church where White was to be buried, having got wind of the events leading up to his death, contacted Wakley, who ordered an inquest. Three post mortem examinations of the body were performed, and whereas the first two were more or less botched, the third was carried out with great professionalism by an independent surgeon. As a result, the jury was perfectly placed to deliver a verdict of death resulting from the effects of a 'severe and cruel' flogging. The jury added as a rider to its verdict its earnest desire to see an end to a barbaric punishment no soldier should be subjected to.[46]

The national outcry over White's death was loud enough to persuade the Duke of Wellington, as head of the British Army, to impose a restriction on military flogging. The number of lashes was not to exceed fifty, and although it would be another thirty-five years before the passing of the 1881 Army Act finally put an end to this type of punishment, the claim made by the *Lancet* in 1849 that it had been 'virtually abolished' was to all intents and purposes correct. Child farming was the target of equivalent restrictions in the form of legislation pushed through by the Poor Law Board that prevented the exploitation of pauper children by private contractors. So the *Lancet* was able to trumpet a double triumph, a double endorsement of the power of medical coroners to expose egregious malpractices, and, importantly, to bring about change.[47]

Chapter Eleven

New Homes

Finding accommodation for the children returning from Surrey Hall was a problem all the parishes had to deal with one way or another. How they did so is in a sense the other part of the story, and it is far removed from the inquests held in taverns, and from the Queen's Bench and the Old Bailey. It is the part of the children's story the newspapers overlooked.

In Holborn the solution to the problem of accommodation had initially been provided by the Royal Free Hospital, but as time went on the pressure on its resources mounted, until, at the end of February, the guardians were obliged to take all the girls back into the workhouse and place all the boys in the house in Greville Street. The new arrangement persisted until the end of March. At that point, to comply with the wishes of the hospital managers, the boys also went into the workhouse. This was bound to displease the Poor Law Board as it seemed that the old problem of having children in adult pauper establishments had never gone away. But one of the guardians, James Bywater Humphreys, who ran the Crown coffee house in High Holborn, made the financial case for keeping accommodation costs to a minimum. As always, it was important not to overburden the ratepayers. Humphreys also maintained that money was not the only factor, because he and his fellow guardians were convinced that the children had always been healthier and happier in the workhouse than in any other place. If by any other place he meant Surrey Hall, then he may well have had a point, as it was not unknown for Drouet's children to say much the same thing.[1]

By the beginning of May, all the children had been returned to the workhouse, and a schoolmaster and a schoolmistress, William Robinson and Elizabeth Sarah Hislop, were appointed on a temporary basis to take charge of them. As these appointments were residential as well as educational, Robinson and Hislop, who were both single, were provided with board and lodging in order to undertake round-the-clock supervision duties. Both had been previously employed in schools, and Robinson, who had at one time been a member of the metropolitan police, struck the guardians as more than adequately qualified for his interactions with the boys.[2]

If proof was needed that working with these rootless and destabilised children, whose most recent experience of education had been the chaos of the schoolrooms in Surrey Hall, would be anything other than challenging, it was ready to hand. For when they had finally been retrieved from the hospital, the damage they had done became the subject of a furious and unedifying row. As it was, the hospital had limited funds, but now the managers were being presented with a catalogue of repairs. The bedding used by the children, although not new, had been in sufficiently good condition to withstand many months of hard treatment but would now have to be thrown away. A hundred beds and an equal number of mattresses and bolsters, well over a hundred pillows, twenty-six counterpanes, fourteen blankets and forty-nine sheets had been damaged. The curtains separating the beds, numbering over a hundred, needed to be washed and repaired. Other expenses were four months' worth of medicines and ointments, seventeen tons of coal, an unspecified quantity of gas, the supply of extra water and the new plumbing for the same, the cleaning, limewashing and general upkeep of the rooms where the children had been kept, and wear and tear to over a thousand additional items of assorted bedding. There was also an entry for broken windows. All hell must have broken loose.[3]

The hospital presented the Holborn Union with a bill for £250, which the guardians considered to be steep: some of the itemised charges seemed exorbitant and others should not have been included. They had it on good authority, namely from Keziah Dimond, who had looked after the children throughout their time in the hospital, that the beds and mattresses had been used prior to their arrival and were already the worse for wear. Also, most of the bedding had been brought up from the workhouse, washing was done in the union building, and the wards had been left in good repair. On the strength of this, William Roberts James wrote to the hospital to make it clear that the guardians declined to do what they assumed the hospital was angling for, which was to buy the beds and the bedding. These were of the wrong size and quality to meet the demands of the workhouse. On the other hand, they were in good enough condition for the hospital to get more use out of them. So instead of accepting the price of purchase, the guardians offered the hospital £150, which would pay not only for wear and tear in the wards but also for the use of the house in Greville Street. They added an extra £50 of donations to the hospital, some of which might be offered as gratuities to Drs Marsden, Peacock and Jackson and other members of the medical staff.[4]

The members of the hospital board were indignant at the implied accusation of overcharging levelled at them by the guardians. The chairman, the Reverend Dr Edward Rice, listed a number of grievances, beginning with the observation that because over half the children had been suffering from cholera, and almost all from itch, bedding had been completely spoilt. Then again, the proposed donation to the hospital was not what he would call generous, and the proposed gratuities hardly covered the expenses incurred by the doctors, who had been obliged to travel in from home every day in order to deal with the influx of new patients. Nor were the guardians being asked to pay the hospital rent. Even so, Rice could see his way to offering discounts on the cost of bedding in line with figures supplied by a wholesaler in Saffron Hill, and these would allow a deduction on the bill amounting to £21 7s. 9d. Other costs could not be reduced, though. An example was the £20 15s. 2d. spent on the new water supply, which, as Rice admitted, would ultimately benefit the hospital but had still diverted money that would otherwise have gone towards paying off its immediate debts.[5]

Over the coming days both sides stuck to their guns. The guardians offered £200 and not a penny more, while the hospital insisted that it could not in all conscience take less than £228 12s. 3d. Rice justified his obstinacy by reminding Holborn that the hospital was run as a charity. It 'literally threw its wards open' in response to the emergency, without waiting for a formal agreement to be drawn up, and at a time when the widespread prevalence of cholera had already placed it under enormous pressure. The hospital asked the Poor Law Board to weigh in on its behalf, but James dug his heels in and defended Holborn's corner. In the first place, the wards had been empty for many months before the children's arrival. Then a third of the cohort had been removed to Greville Street within a matter of days. Finally, cholera and diarrhoea had disappeared in a very short time, and itch had been gradually suppressed, virtually to the point of eradication. The sticking point was the absence of a contract. It took until the end of the year for the two sides to reach a resolution, and even then it was only reached after the hospital threatened legal action. The result was an out-of-court settlement of £220.[6]

*   *   *

The efforts of the Chelsea guardians shine a very different light on the problem of finding accommodation. At first their aim was simply to locate suitable premises, and to this end the guardians placed advertisements in the press, sent out circulars to house agents, and visited addresses that showed promise. They came close to taking the lease on a large plot of land at Cook's Ground off the King's Road, where there was a small house that could be converted into a school, but they were blocked by the Poor Law Board, which considered the site not fit for purpose.[7]

Other boards of guardians also advertised in newspapers and posted bills in suitable areas, which met with varying degrees of success. The Newington board was even approached by Drouet with an offer on Surrey Hall, although there is nothing to indicate that the guardians were interested.[8] These searches for accommodation were always urgent because guardians were reluctant to return children to the workhouse. There was little to reassure them, either, in the Poor Law Board's plans for a system of 'district schools' that would combine cohorts of children from more than union and house them in appropriate buildings in suitable locations. The Board's proposals met with a cautious response. Setting up district schools seemed to be another unwelcome move towards centralisation.

However, Chelsea differed from many parishes in farming its children out to ratepayers, who were paid up to 5s. per child per week for their pains. This was strictly an interim measure born of necessity. It delighted neither the guardians nor the Poor Law Board, involving as it did a whole raft of precautions, the first of which was the careful vetting of householders and their properties by workhouse medical officers. There was no shortage of applications as the scheme was seen as an opportunity to earn money. Some householders even tried to play the system, invariably in vain, by offering their services when they were not even ratepayers, or when they did not live strictly within the boundaries of the parish.[9] One example of a disappointed applicant was a bricklayer's wife, one Catherine Clowser. She had two daughters of her own, but was seemingly happy to take all thirty-five of the girls on the waiting list, offering them instruction in dressmaking as well as accommodation. She had to be turned down because she lived in Merton.[10] Another doomed application, and a rather remarkable one, was submitted by Richard Drouet, who came before the board with details of a house he owned and was ready to let. The Chelsea guardians kept their distance, though relations with the Drouets were not so strained as to prevent the board discussing offers of redundant items from Surrey Hall, such as iron bedsteads at 15s. 6d. each and children's clothing at 5s. a set.[11]

On 23 February seventy-eight Chelsea children were placed with ratepayers and over the following weeks the number rose steadily.[12] The guardians documented every aspect of the operation. They recorded the names and addresses of the ten householders who provided temporary accommodation, along with the numbers each took in and the weekly payments they received to cover the cost of board and lodging and whatever education or training they were able and willing to provide. They also logged the results of their regular inspections of the children, who had to present themselves, together with their carers, in the workhouse yard.

All might seem impressive enough on paper, but in reality these were desperate arrangements. On the one hand, children who by now would have been utterly traumatised were being decanted from the horrors of Surrey Hall into wholly unfamiliar surroundings. On the other, their carers were having to cope with a range of logistical challenges. The household that took on more responsibility than any other was that of William Rendell, a greengrocer, and his wife, Sarah. The Rendells were elderly and lived alone with a single servant, but the size of the cohort they squeezed into their house in Willis's Row on the Fulham Road kept growing. At one point, Sarah, who was in her sixties, was in charge of twenty-three children. Even in the early days, when she was only hosting thirteen children, all of them girls, she had a great deal to contend with. She had to ask the guardians for decent clothes, twice, and was given what she asked for on the first occasion but not on the second. She also had to apply to the workhouse matron, Charity Sutton, for some sort of work, indeed any sort of work, to keep the girls occupied.[13]

The most galling setback came about three weeks into the operation when Sarah was told by a medical officer that all thirteen girls were riddled with itch. The board removed them to the workhouse to be treated and sent Sarah seven girls and four boys to take their place. But the problem repeated itself several weeks later when another two girls were forced to leave, again on account of an eruptive skin disease.[14] Other children left Willis's Row, not to return to the workhouse but to go into employment as domestic servants. They were invariably girls, and Charity Sutton supplied them with clothes appropriate to the households they were about to enter, which would have been respectable though modest. Sarah Rendell took it upon herself to engineer these opportunities, and there are records of two girls, one aged fifteen and the other twelve, being sent to addresses in Plaistow and Kensington. Each would earn 1s. 6d. a week. How the world of work treated them would have depended on the kindness or otherwise of their employers, but they had at least escaped the workhouse, and, of course, they had survived Surrey Hall.[15]

There were other pitfalls awaiting those who took these damaged children into their homes. A householder in Cadogan Street with ten boys under her care was obliged to send one of them back to the workhouse. She complained that the boy, William Wells, was so out of control that she was unable to keep him any longer. He had been caught performing sex acts on the other boys. The board instructed the workhouse master, Daniel Sutton, to flog William and put him on a reduced diet for a week.[16] Then there are records of adult improprieties, which collectively create a worrying impression of what might have been happening to the children behind closed doors. One such case was that of James Morgan, a furniture dealer in his mid-sixties, who had been given responsibility for a cohort of ten boys. Morgan and his wife lived in Exeter Street in a house that must have been reasonably spacious, given that at the time of the 1851 census they had room for seven lodgers along with their grown-up son and daughter, who were both in their twenties.[17]

The first sign of trouble was picked up at the workhouse, where at a routine inspection the children alleged that they were 'very much neglected' and kept in a 'very dirty' state. They were only able to say this because no member of the Morgan household was present at the inspection. This, of course, was incriminating in itself and added weight to the boys' allegations. Two guardians went to the house in Exeter Street to investigate. There they saw with their own eyes that the Morgans were indeed taking very little care of their young charges. It must have seemed to them all too reminiscent of Surrey Hall, if on a smaller scale, and the concerns they laid before the board were real enough to have the boys removed from the Morgans and assigned to other households. Three went to an address in Symons Street, where the householder, Caroline Bell, was caught out three months later. She was in her early thirties with three young children and married to a man who cut firewood for a living. The Bells were probably very poor, and when a guardian came round one evening to inspect the ten children Caroline now had in her care, he was shocked to see that they were sleeping on the kitchen floor.[18]

Another board that farmed children out to the parish, Fulham, had recourse to a single household. Nine girls of all ages were sent from Surrey Hall to Dixon's Farm in Wormholt Scrubs, a remote and isolated spot near a viaduct on the West London Railway, surrounded on all sides by poorly drained ground that was left waterlogged by the winter rains. Though no one from the workhouse was allowed to visit, by order of the guardians, the General Board of Health dispatched a doctor, Arthur Farre, to the farm on a fact-finding mission. He was concerned that the air was damp and miasmatic, that there was nothing in the way of a dry road or even a path leading to the farm, and that the marshy conditions and poor access would make it impossible for the girls to get out into the open to exercise. Moreover, Kite had written ahead to report that three of the girls had been in poor health when they left Surrey Hall. But this was an underestimate, and a local surgeon, Daniel Thomas Roy, examined all nine at the farm and found that seven were unwell.[19]

The children were cared for by a middle-aged couple, Thomas and Anne Ireland, under the direction of another surgeon, George Brown, who visited Wormholt Scrubs every day. Brown lost no time in cracking the whip, ordering the Irelands on his first visit to sort out the familiar Surrey Hall problem of too many beds competing for space in the room where the new arrivals slept. He noticed that the children's clothes and bedding were clean while their persons were filthy, and he insisted that they be given two baths a week. They all had heads crawling with lice, but the diligent doctor managed to control these infestations, along with the inevitable cases of itch, but not before they had passed the torments of their irritated skin on to Anne Ireland. She in her turn passed the complaint on to her husband. Thomas Ireland then passed it back to one of the girls, who promptly came out in a scorbutic rash. Indeed, the Irelands were as much a worry for Brown as the children. At one point, Thomas succumbed to a 'sudden attack' of an unidentified malady, which the doctor treated with medicine and draughts of port wine. Anne was completely exhausted, and he prescribed stimulants, but twice he had to lift her up when she had fainted and fallen to the floor.[20]

Itch and lice were less important than the generally poor health of the girls. Not only did they suffer from diarrhoea, but they developed a persistent cough and a tightness in the chest, which Brown recognised as bronchitis. He insisted that they had brought the disease with them from Surrey Hall, refusing to believe, as Farre did, that it had been waiting for them in the Irelands' musty rooms, lurking in the saturated air. Unlike Farre, who had a low opinion of the farm, he felt that there was ample space outside for the nine girls. 'With regard to the ground they have to play & exercise in now,' he said in a letter to the guardians, 'from their statement, it is nearly as much as 100 had at Tooting.' A few weeks later, as the weather improved, the fields were dry enough to walk across. 'A good opportunity now offers,' he wrote, 'for anyone desirous of seeing this delightful and healthy spot.'[21]

Brown's optimism became something of a motif in his reports on the girls' health. He was encouraged by any signs of progress. On a Thursday in the middle of February, he arrived at the farm to find the girls in the yard. 'They were playing with their skipping ropes out of doors,' he wrote to the guardians, 'and appeared as happy as it is possible for children to be.' One nine-year-old, Margaret Martin, who had struggled with sickness, especially pleased him. She had a long history of attacks of paralysis, which had resulted in the partial loss of the use of her left arm, but by the end of the month she was well on her way to recovery. 'Today I find her knitting,' Brown reported. She was, for the moment, blessed with mobility again.[22]

* * *

The guardians of St George in the East also looked for new premises on the outskirts of the capital. They went south, and early in January they took the lease on The Elms, a property in Mitcham. The arrangement almost fell through when the landlord got it into his head that his property would be turned into a sort of colony for children with cholera. His solicitors offered to pay the guardians £50 to be released from the tenancy agreement, but they refused the offer, agreeing instead that, as a condition of occupancy, no child would be removed to the house unless certified free of disease by the workhouse medical officer. At the end of the month, the first cohort of around a hundred children left Surrey Hall for Mitcham. They did well, and others soon followed. The guardians appointed a matron on a salary of £40 a year: she was Fanny Sharpe, a widow in her mid-forties. They paid a further £40 a year for a local surgeon, Frederick Albert Tipple of Mitcham, to take responsibility for the children's medical needs.[23]

Whereas the appointment of Samuel Harding as schoolmaster, with a salary of £35 a year, caused the guardians great consternation, the appointment of his wife, Sarah, as schoolmistress, with a salary of £25 a year, seems not to have got anyone's hackles up. That said, their tenure was not all plain sailing, and it was, perhaps, only a matter of time before they crossed swords with Mrs Sharpe. The exact cause of the problem was never explained in detail, but a reasonable surmise is that the Hardings had behaved unprofessionally in some way, and that when Mrs Sharpe confronted them, there was a heated exchange of words. She must have felt undermined because she asked the guardians to give their opinion 'as to her duties & authority in her office of matron of the establishment'. The guardians placed 'entire confidence' in her, telling her that she must 'enforce such regulations to be observed by all parties in the establishment as shall be necessary to obtain order, regularity, industry and good conduct throughout the house.' There is more than a suggestion here that the schoolrooms in the Mitcham establishment were no happier than those in Surrey Hall.[24]

The Newington guardians' solution to the problem of their returning children was to send them to the north coast of Kent. They were taking advantage of an arrangement they already had with Robert Perry, who owned the Chateau Belle Vue Sea Bathing Establishment in Margate, a boarding house for invalid paupers. The house stood in Wilderness Road on the chalky outskirts of the town. Perry said that he could take fifteen children, but Newington sent forty-seven. The clerk to the guardians took the little refugees down to Margate on the train that steamed out of London Bridge and rattled its way through slums and suburbs and green countryside. The hardships they must have endured on the journey almost defy description, and it is appalling to think that they were all suffering or would soon suffer from diarrhoea, and that nine of them would go on to develop the symptoms of cholera.[25]

The impact on the Chateau was profound. The population of around a hundred inmates from the Greenwich Union had previously been unaffected by cholera, but within days four Surrey Hall boys and three Surrey Hall girls were showing its unmistakable symptoms. One of the children, little Mary Ann Doddington, had an eleven-hour struggle and then died, and the deaths of two adult male paupers soon followed.[26] A local newspaper, the *Canterbury Journal*, reported that the 'malignant form' of the 'much-dreaded disease' had appeared in Margate, which only succeeded in frightening parents who might otherwise have sent their children to the boarding schools of a seaside town with a reputation for healthiness and bracing air. As it turned out, the newspaper's use of lurid prose had given a misleading impression, as no cases of the cholera that had blazed forth briefly in Perry's boarding house were recorded anywhere in the town.[27]

Since not all of Newington's children were taken down to Margate, this was at best a partial solution. Those who remained were initially taken back into the workhouse in Walworth Road, where of course they caused the board of guardians acute anxiety, not least because the ideal maximum of 320 inmates had been exceeded by some margin. By the middle of February, it was reported that the population of the workhouse numbered 400. This was a potentially dangerous situation, but it had been seen coming for several weeks, and the board had already looked at plans to expand the existing premises. Such a programme, it was argued, would be cheaper than paying for the extra staff a new site would need, and it had the added advantage that the children would be observed constantly by the guardians. However, the Poor Law Board refused to sanction the proposal, its objection being that erecting new structures would reduce the amount of air and light reaching the main workhouse. The proposed building programme would also leave too little space for the exercise yards that were essential to the wellbeing of the children.[28]

With their plans for keeping the children in Newington frustrated, the guardians considered accommodating them in a remote location. The final decision was to take Alfred Charles Drouet up on his offer, made in May, to farm all their children over the age of three. At the time, Alfred was running Grove House in Brixton, and although there may have been some reluctance on the part of the guardians to continue their association with the Drouets, he could see that they were in a difficult position. He designed his business proposal cannily. Not only would he provide the full range of services, and submit his dietary for Newington's approval, but also, in the event of other parishes sending their children to Brixton, he would impose a strict cap on numbers. The impression was that the lessons of Surrey Hall had been learnt. Furthermore, whereas the rate at Surrey Hall had been

4s. 6d. per child per week, at Grove House it would be 5s., almost as if the extra cost brought with it a guarantee of sorts. The guardians made noises about the 5s., but Drouet pointed out that tighter government regulation of pauper establishments was making it an expensive occupation, and they failed to beat him down.[29]

Inspections of the premises, both by Newington and by the Poor Law Board, revealed that the schoolroom earmarked for the girls had a defective roof and was very damp, and that the privies were in an unsatisfactory state. In addition to the necessary repairs, the Poor Law Board demanded an even more stringent limit on numbers, and stipulated that all adult inmates had to be sent elsewhere before any child set foot on the premises. Appointments of an 'efficient' schoolmaster and schoolmistress and medical personnel were to be made with circumspection. At all costs the sins of the recent past must not be repeated. But the Poor Law Board was persuaded that these were the best arrangements and indeed the only arrangements the emergency allowed, and in June all the Newington children, including those returning from Robert Perry's establishment in Margate, were consigned to the care of Alfred Charles Drouet of Grove House in Brixton.[30]

*   *   *

Meanwhile, Alfred's half-brother Bartholomew was facing ruin. He wrote to the parishes, hoping to persuade them to compensate him for the extra costs the crisis had inflicted on him. He had bought wines and spirits and other 'remedies' for the ailing children. He had made alterations to their diet. He had recruited many doctors and nurses. It had all cost him money and he wanted the money back. He met with stony-faced refusals. The Strand guardians were a notable exception, though. They agreed to pay him 9d. per head per week for the care of over a hundred sick children, and another 9d. for the supply of flannel clothing.[31]

As Surrey Hall had by now been comprehensively abandoned by the parishes, it was no longer a going concern. Drouet put his property on the market, but it was tainted, and there seemed to be little appetite for a house with such bleak associations. The Strand guardians alone gave Drouet's offer serious consideration. At the time, they still had the use of the House of Refuge in Little Ogle Street, a strictly temporary measure dating back to 9 January, when the first children fit enough to travel had been brought up from Lower Tooting in omnibuses, accompanied by three guardians and two medical officers. There were eighty-nine in that cohort: in a month's time the number would rise to a hundred or so.[32]

In terms of bricks and mortar, the House of Refuge was everything Surrey Hall had so conspicuously proved not to be. It was spacious, having room for many more beds than were actually needed to meet the immediate crisis, and it was comfortable in that its dormitories and day wards were well ventilated and heated by means of large stoves. There were warm and cold baths and the gas supply extended to all the rooms. The children were given a diet of meat with bread and rice, and milk thickened with arrowroot, and coffee and wine. Supplies came from the workhouse, which was only a short distance away in Cleveland Street, and the establishment was operated by a matron and assistant matron, nurses from the workhouse, a labour master for the boys, and a doorkeeper.[33] The union medical officers supervised medical matters, keeping the children in strict quarantine while they treated the many cases of skin diseases and ophthalmia. One of the children had a condition that resembled leprosy, and several fell ill in the first week with the symptoms of the cholera that had travelled up with them from Surrey Hall.[34] Most recovered, but one died, Margaret Kingham, who was eleven years old. She had been seized by the illness in the night, and from that point on her condition had swung between extremes, showing the symptoms of a painful disintegration one minute and false signs of recovery the next. The two attendant surgeons, Benjamin Brookes and Samuel Lovett, ordered hot baths and stimulants, but Margaret's fight was over in forty-eight hours.[35]

The use of the House of Refuge met with opposition. The day after the children arrived, an angry letter was sent to the *Morning Chronicle* by a subscriber to the Society for the Relief of the Destitute Houseless Poor. The Society owned the building, and yet it had been closed to the very people who would have most need of it over the winter, which the writer regarded as a 'breach of faith' towards those who supported the refuge financially. Furthermore, it was a 'very hazardous experiment' to bring victims of cholera into the neighbourhood, which was poor and densely populated.[36] The Poor Law Board also had serious reservations, and these came to a head three months after the children's arrival, when the inspector, Richard Hall, visited the premises. Hall's report was highly critical. The children had no yard for exercise and had to be walked through the streets by the labour master, the doorkeeper, and assorted inmates of the workhouse. They were given books and slates, but they had no teachers and did no learning. In a word, the children ruled the roost. Indoors, packed into a single room, they behaved in a wild manner, shouting obscenities. Those who would otherwise have worked for a wage, such as the two boys who had been trained up as pupil teachers in their time at Surrey Hall, or the girls who had been taught to do needlework, withdrew their labour when they were told that they would not be paid. Boys and girls, some of whom were as old as fourteen or fifteen, shared the same sick ward.[37]

Hall was unhappy about the absence of disciplinarians. The sexes were allowed to mix in all areas of the building, and he believed that their unregulated behaviour might have regrettable consequences. To make matters worse, the taskmaster, Richard Woolfall, who was paid to supervise the boys, was proving to be a liability. Recently he had been drunk on a daily basis and to the point where he could barely keep control. Several witnesses were prepared to testify to his woeful performance, and he must have got wind of their statements because he tendered his resignation, which the guardians accepted, probably with relief.[38] The problem of the mixing of the sexes was dealt with, but only in the short term, by sending the boys back to Cleveland Street and reserving Little Ogle Street for the girls, who were joined there by any female infant who could be separated 'with propriety' from a mother in the workhouse.[39] The guardians ensured that the children had the materials they needed to resume their education and advertised for a schoolmaster and schoolmistress. Among the applicants were Samuel and Sarah Harding and Joshua and Mary Brown. At the time, the Hardings were working down in Mitcham and must have been looking to escape from a situation that had turned sour, but neither they nor the Browns stood a chance with the Strand guardians, who were appalled, and with good reason, by the abuses the two men had handed out in the schoolrooms of Surrey Hall. Sarah Shambler also applied, and seems to have been highly rated, but was at a disadvantage because she was not married.[40] The jobs were given to a Mr and Mrs Samuel Hind, the latter repaying the trust placed in her by locking two girls she deemed to be insubordinate in an upstairs room for two nights. When a third girl earned her displeasure, Mrs Hind, in clear contravention of Poor Law regulations, caned her in the presence of her husband. His motive for observing the caning was complex: a desire to see the punishment properly administered suffused with a dark and unwholesome gratification.[41]

The appointment of Samuel Hind and his wife coincided with the decision of the board of guardians to reject Drouet's offer of Surrey Hall. On the face of it, though, the proposal was perfectly viable, and his acres in a Surrey village at a healthy distance from the cramped streets of Marylebone must have had more than a little appeal. For one thing, there was reason for the guardians to believe that they might realise their vision of an ideal arrangement, namely fully staffed premises in extensive grounds, where they might accommodate up to 250 children and separate them by age and sex. Then again, their search for new premises had so far drawn a blank: they had recently viewed the George Inn at Hounslow and the Red Lion Inn at Barnet, but one was in poor repair and the other was pricey.[42]

Not everyone was happy, though. One of the parishes that made up the union, St Anne's in Soho, was concerned that what they called 'the pest house at Tooting' had a strong odium attached to it, that it was far too large for their purposes, and that it would therefore be an unjustifiable burden on the ratepayers.[43] These objections notwithstanding, when it came to a boardroom vote, those against accepting Drouet's proposal were outnumbered fourteen to eight. The fourteen were intent on beating him down from a sale price of £4,000 to £3,500, and the deal got as far as a meeting at which the plans of the premises, the garden and the land were scrutinised. Drouet, who was ill, did not attend the meeting. He was represented by his half-brother Richard.[44]

The Poor Law Board, having the final say on the sale, engaged two highly qualified medical men, Joseph Hodgson and Edward Rigby, to submit a report on the state of the property. They went down to Lower Tooting on 23 June. It is not known who took them round, but it is a safe assumption that they were disgusted, and not only in the figurative sense. They wrote in their report that they had barely been able to stomach the stench wafting over the yard from the privies, the rabbit and ferret pens, and the drains. The filth might have been reason enough on its own to block the sale, but it was the state of the buildings that settled the matter, even though they were empty of starving children and were therefore being seen in the most favourable light. The main house had been patched up and painted, but Hodgson and Rigby were quick to point out that it 'would appear very different when in full operation' with a teeming population of children and adult staff, even if the Strand guardians were to send only a quarter of the numbers Drouet had herded through the establishment's doors. The White House was also worrying. It was not included in the proposed purchase, and there was every chance that it might revert to what it had previously been, namely a private lunatic asylum, which, in the frank opinion of the two doctors, would be a 'very undesirable' neighbour. In their summing up the writers of the report gave full vent to their displeasure:

> The locality is so low & flat; the surrounding nuisances in the form of open ditches & drains are so numerous, extensive, & unwholesome; some of the out-buildings are so slightly constructed, some of the rooms are so ill supplied with means for ventilation & warmth; the privies are so ill constructed & offensive, & there is such a want of proper accommodation for the sick, that we do not consider the premises suitable for the residence of pauper children: nor do we believe that they can be rendered so even by a large outlay of capital, which, in our opinion, it would be more humane & prudent to add to the amount required for the present purchase & to employ in the erection of really efficient accommodations in a more suitable & decidedly healthy locality.[45]

The Poor Law Board withheld its approval, and the Strand guardians wrote to the ailing Drouet to inform him that they were pulling out of the process.[46] Drouet's reply to the guardians, fuelled by a combination of disappointment and annoyance, in places verged on the incoherent:

> Gentlemen,
> I feel great disappointment at the contents of your letter in reference to this establishment, received this morning, after waiting so long, and I am inclined to believe the Poor Law Board would be placed very awkwardly if their answer was brought before the public, Mr Hall having told me there was no objection on the part of the Poor Law Board against the Tooting establishment, & I know the same expression has been made at the Strand Union Board.
> I consider it anything but justice to me after it has gone the round of every parish that the Strand Union had bought it, and very cheap, that it should now turn out not to be true, great will be the surprise by every parish at the result.
> I am at a loss what to do, but feel inclined to do business & if I can be informed what alterations are required by the two doctors who visited the establishment on the part of the Poor Law Board, I would do them.
> I am sure it would bother doctors, guardians, & the Poor Law Board to find a place better suited for the purpose, and I may add, few villages, if any, have larger schools, or of greater respectability than Tooting.

I hope I shall not offend any guardians at the Board, when I make use of his or their expressions, that of the parish not affording their share of £3500 for everything an establishment requires, what will they afford when called upon for a share of three times the amount for an establishment they may build; but persons are to be found to lend themselves to anything.[47]

In the late summer, the guardians bought premises at Edmonton in Middlesex at a cost of £4,000.[48] Edmonton was at least as far to the north of the capital as Lower Tooting was to the south, so it was as if they were turning their backs, symbolically, on the past. However, this did not prevent them buying a lot of clutter from Surrey Hall. They had been contacted by Alfred Charles Drouet: Bartholomew was dead, the children had gone, and he was selling off beds and bedding, school desks, dining tables and other redundant stuff. Everything came at a price, of course, down to a slipper bath worth 4s., a quantity of cutlery worth 7s. 6d. the lot, and chamber pots in a range of sizes and designs worth 1½d. each.[49]

Chapter Twelve

After Surrey Hall

Drouet's notoriety as a man who almost literally got away with murder was established early on. The story of Jane Matthews illustrates this well. She was the accomplice of a London swell mob, and on 17 April, three days after Drouet's acquittal, she went on trial at the Old Bailey charged in connection with the attempted theft of a large sum of money at a coaching inn in Clerkenwell. In spite of the best efforts of her counsel, who happened to be William Ballantine, she was found guilty and sentenced to be transported for ten years. 'I am innocent,' she declared to the court, 'but had I committed as many murders as Mr Drouet I should have been acquitted.'[1]

Many might have agreed with Jane Matthews that Drouet was on some level a murderer. As assessments go, it lacked logic, but it reflected the scale of the tragedy, the number of deaths, and the innocence of the victims. It also persisted long after the events of January 1849, and a striking example of Drouet's lasting relevance is to be found in newspaper accounts of another tragedy, and a real murder, that occurred in March 1850. The guilty parties were a married couple, Robert Courtice Bird and Sarah Bird, and their victim was a fifteen-year-old girl, Mary Ann Parsons.

It was an appalling story. The Birds, who were in their early to mid-thirties, lived on an isolated farm in North Devon, and Mary Ann, an inmate of the workhouse in Bideford, had entered their service in the autumn of 1849. Officially she was a parish apprentice, but in practice she was little more than a drudge, and as her father had left the country and her mother was still in the workhouse, she was completely at the disposal of the Birds. They treated her brutally, later claiming that she had been dishonest and could not keep herself clean, and that the master of the workhouse had recommended that Sarah Bird exercise her legitimate authority to keep the girl in line. Workers on the farm had heard the angry shouts and the cries of pain and distress, but nothing was said or done, until, that is, Mary Ann died after three months of ill treatment and her body was examined by a surgeon. He found bruises and marks on her face, on her back, and on her arms and legs. Some had been caused by kicking or punching; others had been inflicted with a leather scourge, or a hazel stick, or a birch. Abscesses had formed above and below her elbows, and some had burst. In the extreme cold of winter, her hands had been so badly frostbitten that four fingernails had dropped off, and the bone of her left middle finger had worked its way through the damaged skin. She had died as a result of a blow to the back of her head, as evidenced by the pooling of blood at the base of her brain.[2]

The Birds were charged with murder, but at their trial, which was held in Exeter, they were acquitted. Although no one disputed that they had been monstrously cruel to Mary Ann, it could not be established that they had been responsible for her fatal injury, which the defence argued might have been a consequence of her falling down the stairs or falling in the kitchen against the fender. Their acquittal was greeted with disbelief, which erupted in the streets outside the courthouse, forcing the Birds to run the gauntlet of an angry mob who sent them on their way with hisses and curses.[3] Many newspapers discussed the outcome of the trial and they agreed that the line dividing moral and legal guilt was in this instance exceptionally thin. The *Examiner* referred the discussion back to the previous year's scandal at Surrey Hall, proposing that something very similar had happened when Drouet escaped the charge of manslaughter thanks to the outbreak of cholera, which obligingly killed James Andrews before the boy could be starved or beaten to death. The newspaper that had provided the platform for Dickens's four thunderous articles on the Tooting tragedy was in no rush to forget Drouet.[4]

However, there is no getting around the fact that, in the case of Drouet, emotions were driven by the age and innocence of the children. 'When the children were dying by dozens,' the *Daily News* observed, 'there was intense excitement and vehement denunciation.'[5] But as the *News* went on to say, these were emotions of the moment. The story gripped the reading public only until the next story and the next trial came along, which, as it happened, was the trial of James Blomfield Rush, who really was a murderer. The brutal deaths of his victims caused a media sensation, and Rush's court appearances, which extended from 28 March to 4 April and were followed by his execution on 21 April, very much took over where the reporting of the Surrey Hall scandal had left off. Also, and at much the same time, belated news was beginning to emerge of the loss of the *Forth*, a Royal Mail steamship wrecked off the north coast of Mexico in January.[6] The *News* was under no illusion as to the ease and rapidity with which these stories came and went, and it regretted the fact that 'the last new topic for gossips, whatever it might be, soon effaced all recollection of the children's agonies'.

It is perhaps no surprise that the most moving comment came in the form of a letter written by a private individual. Although its authenticity may reasonably be questioned, the letter, which was submitted to *The Times* a few days after Drouet's trial, throws a light as does no other source on the feelings of an impoverished parent, real or imagined, with acute concerns for the wellbeing of her children. The writer, who signed the letter with the abbreviation 'A. B.' rather than with her full name, was responding, or purporting to respond, to an editorial in *The Times*.

The editorial pilloried the trial. It objected to the way Thesiger and Ballantine had attempted to derail the prosecution case. But it also pointed out that had the law given pauper children proper protection, then Drouet would have been found guilty. In many places the language it used was emotive, resorting to ridicule one moment and to pathos the next. The 'tender-hearted, child-loving Drouet' was 'the keeper of the Tooting pesthouse', while the children, in an ironic reference to the price charged for their upkeep, were 'the four-and-sixpenny boys and girls'. James Andrews was 'the little unfortunate'. Throughout, the tone of the writing was properly indignant, leading A. B. to hail *The Times* as a champion of the poor:

Sir, – Will you permit an humble individual to offer you her mite of thanks for your noble and benevolent remarks on the conduct of Mr Drouet? Believe me, Sir, many a mother's heart was warmed, and her eyes have overflowed with tears of gratitude to see the view you have taken of this melancholy affair. Your valuable advocacy of the unhappy class "the pauper child" reflects credit equally on your heart and your head. Does poverty crush the anxious solicitude of a mother? Does it render the body less sensible to cold, hunger, and privation? These last events will prove how far this is from being the case. Though the daughter of a professional man, the sister of clergymen, I am, from sad reverses, exposed to see my children ranked among these poor unfortunates; and are my feelings as a mother less acute than when surrounded with comfort and plenty I watched and tended my infant family? Certainly the reverse is the case. The verdict of the jury cannot alter the facts of the case. Long may your pages continue to denounce injustice and crime, however upheld, thus proving a blessing to all classes – the poor as well as the rich.[7]

A. B. may have been a fiction, but whoever she was, the letter expressed with eloquence what many must have been thinking and feeling. It had caught the public mood.

*   *   *

Once the trial was over, Drouet attended to his failing health. In June, when the sale of Surrey Hall was still under discussion, Richard deputised for him at a meeting with the Strand guardians, excusing his half-brother's absence on account of illness.[8] Bartholomew was away from home at No. 5 Cliff Terrace in Margate, where he had a seaside retreat and the company of Sarah Jane Day, who was there, officially, as his housekeeper. He was writing letters to the guardians and the Poor Law Board almost to the end, but the last sighting of him was in the middle of May in Lower Tooting, when he attended meetings of the vestry. At one of these meetings, he was given a reduction in the rating of his property from £209 to £100 'in consideration of its unemployed state'. A week later, an irritation over one of his fences, which encroached on Garratt Lane, was brought up. The issue had been allowed to rumble on because of his declining health, but now, finally, he agreed to have the fence moved. The date of the meeting was 17 May and it was Drouet's last recorded appearance.[9]

It is possible that the Drouets first became familiar with Margate in connection with their work in pauper administration. Cliff Terrace was a short distance from Robert Perry's Sea Bathing Establishment in Wilderness Road, and an even closer neighbour was John Weekley's Metropolitan Establishment in Clifton Place, where the London workhouses sent children with scrofula to enjoy the therapeutic benefits of sunlight, clean air and sea water. Then again, they may have come to Margate for no other reason than that it had long been a fashionable seaside resort, a draw for the well-to-do and the respectable, and increasingly a popular destination for Londoners, who would travel down through Kent on the South Eastern railway, or along the Thames estuary on a steamboat.

The appeal of this coastal town was captured perfectly in a guidebook published in 1850: 'Margate being a weather-shore, during the greater part of the summer in consequence of the southerly winds, which generally prevail in that season, blowing off the shore, the sea is rendered perfectly smooth and the water clear to a considerable depth.'[10]

In Margate the visitor could breathe, walk up and down the gentle slopes, and bathe in the emerald green waters of the harbour in search of relaxation and health. The Clifton Baths, carved into the chalk of the cliffs, offered terraces, subterranean chambers, bathing machines, and a waiting room with newspapers, books, pianos and views over the sea. The promenade, almost 900 feet long, was brassy with military bands by day, and brilliant with the chemical colours of gas lighting when evening fell. At night the sound of the waves was soft and soothing, borne to land from remote reaches lying unseen on the far side of the dark.[11]

Behind the seafront and its hotels and large houses, in the town itself, were the Assembly Rooms, the Theatre Royal, and the Literary and Scientific Institution with its reading room and lecture room, and its museum collections of insects, minerals and native birds. Also there were the circulating libraries and the bazaars in the High Street. Jolly's French Bazaar was filled with music and singing and stocked with costly china and porcelain, shawls and muslin, bottles of scent and jewellery. At the Boulevard de Paris, ladies dressed in white muslin played pianos, while customers with cash to lose threw dice or tried their luck with the wheel of fortune.[12]

The houses in the Drouets' corner of Cliff Terrace were built on three storeys, and made a fine display of brickwork and tall windows that flooded the rooms with light. Paths ran from the street through planted areas up to the front doors. Behind the houses there were little gardens with trees and shrubs. No. 5 was occupied after the Drouets by a Peter Truefitt, who had made money in perfumery, along with his sister and his niece and two female servants.[13]

Samuel Taylor Coleridge's daughter, Sara, visited Margate in the 1840s. A writer herself, Sara recorded her impressions as they swung from disgust at the smell of the drains in the centre of the town to delight in the little gardens on the cliffs planted with carnations and pinks, stocks and gillyflowers, roses and southernwood. She went there for 'refreshment and bracing sea-breezes', and at a time when she was grieving for her husband, Henry Nelson Coleridge, she chose Margate over neighbouring towns for the 'greater cheapness' of its accommodation. In the summer of 1847 she was caught in a storm, and as she sheltered behind a hedge, it struck her that the town looked 'really fine' under its canopy of dark clouds. She preferred it to Herne Bay and Broadstairs. 'There is more to see,' she noted, 'more of human life in this long-established, half-new, half-old town.' To her way of thinking, Margate was less genteel, less mannered than other coastal towns.[14]

Later in the same year, Sara put up in a house where her sitting room had a pleasant view, but it was poky, and she disliked the rose design of the wallpaper. Worse, the family who owned the house brawled incessantly. She did better when she visited the town again in 1849, staying in congenial lodgings just round the corner from Cliff Terrace in Zion Place. She walked twice a day with her sixteen-year-old daughter and was at peace and felt content. In a letter to a friend, she wrote: 'I enjoy the quietness of this place. Very few visitors are here. We have the cliff all to ourselves for the most part, or share it only with the carolling larks.' But a few lines later the tone is more sombre: 'Who can be very *gleeful*, for more than a few minutes at a time, in such a world as this, dear friend, so full of sorrow and misery and crushing want, spiritual and physical, and so surrounded by impervious shadow, the awful mystery of the world to come?' Had she known that Bartholomew Peter Drouet would live out the last days of his life only yards away, she might have recognised a disturbing aptness in her brooding and pessimistic thoughts.[15]

*   *   *

It was suggested that the true start of the tragedy was Maria's death on 4 October 1848. She had spent her final hours far from Lower Tooting at the house in Cliff Terrace, and there she suffered a stroke. Her husband was not at her side but their son William Charles was. He was twenty-six, and it was left to him to provide for his mother whatever comfort he could. Her death certificate shows that there was no doctor in attendance, and that when the end came, it came quickly. The deadly drama had finally begun.[16]

An article published in *Bell's Life in London* in February 1849 offered a sympathetic view of Maria:

It is due to state that Mr Drouet, about the middle of last year, had the misfortune to lose his wife, upon whom a great portion of the domestic arrangements for the comfort of the children had depended. She was an active, kind-hearted woman, herself a parent, and universally beloved by the whole establishment, and more especially by the infants, who evinced towards her unmistakable affection. This was indeed a severe loss, not only to Mr Drouet himself, but to those poor little things entrusted to his care.[17]

Bell's glowing testimonial sits rather unhappily with the many denunciations of the regime at Surrey Hall. The charming image of little children clustering around a beaming Maria seems out of kilter with the plentiful evidence of a culture of indifference in the asylum and the many documented instances of cruelty and neglect. However, there is no reason not to believe that Maria was an effective matron, and that the management of the asylum relied heavily on her organisational skills. She was very experienced, having held the office of matron at the workhouses in Alverstoke and Lambeth, where her duties, as defined by the Poor Law Commissioners, would have been exacting. She would have had sole charge of the female paupers, and this would have entailed not only overseeing their conduct and ensuring that they kept to regulation hours in the sleeping wards, but also supervising the making and mending of workhouse uniforms and the constant laundering of bedding and clothes. She would have cared for sick paupers, and for children, and for mothers with infants at the breast, and she would have seen to it that their diet suited their needs.

Moreover, Maria's importance would not have been limited to these roles. As a workhouse matron, she would be required to act as the master's deputy in his absence, and at all times she would share his responsibility for the state of the 'house' and the good behaviour of the inmates, and assist him in buying in stores and provisions. It is hard to imagine that a woman with the competence and energy to meet such taxing demands took a back seat at Surrey Hall. She may well have left business matters to her husband, and the correspondence flowing endlessly between Surrey Hall and Poor Law administrators at parish and government level makes it abundantly clear that in this respect Drouet was a busy man. But in every other department of the asylum, Maria would have been vitally important.

In the middle of July, Drouet was feeling the full effects of his illness, which was worsening by the day. He was treated by a local doctor, David Price, who recognised that the end was not far off, and must have been perfectly open on this point because on 18 July Drouet summoned a solicitor and his clerk to witness the signing of his will.[18] If he had been well enough to leave the house, he would have found the Margate summer season in full swing. Records show that almost 800 visitors arrived on the steamboats on the previous Saturday.[19] He would have heard the holiday sounds coming up from the Clifton Baths, the music of street organs and hurdy-gurdies, the cries of fish hawkers and shrimp sellers, and the clanging of the bell of the blue-coated town bellman. Had he been strong enough to go further, down to the promenade, he would have seen the crowds of Londoners enjoying the sight of the sea and mingling with the conjurors, the tumblers, the animal entertainers with their bears and their monkeys, the fortune tellers and the pedlars of cheap plaster statuettes.[20]

On the morning of 19 July, which was a Thursday, he died. The official cause of death was heart disease, and although it is possible that he was carried off by a sudden episode, it may just be that his life had petered out in the lingering final phase of his illness. At the critical moment, Richard was at his bedside, and it was Richard who informed the local registrar, Henry Wootton, that his half-brother Bartholomew had died, that his occupation was that of a gentleman, and that he was fifty-four years old.[21] Richard may well have been the source of the rumour that Bartholomew's decline had been hastened by his disappointment at having the sale of Surrey Hall to the Strand Union blocked by the Poor Law Board.[22]

Drouet was brought back from Margate for burial, and on 27 July he was laid to rest alongside Maria in the fashionable South Metropolitan Cemetery in West Norwood. He had bought a plot a week after her death back in October.[23] If things had turned out differently, he would have secured that most cherished of Victorian acquisitions, which was to be thought of in death as having been respectable in life. That was now all but impossible. When a notice in *The Times* announced that 'a very numerous circle of friends' were distressed at his passing – which may well have been true – the *Satirist* pounced:

> We imagine the numerous circle does not include any of the fathers or mothers, brothers or sisters, uncles or aunts, of the unfortunate children committed to Mr Drouet's charge when he "farmed" the pauper establishment at Tooting, and where the miserable victims were allowed scarcely the benefit of God's air, or of proper nourishment. Amongst this "numerous circle of friends" are not surely to be reckoned any of the indignant jurymen before whom the various

cases of the victimised pauper children were investigated. Oh, no! far from it: the above announcement is quite wrong; it must be a misprint. It should have read thus:— "Scarcely regretted by the *small* circle of his *private* friends!" This one might understand; but the matter as it really stands recorded in the *Times*, is much more calculated to provoke the smile of contempt than the tear of regret.

The *Satirist* then took aim at the notion that it was 'an affection of the heart' that had been the cause of his long illness and ultimate death. Drouet must have 'kept all the "affection" to himself,' the *Satirist* suggested, playing on the ambiguity of the word, 'for none of the hapless infant inmates of his starvation prison-house ever felt any of his paternal kindness.'[24]

The will was proved on 3 August at the Prerogative Court in London. Drouet had named as his executors the oldest of his half-brothers, Alfred Charles, and the Kennington butcher Jonathan Gain, who was married to his half-sister Margaret Elizabeth. They were men he was able to trust. Alfred was running the Grove House operation, where the Newington children had been sent, and he actively assisted in tying up loose ends of Surrey Hall business, contacting the Strand guardians in March with a demand for payment in relation to the cost of burying children in the Tooting churchyard.[25] Gain had been a regular supplier of meat over a period of three years. He was also one of the four sureties who had paid £50 each towards Drouet's bail.[26]

It was the responsibility of the executors to dispose of Drouet's property. Three-fifths was assigned in joint ownership to Alfred, Richard and a third half-brother, Robert Creak. The remaining two-fifths was invested on behalf of Margaret and Drouet's other half-sister, Miriam. Although as a girl Miriam had occupied the lowly position of assistant matron at Surrey Hall, in her early twenties she had married a 'gentleman' of Stockwell, Henry Seymour Conway. Thanks to her marriage, she enjoyed a rise in status that enabled her before very long to live in Upper Tooting with two daughters and five servants.[27] Since Conway had been another of Drouet's four sureties at the time of his arrest, it may be that there were connections between the two men that went beyond being brothers-in-law.

Drouet made a number of cash gifts. He gave £100 to his widowed sister, Elizabeth Sarah Willson, and £10 each to his brother, William Leonard, and another half-brother, Alexander, who worked as a licensed victualler. These were generous gestures, and in the case of Elizabeth, who was living with her three children in Newington and working as a schoolmistress, Drouet may well have been influenced by the beneficiary's circumstances.[28] But even these not inconsiderable sums of money were overshadowed by the remarkable £1,000 Drouet left Sarah Jane Day. The question this raises is just what Sarah meant to him, and the answer would seem to be that their relationship had to have been more than that of employer and employee. Certainly she had been a valued assistant matron to his wife in Surrey Hall, and had stayed loyal to him in his darkest hours, but she was benefiting significantly more from his will than his own flesh and blood. Faced with this fact, it is hard not to wonder if Sarah had been not just an indispensable member of the Surrey Hall team but Drouet's mistress as well. Whatever lay behind it, though, his bequest left her comparatively well off, and within four years she had married a widower, Thomas Webber, who brought with him four children and four servants, a successful baker's business that employed three other men, and a comfortable house in Stockwell.[29]

A more complicated arrangement was the 30s. allowance Drouet settled on his son, William Charles. He stipulated that the money was to be paid every Monday, starting from the first Monday after his death, and continuing in perpetuity. William, who was in his twenties at the time of his father's death, had worked as a cheesemonger in Lambeth and as a victualler with a licence for the Nile Tavern in Hog Lane in Woolwich, and had married Hannah Copping, a governess at Surrey Hall.[30] Hannah had given birth to two children in the two years following their marriage, and in 1850 she would give birth to a third. Curiously, when his father's will was drawn up in 1849, William was living on the French coast in Boulogne. A plausible explanation for his temporary move abroad is that he was looking for a place where he could live more cheaply than in England. Again, the fact that he transferred his victualler's licence to a new landlord of the Nile Tavern early in 1848 certainly hints at money problems, and it is possible that his French adventure was little more than a bid to escape his creditors. Now that the Continent had thrown off the restrictions imposed by the Napoleonic Wars, Boulogne would have been an appealing place of refuge. In 1854 a handbook for travellers in France commented that the town

has become, since the peace, one of the chief British colonies abroad; and, by a singular reciprocity, on the very spot whence Napoleon proposed the invasion of our shores, his intended victims have quietly taken possession and settled themselves down. The town is enriched by English money; warmed, lighted, and smoked by English coal; English signs and advertisements decorate every other shop-door, inn, tavern, and lodging-house; and almost every third person you meet is either a countryman or speaking our language; while the outskirts of the town are enlivened by villas and country-houses, somewhat in the style and taste of those on the opposite side of the Channel.[31]

Boulogne was very accessible to the English. The journey time by steamboat was ten to twelve hours from London Bridge Wharf or two hours from Dover.

Money problems may well account for Drouet's decision to set up a weekly allowance for William. In his years in pauper management he had proved himself to be nothing if not financially astute, and if he could not trust his son to handle his affairs competently, he may have been reluctant to make him a one-off pecuniary gift. But William might have had other reasons for living in Boulogne. Conceivably, he was already dogged by the medical condition that would force him into a workhouse infirmary in 1853. It would eventually manifest itself as heart disease and kill him in 1858 when he was still a young man.[32] He may have feared dying the way his mother and father had died, and he may have decided to spend time in a French coastal resort, where sea bathing was an established activity, for the sake of his health.

Living in Boulogne may also have made it easier for William to keep his father's disgrace at arm's length. That said, there is nothing to indicate that he suffered anything more than embarrassment as a result of the scandal, and on his return to England he carried on much as before, working first as a butcher in Norwood and then as an innkeeper in Fleet Street.[33] Other members of the Drouet family also continued in their various lines of business. William Leonard Drouet, for example, was a registered coal and corn merchant when cholera broke out in Surrey Hall, and had recently been admitted into the Freedom of the City of London in the Company of Loriners, who were makers of horse bits and bridles. The privilege cost him £2 6s. 8d.[34] For a time he worked with his son-in-law, Frederick Battcock, on the dusty wharves along the Chelsea Embankment. Frederick was related to the Rubergalls, a family of Chelsea market gardeners, and when William died in 1869, at the age of seventy-seven, he was not at home with Rebecca but in a house where three Rubergall sisters lived. They were all less than half his age.[35]

Richard Drouet, who was a butcher by trade, worked in Walworth until 1852, when he moved to Tranquil Vale in Blackheath as landlord of the Crown Hotel and married Emma Jane Hall, whose father, Robert Hall, carved figureheads in the shipyards of Rotherhithe. Emma gave birth to a daughter in 1856, and one wonders if the man who had inflicted so much violence on the young inmates of Surrey Hall might have been softened by fatherhood. But the child died shortly after birth. The following year a boy was born, but he also died. Emma had no more children, and Richard, a Drouet to the very end, was still managing the Crown when he died of tuberculosis in 1867 at the age of forty-nine.[36]

Alfred Charles Drouet managed the Grove House operation from late 1848 with his wife, Mary Ann, but in the summer of 1851, for reasons that are not entirely clear, he closed it down.[37] It was the end of a career in pauper management that had started in 1836 with his appointment as an assistant clerk at the Lambeth workhouse under the management of Bartholomew Peter and Maria Drouet.[38] He was master of the Camberwell workhouse with his wife as matron for ten years. Their sustained service earned them the praise of the guardians, much to the annoyance of Richard Hall, whose inspections had raised questions about the state of the premises. When the guardians proposed a £50 gratuity for the departing Drouets, Hall objected. He felt that their salary of £120 a year, with other emoluments, was reward enough. The Poor Law Board bowed to the will of its inspector by refusing to sanction the gratuity.[39] Alfred had formerly put himself forward as a trustee and treasurer of a provident society that had been established 'to ameliorate the condition' of Poor Law officers, and in the light of Hall's spiteful intervention, this must now have seemed to him to have been a wise decision.

Early in August 1851 the contents of Grove House were put up for sale by public auction. The extensive catalogue embraced a bewildering range of items from beds and bedding to washing troughs, brass taps, a patent mangle, and an iron garden roller.[40] Thereafter, Alfred threw himself into the family tradition of earning his daily bread as a licensed victualler, first at the Lansdowne Arms in Lambeth and later at the King's Head in Norwood. His personal life was in turmoil, though, and in 1861 his marriage of almost twenty-five years ended in divorce.

Alfred had met his future wife, Mary Ann Mott, during the time of his employment at the Lambeth workhouse. It was very much a Poor Law affair, as Mary Ann was the niece of Charles Mott, who held the contract in partnership with Bartholomew Peter Drouet. At the time of their marriage, which took place in 1837, they were both in their early twenties, and they went on to have seven children. The seventh, Betsy, was only three years old in 1856 when Mary Ann eloped with a man by the name of William Stevens, an omnibus conductor living not far from Grove House in Brixton. When Mary Ann left with Stevens, she took Betsy with her. Nothing was heard of them for over a year, but finally, in the summer of 1857, Mary Ann began sending letters to William and Amelia Wright, friends from the old days who had at one point been the master and matron of the Camberwell workhouse. It emerged later that she and Stevens had been cohabiting at various addresses: the letters came from Old Swan on the eastern outskirts of Liverpool.[41]

Mary Ann expressed remorse for her behaviour, but she also confessed that she was in great distress and begged the Wrights to ask Alfred if he would help her. He did, by sending small amounts of money to Liverpool, partly because he felt sorry for Mary Ann and Betsy, and partly in the hope of persuading his estranged wife to send their daughter back home. Time passed, but the day came when Betsy was put on a train in Liverpool and travelled down to Euston in the company of a protective railway guard. Eventually Mary Ann and Stevens were traced, and the dissolution of the Drouets' marriage went ahead, but whether there were sins on both sides is impossible to determine as the divorce papers only represent Alfred's version of events.[42] Exactly what motivated Mary Ann to run off with another man can only be a matter of speculation. It may be relevant, though, that a year after the divorce Alfred married a cousin, Sarah Ann Middleton, who had been living with him as his housekeeper for at least a year.

*   *   *

Before long, in October, the clearing out of Surrey Hall went public with an auction of the freehold property at Garraway's Coffee House, which was tucked between Cornhill and Lombard Street in Change Alley. The notices in the newspapers gave the place a glossy write-up that reached out to 'Capitalists, Manufacturers, Engineers' and generally to developers and investors who might be able to take advantage of the buildings in the yard. At a separate auction, which was held on the premises, the furniture and miscellaneous contents of the household went under the hammer. Among other items, the catalogue listed:

> 400 iron bedsteads, besides others, 400 pairs of new blankets, 400 pairs of new sheets, 600 beds, bolsters, and pillows, a very expensive steam-cooking apparatus with large wrought-iron boiler, furnace, etc. erected at a cost of £400 and one other large steam boiler, all the fixtures and fittings-up of the school-rooms, desks, forms, tables, etc. about 200 suits of boys' clothes (new), etc.

So much of the story of Drouet's children could be told by perusing this list. There were also reminders of the agricultural work and training that went on at Surrey Hall: four acres of rich meadowland and two generous stacks of meadow hay were on sale along with two cows, a horse, two carts, and 'numerous other useful effects'.[43]

The property was duly auctioned and was bought by Joseph Lucas, a London solicitor with an office in Charing Cross and a house in Upper Tooting.[44] But it had no future, and in the spring of the following year, it was pulled down. There was a final sale, by which time every last trace of the tragedy had gone. Where before there had been a structure with a discernible purpose, now there was only the stuff of which it was made: the bricks and the tiles, the roof rafters and the floors, the glazed sash windows, the lead gutters and pipes and cisterns, the doors to the rooms, the cupboards, the stoves and the ranges and the kitchen coppers, the paving, the fences, the railings and the gates.[45] The *Illustrated London News* reported the dismemberment of Surrey Hall in a notice in which overt relief that a line had finally been drawn under the tragedy is tinged with a sense of melancholy, a yearning for a prelapsarian past: 'Thus, we hope, will be effaced all recollection of the fearful events that happened at Drouet's, at Christmas, 1848, and which tended to injure the village, inasmuch as, prior to those events, Tooting was highly esteemed as a locality enjoying pure air and many other advantages.'[46] As the *News* pointed out, the registrar, Henry Withall, had given evidence at the Holborn inquest that deaths from cholera had been confined to Surrey Hall. This was taken as proof 'that Tooting was' or had been 'one of the healthiest districts in Surrey'.

Lucas removed the offending buildings and was thanked by the vestry. He also proposed building a terrace along the upper boundary of the site and widening Garratt Lane where it ran alongside what had once been the children's yard. These projects he would fund at his own expense, as if he wanted not only to improve public facilities but also, somehow, to diminish Drouet and the memory of the terrible things he had done.[47] Then in 1853 he sold the land to Richard Wilson Greaves for £250.[48] Greaves, who had buried so many of Drouet's children, was now pressing to have a Church of England parochial infants' school built. He argued that the need was very great, as the catchment area of the parish of Tooting, which measured roughly two and a half square miles, supported a population of 2,200 residents, of whom those at the lower end of the economic scale were in the main employed as agricultural labourers. He insisted that there was local enthusiasm for the school, and that it could be funded by means of annual subscriptions and grants from the National Society for Promoting Religious Education and the Council on Education. There would be room for 150 infant pupils, and the schoolmistress would be housed on site.[49]

The school was built in Kentish ragstone to the design of Joseph Peacock of Bloomsbury. Peacock was one of the 'rogue' architects who took the Gothic Revival style to new heights of flamboyance, and even in designing a humble infant school he rejoiced in steep roofs and gables and pointed trefoil windows. So much had changed, and above all, in striking contrast to the indifference of the Drouet days, rigorous checks were carried out to ensure that there were no 'noxious or noisy trades or works' in the neighbourhood, no foul ditches, no uncovered drains, no stagnant pools that might be injurious to the health of children.[50] In another change from less happy times, the children flourished. A government inspector visiting the school in 1859 reported that it was 'conducted with animation, good temper, and intelligence' by the schoolmistress and her two apprentices. The fifty boys and forty girls who were in the school on the day of the inspection presented a picture of cleanliness and good cheer. Where ten years earlier there had been cruelty and degradation in the schoolrooms of Surrey Hall, the inspector, who was also a clergyman, now found kindness and hope.[51]

In 1874 the then Rector of Tooting, John Congreve, handed over the lease of the building to the London School Board. However, it could no longer satisfy the educational demands of an expanding local population, and when a new school was built on the other side of the road, it was returned to the parish to be used as a vestry hall.[52] It was photographed in 1887. The walls are clothed in ivy, and a four-horse omnibus stands in the road, its passengers dressed in suits and sporting hats.[53] They are solid and substantial men, and there was a time when men of that kind would have come down to Lower Tooting from the metropolitan workhouses to check on the children in Surrey Hall.

At the turn of the century, with the creation of the Metropolitan Borough of Wandsworth, the vestry became a thing of the past. The vestry hall, although now dilapidated, was a local asset, and in order not to be gifted to the borough it needed a new local purpose. The first proposal was for a public library, but it was rejected in favour of a rival project funded by Sir William Lancaster, the philanthropic Mayor of Wandsworth. Instead, plans were put forward to convert the old vestry hall into public baths. Given that many working-class homes had been built without running water, these would serve a genuine need. The building now lost its Gothic Revival form to a utilitarian box-like structure, but it acquired a curious distinction as the first establishment in London to install a type of spray bath popularised on the Continent by Oscar Lassar, a distinguished German dermatologist. Entry cost 2d., and in the words of the *South Western Star*, patrons would be able to 'recline beneath a gentle tepid shower, which luxuriously facilitates the hygienic progress of the bath'.[54]

In this way, Drouet's former establishment assumed new life. Alongside it, where once the White House had stood, shops were built. Behind it houses sprang up, their gardens covering what in bleaker times had been the animal pens and the children's privies in the yard.

Epilogue

To echo the *Hampshire Telegraph*, it's an ill wind that blows nobody any good, and in the case of the disaster at Surrey Hall, the saying held true.[1] The system of farming pauper children out to private contractors could not survive. Too many abominable practices rooted in greed and cynicism had come to light. Too many failures on the part of the workhouse guardians to keep a careful watch on the contractors' establishments had been revealed. There simply had to be a better way of caring for children who were among the most vulnerable members of society.

However, the dismantling of the system, though timely, was not a complete solution. The contractors may have been discredited, but there was still the problem of what to do with the children. At all costs, they had to be kept out of the workhouse. They had to be cared for, and not only cared for but educated against pauperism and the temptations of crime, and trained up to take their place in society and engage in some form of productive employment. This was the agenda, and the Poor Law Board now had every reason to push ahead with its plans for district schools. The ground had already been laid in an Act of Parliament passed in 1844 allowing boards of guardians to form district unions for the purpose of building schools and training establishments in suitable locations. But it needed the shock, and the shame, of the events in Lower Tooting for the plan to become a reality, and by the end of 1849 three district schools had been established in the vicinity of the metropolis. More would be formed as the years and decades passed.

These were ambitious projects, and one of the earliest, the North Surrey District School, was hailed by the *Illustrated London News* as a model establishment. Five unions had combined to buy land near the Croydon Railway at Anerley, and they commissioned a London architect to design a building that would accommodate 600 children. The *News* listed its many amenities, and these ranged from schoolrooms and workshops to areas given over to administrative and domestic activities. The entire building was heated and a system of flues and shafts guaranteed a flow of fresh air. It was a far cry from Surrey Hall with its filthy rooms and its even filthier yard.[2]

It is a mistake to think of the children who survived Surrey Hall as defined by its lamentable history. Drouet's children were more than just victims of his asylum. They had other lives. But they are hard to trace after 1849, and it is a sad truth that in many cases the most we know about them is what they said at one of the parish inquests or at Drouet's trial, or the comments the guardians made about them in their copious written records.

But sometimes, with persistence, or more likely with luck, they can be found. Take Henry Hartshorn. He was the Holborn boy who used the money he earned in the shoemaker's workshop to buy food from the nurses.[3] But the skills he acquired in turning out 'five pair of uppers for a penny' stayed with him, and in the late 1860s, after a protracted silence lasting the best part of two decades, his name suddenly emerges in a local newspaper.[4] He was working for a shoemaker, Benjamin Hackshaw, in Sittingbourne in Kent. He must have moved in occupational circles, because at the age of forty-six he married a widow, Mary Ann Cogger, whose first husband, William, had been a shoemaker too. When not making shoes, both Henry and William were active in the local temperance movement.[5] They also helped publicise the movement, and Henry, in the 1881 census, was a newsagent and stationer in Spital Street in Dartford.[6] He had no children of his own, but Mary Ann, who was aged fifty-nine when they married, was the mother of seven. The three youngest, all in their twenties, lived in Spital Street for a time, and Henry, who had been one of the Surrey Hall orphans, must have enjoyed having his new family around him. He had no brothers or sisters, and in those vital childhood years he had been all alone.

There are still traces of the Drouets. Cliff Terrace in Margate is a short walk up from the Harbour Arm and the old customs house, less than half a mile from the six white blocks of Turner Contemporary and an Antony Gormley cast-iron man looking out to sea. One would have thought that South London would offer richer pickings, but it is hard to picture old Surrey Hall in the bustling centre of modern Tooting. Where it once stood, there is now a bank, and next to the bank there is a pub. The Drouets, a family of licensed victuallers, would no doubt have approved.

The site of the Hall can still be seen on a map, or on Google Earth, clipped between Garratt Lane and Garratt Terrace. The naming of Garratt Terrace postdates Drouet: in his day it was the final stretch of Garratt Lane. It is now a quiet residential street lined with houses and parked cars, but back then it skirted Drouet's dismal yard. You would not know it now. You can only picture in your imagination the workshops, the shoddy schoolrooms, the children blasted by the winter winds.

The one place that has not changed is St Nicholas Church. It stands off the busy Mitcham Road, and it is a strange thought that had you been there in January 1849, you would have seen the carts bringing the coffins from Surrey Hall to be buried at nightfall in unmarked graves. However, Drouet's children at least have a memorial: a stone plaque commemorating the loss of all those young lives. The plaque was set up by Wandsworth Borough Council and unveiled by Princess Alexandra in 1989. It is a moving tribute, the more so because it was local children, the pupils of Broadwater Junior High School, who asked to have it installed.[7]

Notes

Prologue
1. The National Archives, PCOM 2/211, p. 440
2. oldbaileyonline.org/record/t18490409-916
3. oldbaileyonline.org/record/t18490409-918
4. oldbaileyonline.org/record/t18490409-917
5. *Satirist*, 14 April 1849
6. Knight, 1851, p. 681

Chapter One: Elizabeth Frost
1. The National Archives, HO 107/664/7, Adelaide Square
2. The National Archives, HO 107/1502, Adelaide Square
3. Registrar-General, 1854, p. 329
4. *Builder*, 19 March 1859, p. 212
5. Lewis, 1854, pp. 52–3
6. Lewis, 1854, p. 62
7. *Builder*, 26 March 1853, p. 201
8. *Builder*, 26 March 1853, pp. 201–2
9. Mayhew, 1861, passim
10. Doré, 1872, pp. 116, 124/5, 158/9
11. *Builder*, 26 March 1853, p. 201
12. *Ragged School Union Magazine*, February 1850, p. 56
13. *Ragged School Union Magazine*, September 1851, p. 207
14. General Register Office, death certificate, Henry Frost, 20 November 1843
15. *Lancet*, 29 July 1865, p. 133
16. *Leicestershire Mercury*, 30 June 1849; *Morning Herald*, 17 September 1842; *Morning Advertiser*, 24 November 1845
17. *Morning Herald*, 13 November 1841
18. *Essex Herald*, 26 July 1842
19. The London Archives, P83/MRY1/0793-7, passim
20. Late Relieving Officer, 1859, p. 78
21. Late Relieving Officer, 1859, p. 78
22. Late Relieving Officer, 1859, p. 78
23. The National Archives, HO 107/652/9, Islington Infant Poor House
24. Lewis, 1842, pp. 138–9
25. Dickens, 1838, p. 9
26. The London Archives, P83/MRY1/0735, passim
27. Lewis, 1842, pp. 138–9
28. *Morning Chronicle*, 16 January 1849
29. The London Archives, P83/MRY1/0796, pp. 104, 109–10

30. The London Archives, P83/MRY1/0796, pp. 197–8, 201–2
31. The London Archives, P83/MRY1/0797, p. 161
32. Pigot, 1839
33. London Picture Archive, St Nicholas, Tooting, 1832
34. Morden, 1897, p. 200
35. *Law Times*, 29 September 1849; *Morning Chronicle*, 8 January 1849
36. *Morning Chronicle*, 20 January 1849
37. *Morning Chronicle*, 20 January 1849
38. The London Archives, WEBG/ST/006, letter, 8 August 1842; KBG/010, minutes, 4 January 1847
39. *Manchester Times*, 25 September 1841; *Morning Post*, 19 January 1849

Chapter Two: Bartholomew Peter Drouet
1. *Royal Kalendar*, 1814, p. 260
2. Guildhall Library, binding records 1692–1949, Bartholomew Peter Drouet
3. *Morning Herald*, 19 February 1849
4. Hampshire Record Office, PL2/1/3, letter, 8 January 1823; minutes, 6 February 1823; deed, 20 February 1823
5. Post Office London Directory, 1820; *Law Chronicle*, 6 June 1816
6. Hampshire Record Office, PL2/1/3, minutes, 18 April 1826
7. Hampshire Record Office, PL2/1/3, letter, 6 January 1825
8. Hampshire Record Office, PL2/1/1, vestry records, 26 March 1826 to 26 March 1827
9. Hampshire Record Office, PL2/1/3, letter, 22 December 1826
10. Poor Law Commissioners, 1834, p. 180
11. Poor Law Commissioners, 1834, pp. 197–8
12. *Morning Advertiser*, 16 December 1831
13. *Satirist*, 17 February 1849
14. Poor Law Commissioners, 1834, pp. 180–1
15. Poor Law Commissioners, 1834, p. 181
16. Poor Law Commissioners, 1834, p. 181
17. *Morning Chronicle*, 17 March 1832
18. The National Archives, MH 12/12457, letter, 18 January 1838
19. *True Sun*, 21 January 1836
20. *Globe*, 18 August 1837
21. *Evening Mail*, 29 January 1838
22. Poor Law Commissioners, 1834, p. 194
23. *The Times*, 3 and 4 July 1835
24. The National Archives, MH 12/12457, undated communications, 3571, 4008, 4009
25. *West Kent Guardian*, 25 August 1838
26. The London Archives, LABG/002, letter, 1 May 1838
27. The National Archives, MH 12/12456, letter, 29 April 1836
28. *Morning Herald*, 19 February 1849
29. https://blog.nationalarchives.gov.uk/george-sangliers-petitions-two-sides-every-petition/
30. *Morning Advertiser*, 21 January 1834
31. Pettigrew, 1836, p. 9
32. The London Archives, P92/MRY/295, letter, 27 May 1835
33. The London Archives, P92/MRY/295, letter, 1 June 1835
34. The London Archives, P92/MRY/295, letters, 27 and 29 May, 1 June 1835

35. The London Archives, P92/MRY/295, letters, 27 May, 1 June 1835
36. The London Archives, P92/MRY/295, minutes, 5 June, 7 July 1835
37. *Salisbury and Winchester Journal*, 20 February 1832; *Wiltshire Independent*, 1 December 1836; *Hampshire Chronicle*, 23 October 1837
38. *Weekly Chronicle*, 14 December 1845
39. *Sun*, 13 December 1845
40. The National Archives, MH 32/49, minutes, 25 August 1837
41. The National Archives, MH 32/49, minutes, 25 August 1837; MH 12/12456, letter, 11 September 1837
42. The National Archives, MH 32/49, minutes, 25 August 1837
43. The National Archives, MH 32/49, minutes, 25 August 1837
44. The National Archives, MH 32/49, minutes, 25 August 1837
45. The National Archives, MH 32/49, minutes, 25 August 1837
46. The National Archives, MH 12/12456, letter, 11 September 1837

Chapter Three: Surrey Hall

 1. Stanley, 1909, p. 10
 2. Wandsworth Heritage Service, TP/1/1/4, passim.
 3. *Morning Chronicle*, 8 January 1849
 4. The National Archives, MH 12/7837, letter, 28 June 1849; *Public Ledger*, 18 August 1832; *Morning Advertiser*, 3 April 1833; *Law Times*, 29 September 1849
 5. The National Archives, MH 12/7837, letter, 28 June 1849
 6. *Morning Chronicle*, 8 and 13 January 1849
 7. The National Archives, MH 12/12692, report, 28 February 1846; *Morning Post*, 20 January 1849; *Morning Chronicle*, 31 January 1849
 8. The National Archives, MH 12/7288, letter, received 14 June 1848
 9. *Morning Post*, 13 January 1849
10. *The Times*, 26 January 1849
11. *Daily News*, 12 January 1849
12. Local Government Board, 1874, pp. 247–59; Higginbotham, 2012, p. 41
13. *Morning Chronicle*, 20 January 1849
14. The National Archives, MH 12/7288, report, 9 December 1848
15. Rogers, 1889, p. 9
16. Glen, 1847, pp. 92, 148
17. *Morning Chronicle*, 19 and 20 January 1849
18. *Morning Chronicle*, 19 January 1849
19. The London Archives, CHBG/002, minutes, 21 and 28 June 1843
20. The London Archives, CHBG/002, minutes, 24 May, 14 June 1843
21. *Morning Chronicle*, 13 January 1849
22. *Morning Chronicle*, 14 April 1849
23. *Manchester Times*, 25 September 1841
24. The London Archives, WEBG/ST/006, letters, 22 April, 21 May 1842
25. *Manchester Times*, 25 September 1841
26. *Morning Post*, 11 December 1841; *Era*, 12 December 1841
27. The London Archives, WABG/008, report, 12 November 1846
28. The National Archives, MH 12/7837, letter, 28 June 1849
29. *Morning Chronicle*, 31 January 1849
30. *Illustrated London News*, 20 January 1849

31. *Examiner*, 20 January 1849
32. *Morning Chronicle*, 20 January 1849
33. The London Archives, WABG/009, minutes, 9 March 1848
34. Glen, 1849, p. 62
35. The London Archives, WABG/009, minutes, 19 October 1848
36. The London Archives, WABG/009, letter, 23 November 1848
37. The London Archives, WABG/009, letter, 23 November 1848
38. Baly, 1854, p. 307
39. *Morning Chronicle*, 8 January 1849
40. *Morning Chronicle*, 5 and 24 January 1849
41. Ancestry: St Mary, Islington, burial register, 5 January 1849
42. The National Archives, HO 107/1505, Park House, Church Street
43. The National Archives, HO 107/1068/6, Merton Road
44. The National Archives, MH 12/7837, report, 9 August 1848
45. The London Archives, WEBG/ST/006, letter, 22 April 1842
46. The London Archives, WEBG/ST/006, letter, 22 April 1842; minutes, 3 May 1842
47. The London Archives, WEBG/ST/006, letter, 21 May 1842

Chapter Four: Drouet's Children

1. The London Archives, P92/MRY/358, pp. 1, 12
2. The National Archives, MH 12/7837, report, 9 September 1847; The London Archives, WEBG/ST/010, minutes, 21 September 1847
3. The London Archives, WEBG/ST/011, minutes, 13 and 20 June, 17 October 1848
4. *Morning Chronicle*, 13 January 1849
5. *Morning Chronicle*, 13 January 1849
6. *Morning Chronicle*, 31 January 1849
7. The London Archives, CHBG/003, minutes, 24 April 1844
8. *Morning Chronicle*, 19 January 1849
9. *Morning Chronicle*, 13 January 1849
10. *Morning Chronicle*, 20 January 1849
11. The London Archives, KBG/010, minutes, 8 July 1847
12. The London Archives, KBG/010, minutes, 4 January 1847
13. *Morning Chronicle*, 19 January 1849; *The Times*, 31 January 1849
14. *The Times*, 31 January 1849
15. *Morning Chronicle*, 19 and 31 January 1849; *The Times*, 20 January 1849
16. *The Times*, 19 January 1949
17. *Morning Chronicle*, 20 and 31 January 1849; *The Times*, 20 January 1849
18. British and Foreign School Society, 1856, p. 142
19. *Illustrated London News*, 13 May 1843
20. *Morning Chronicle*, 13 January 1849; *The Times*, 11 January 1849
21. *Morning Chronicle*, 19 and 20 January 1849
22. *Daily News*, 20 January 1849
23. The National Archives, MH 12/7103, report, April 1850; The London Archives, STBG/SG/003, minutes, 27 July 1849
24. *Derby Mercury*, 24 January 1849
25. *Ragged School Union Magazine*, March 1849, p. 55; July 1849, p. 128; November 1849, p. 205
26. *Daily News*, 12 April 1850

27. *Daily News*, 12 April 1850
28. *The Times*, 19 January 1849
29. The National Archives, MH 12/7103, letter, received 24 February 1849
30. General Register Office, death certificate, William Baker, 13 November 1844
31. *Daily News*, 20 January 1849
32. *Morning Chronicle*, 24 January 1849
33. *The Times*, 20 January 1849
34. *The Times*, 26 January 1849
35. The National Archives, HO 107/1055/3, Kennington Row; Post Office London Directory, 1851; Ancestry: St Mary, Lewisham, marriage register, Richard Drouet and Emma Jane Hall, 8 December 1852
36. *Era*, 28 January 1849
37. *Morning Chronicle*, 20 January 1849; *The Times*, 20 January 1849
38. The London Archives, KBG/011, minutes, 6 and 8 November 1848
39. *Morning Chronicle*, 14 November 1848
40. The London Archives, KBG/011, minutes, 6 and 8 November 1848
41. *Weekly Dispatch*, 19 November 1848
42. *Morning Chronicle*, 14 November 1848
43. Romero Ruiz, 2010, pp. 148, 153, 155
44. Lock Asylum, 1810, p. 3
45. The London Archives, KBG/011, minutes, 12 October 1848; KBG/012, minutes, 31 May 1849
46. General Register Office, death certificate, Margaret Dawley, 11 August 1852

Chapter Five: An Awful Visitation

1. *Morning Chronicle*, 20 and 31 January 1849
2. *Bell's*, 4 February 1849
3. The National Archives, MH 13/245, government information poster, 21 October 1848
4. London and Provincial Medical Directory, 1851
5. *Lancet*, 4 March 1848, p. 257
6. *Morning Chronicle*, 13 January 1849
7. *Morning Chronicle*, 13 January 1849
8. *Morning Chronicle*, 20 January 1849
9. *Daily News*, 20 January 1849
10. The National Archives, MH 12/7837, letter, 28 June 1849; *Morning Chronicle*, 13 and 20 January, 16 April 1849; *Morning Post*, 20 January 1849
11. *Morning Chronicle*, 19 and 20 January, 16 April 1849
12. *Morning Chronicle*, 20 January, 16 April 1849
13. *Morning Chronicle*, 20 January, 16 April 1849
14. *Morning Chronicle*, 13 January 1849
15. *Morning Chronicle*, 13 January 1849; *Morning Post*, 13 January 1849
16. The National Archives, MH 12/7837, letter, 28 June 1849; *Morning Chronicle*, 13 January 1849; *The Times*, 10 January 1849
17. *Morning Chronicle*, 6 and 13 January, 4 April 1849
18. The National Archives, MH 12/7837, letter, 28 June 1849
19. *Bell's*, 29 October 1848, 7 January 1849
20. Pigot, 1839
21. *Morning Chronicle*, 24 January 1849

22. *Morning Chronicle*, 8 and 24 January 1849
23. *Morning Chronicle*, 13 January 1849
24. *Morning Chronicle*, 5 January 1849
25. The London Archives, WABG/009, letter, 4 April 1849
26. *Daily News*, 20 January 1849; *Morning Chronicle*, 20 January 1849; *Morning Post*, 20 January 1849
27. *Daily News*, 20 January 1849; *Morning Chronicle*, 20 January 1849; *Morning Post*, 20 January 1849
28. *Morning Chronicle*, 13 and 20 January 1849; *Morning Post*, 20 January 1849
29. *Morning Chronicle*, 13 and 19 January 1849
30. *Morning Chronicle*, 13 January 1849; *Morning Post*, 20 January 1849
31. *Morning Chronicle*, 4 January 1849
32. The National Archives, MH 12/7837, letter, 28 June 1849; *Morning Chronicle*, 20 January 1849
33. *Morning Chronicle*, 5 January 1849
34. *Morning Chronicle*, 5 January 1849
35. *Daily News*, 5 January 1849
36. The London Archives, WABG/009, minutes, 6 January 1849; *Morning Chronicle*, 13 January 1849
37. *Morning Chronicle*, 4, 8 and 13 January 1849
38. *Bell's*, 7 January 1849
39. *Morning Chronicle*, 13 January 1849
40. *Daily News*, 6 January 1849; *The Times*, 8 January 1849
41. *The Times*, 4 January 1849
42. *Morning Chronicle*, 13 January 1849
43. *The Times*, 19 June 1849
44. *Morning Chronicle*, 10 January 1849
45. *Daily News*, 10 and 16 January 1849
46. The London Archives, STBG/SG/003, minutes, 1, 8 and 15 December 1848
47. *The Times*, 26 June 1849

Chapter Six: The Parishes Act
 1. *The Times*, 19 January 1849
 2. *Morning Chronicle*, 6 January 1849
 3. *Bell's*, 7 January 1849; The London Archives, WEBG/ST/011, letter, 6 January 1849
 4. *Morning Post*, 16 April 1849
 5. *Morning Chronicle*, 16 April 1849
 6. *Morning Chronicle*, 8 January 1849
 7. *Morning Chronicle*, 4 and 8 January 1849
 8. *Morning Chronicle*, 13 January 1849
 9. *Morning Chronicle*, 8 January 1849
10. *Daily News*, 7 and 13 February 1849
11. *Morning Chronicle*, 8 January 1849
12. *Morning Chronicle*, 13 January 1849
13. *Morning Chronicle*, 13 January 1849
14. *Morning Chronicle*, 9 January 1849
15. *Morning Chronicle*, 5 January 1849
16. *Morning Chronicle*, 24 January 1849

17. *Northern Star*, 13 January 1849
18. *The Times*, 25 January 1849
19. *Morning Advertiser*, 31 January 1849
20. *Morning Chronicle*, 4 and 10 January 1849
21. *Morning Chronicle*, 20 January 1849
22. *Morning Chronicle*, 19 January 1849
23. *Morning Chronicle*, 10 January 1849
24. The London Archives, WABG/009, minutes, 4 January 1849
25. The London Archives, CHBG/007, minutes, 8 January 1849
26. The London Archives, FBG/003, letters, 4 and 5 January 1849
27. *The Times*, 4 January 1849
28. The London Archives, WEBG/ST/011, minutes, 5 January 1849
29. *Morning Chronicle*, 19 January 1849; *British Medical Journal*, 24 February 1872, p. 226
30. *Morning Chronicle*, 13 January 1849
31. *Morning Chronicle*, 13 and 20 January 1849
32. General Register Office, death certificates, Sarah James, 10 January 1849, William Grafton, 11 January 1849, Horatio Fuller, 7 January 1849, Robert Banks Penny, 18 April 1849; Ancestry: St Mary, Newington, burial register, 10 and 12 January, 24 April 1849
33. *Morning Chronicle*, 31 January 1849; *The Times*, 31 January 1849
34. *The Times*, 24 January 1849
35. Ancestry: St Nicholas, Tooting Graveney, burial register 8, 10, 12, 18 and 31 January 1849; General Register Office, death certificate, Elizabeth Bazznoe (i.e. Bazzone), 28 January 1849
36. The London Archives, WABG/009, minutes, 4 January 1849
37. *Morning Chronicle*, 6 and 13 January 1849
38. *Morning Chronicle*, 6 and 13 January 1849
39. *Morning Chronicle*, 8 and 10 January 1849
40. The London Archives, WABG/009, minutes, 4 January 1849; FBG/003, minutes, 6 January 1849; *Morning Chronicle* 6 and 10 January 1849
41. *Morning Chronicle*, 6 and 13 January 1849
42. The London Archives, WEBG/ST/011, letter, 6 January 1849
43. *Daily News*, 8 January 1849; *Morning Chronicle*, 10 January 1849; *The Times*, 31 January 1849
44. The London Archives, WEBG/ST/011, minutes, 7 January 1849; FBG/003, minutes, 6 January 1849
45. The London Archives, CHBG/007, letter, 8 January 1849 (with some changes to the punctuation)
46. General Register Office, death certificates, Sarah Jordan, 6 and 7 January 1849
47. *Morning Chronicle*, 8 January 1849
48. *Northern Star*, 13 January 1849
49. The London Archives, KBG/012, minutes, 11 January 1849; KBG/192/007, letter, 29 January 1849; *Morning Chronicle*, 19 January 1849
50. The London Archives, WABG/009, minutes, 6 January 1849

Chapter Seven: James Andrews
1. General Register Office, birth certificate, James Andrews, 20 July 1842; death certificate, Joseph Andrews, 24 January 1849
2. The National Archives, HO 107/724/4, Union Court; Post Office London Directory, 1844, 1849

3. Mayhew, 1861, iv, pp. 366–7, 370–3

4. Mayhew, 1861, iv, pp. 366–7, 370–3

5. *Morning Chronicle*, 17 January 1849; *Morning Post*, 14 April 1849

6. workhouses.org.uk/life/classification.shtml

7. The National Archives, MH 12/7288, letter, 8 November 1847; The London Archives, HOBG/138, minutes, 2 and 9 August, 13 and 27 September, 25 October 1848; *Morning Chronicle*, 16 April 1849

8. The National Archives, MH 12/7288, reports, 3 August, 11 September, 7 October 1848

9. *Morning Chronicle*, 14 April 1849

10. *Morning Chronicle*, 14 April 1849

11. *Morning Chronicle*, 14 April 1849

12. *Morning Chronicle*, 14 April 1849

13. *Morning Chronicle*, 14 April 1849

14. *Morning Chronicle*, 24 January 1849

15. The London Archives, HOBG/138, minutes, 5 January 1849

16. *Morning Chronicle*, 17 January 1849

17. *Morning Chronicle*, 6 January 1849

18. The London Archives, MH 12/7289, letter, 23 August 1849

19. *Morning Chronicle*, 17 January, 14 and 16 April 1849

20. *Daily News*, 17 January 1849

21. *Daily News*, 17 January 1849; *Morning Chronicle*, 9 and 24 January, 16 April 1849

22. *Morning Chronicle*, 20 and 24 January 1849

23. oldbaileyonline.org/record/t18490409-919?text=drouet

24. *The Times*, 26 January 1849

25. The London Archives, HOBG/138, minutes, 5 January 1849

26. oldbaileyonline.org/record/t18490409-919?text=drouet

27. *Daily News*, 14 April 1849; *Morning Chronicle*, 16 April 1849

28. The National Archives, MH 12/7289, letter, 23 August 1849; *Morning Post*, 11 January 1849; *Morning Chronicle*, 16 April 1849

29. *Morning Chronicle*, 13 and 24 January 1849

30. *Examiner*, 13 January 1849; *Morning Chronicle*, 13 January 1849

31. oldbaileyonline.org/record/t18490409-919?text=drouet; *Morning Chronicle*, 24 January 1849

32. *Morning Chronicle*, 16 April 1849

33. *Morning Chronicle* 13 and 24 January, 16 April 1849

34. *Morning Chronicle*, 24 January 1849

35. *Daily News*, 13 January 1849; *Morning Post*, 13 January 1849

36. *Morning Chronicle*, 13 and 24 January 1849; *Morning Post*, 13 January 1849

37. Ancestry: Holy Trinity, Gray's Inn Road, burial register, 9 January 1849; *Daily News* 16 April

38. *Morning Chronicle*, 9 January 1849; *Morning Post* 16 April 1849

39. oldbaileyonline.org/record/t18490409-919?text=drouet

40. *London Journal of Medicine*, May 1849, p. 424

41. *London Journal of Medicine*, May 1849, pp. 422, 424; oldbaileyonline.org/record/t18490409-919?text=drouet

42. *London Journal of Medicine*, May 1849, pp. 422, 424; oldbaileyonline.org/record/t18490409-919?text=drouet

43. oldbaileyonline.org/record/t18490409-919?text=drouet

44. Ancestry: Holy Trinity, Gray's Inn Road, burial register, 9 January 1849

Chapter Eight: Burying the Dead

  1. *London Journal of Medicine*, May 1849, pp. 409–37
  2. *The Times*, 20 January 1849
  3. *Morning Chronicle*, 31 January 1849
  4. *Lloyd's*, 14 January 1849
  5. *Morning Post*, 12 January 1849
  6. The National Archives, MH 12/7288, letters, 13 and 22 January 1849; The London Archives, HOBG/138, minutes, 10 January 1849
  7. Baly, 1854, pp. 182, 296–7
  8. *Morning Chronicle*, 24 January 1849
  9. *The Times*, 24 January 1849
 10. The National Archives, MH 12/7288, report, 18 January 1849
 11. *The Times*, 20 January 1849
 12. *The Times*, 20 January 1849
 13. *Morning Chronicle*, 22 and 31 January 1849
 14. *Morning Chronicle*, 8 January 1849
 15. *The Times*, 13 January 1849
 16. Ancestry: St Nicholas, Tooting Graveney, burial register, 5 January 1849
 17. *Morning Chronicle*, 5 January 1849
 18. The London Archives, WABG/009, minutes, 4 January 1849
 19. The London Archives, CHBG/007, minutes, 8 January 1849
 20. *Morning Chronicle*, 8 January 1849
 21. Ancestry: St Nicholas, Tooting Graveney, burial register, 6 and 8–10 January 1849
 22. *Morning Chronicle*, 20 January 1849
 23. *The Times*, 27 January 1849
 24. *Morning Chronicle*, 20 January 1849
 25. *Morning Chronicle*, 20 January 1849
 26. *Morning Chronicle*, 20 January 1849
 27. *Morning Chronicle*, 20 January 1849
 28. *The Times*, 17 January 1849
 29. *Morning Chronicle*, 11 January 1849
 30. *Tait's Edinburgh Magazine*, December 1848, p. 847
 31. *York Herald*, 5 April 1845
 32. Dickens, 1853, pp. 159–60
 33. *Daily News*, 13 January 1849
 34. *Morning Chronicle*, 21 July 1832
 35. *Taunton Courier*, 22 August 1849
 36. *Monmouthshire Beacon*, 15 September 1849
 37. *Durham Chronicle*, 28 September 1849
 38. *Morning Chronicle*, 11 January 1849
 39. *Annual Register*, 1849, chronicle, pp. 449–51
 40. Shapter, 1849, pp. 145–6
 41. *Morning Chronicle*, 12 January 1849
 42. Ancestry: St Luke, Chelsea, burial register, 17 January 1849; The London Archives, CHBG/007, minutes, 11 January 1849; CHBG/158/003, letter, 11 January 1849
 43. Ancestry: St Nicholas, Tooting Graveney, burial register, 12 January 1849
 44. The London Archives, WEBG/ST/011, minutes, 11 January 1849
 45. The London Archives, WEBG/ST/011, minutes, 11 January 1849

46. The London Archives, WEBG/ST/011, minutes, 11 January 1849
47. Ancestry: St Nicholas, Tooting Graveney, burial register, 13, 16 and 18 January 1849
48. *Morning Chronicle*, 5 January 1849
49. *Morning Chronicle*, 13 January 1849
50. *Morning Chronicle*, 20 January 1849
51. *Lancet*, 2 November 1839, p. 206; *Morning Chronicle*, 13 January 1849
52. *Morning Chronicle*, 20 January 1849
53. The London Archives, CHBG/007, minutes, 28 February 1849; WEBG/ST/011, minutes, 6 March 1849
54. The London Archives, WEBG/ST/011, minutes, 6 March 1849
55. *Hampshire Telegraph*, 27 January 1849
56. The National Archives, MH 12/7837, letter, 8 March 1849
57. The National Archives, MH 12/7837, opinion, 12 March 1849
58. The London Archives, WEBG/ST/011, minutes, 12 June 1849

Chapter Nine: Investigating Drouet
 1. *Morning Post*, 13 January 1849
 2. *Medical Times*, 3 July 1847, p. 384
 3. *The Times*, 13 January 1849
 4. Sprigge, 1897, p. 354
 5. Burney, 2000, p. 4
 6. *Morning Chronicle*, 27 January 1849
 7. *Morning Chronicle*, 20 January 1849
 8. Burney, 2000, p. 4
 9. *Morning Chronicle*, 10 and 19 January 1849
10. Burney, 2000, p. 5
11. *Daily News*, 24 January 1849
12. *Daily News*, 26 January 1849
13. *Morning Chronicle*, 19 January 1849
14. *Morning Post*, 20 January 1849
15. *Morning Chronicle*, 20 January 1849
16. *Morning Chronicle*, 20 January 1849
17. *Morning Chronicle*, 24 January 1849
18. *Morning Chronicle*, 16 January 1849
19. *Morning Chronicle*, 13 January 1849
20. *Morning Chronicle*, 16, 20 and 24 January 1849
21. *Daily News*, 26 January 1849; *Morning Chronicle*, 31 January 1849
22. *Morning Chronicle*, 24 January 1849
23. *Daily News*, 25 January 1849
24. *Bell's*, 4 February 1849
25. *Morning Chronicle*, 31 January 1849
26. *Morning Chronicle*, 24 February 1849
27. *The Times*, 1 February 1849
28. *Morning Chronicle*, 24 February 1849
29. *Morning Chronicle*, 24 February 1849
30. *The Times*, 20 January 1849
31. *Morning Chronicle*, 24 January 1849
32. *Morning Chronicle*, 24 January 1849

33. *Era*, 28 January 1849
34. *Morning Chronicle*, 17 January 1849
35. *Examiner*, 20 and 27 January, 3 March, 21 April 1849
36. Letters to John Forster, 31 December 1848; Catherine Dickens, 8 and 9 January 1849
37. *Examiner*, 20 January 1849
38. *Examiner*, 27 January 1849
39. *Examiner*, 3 March, 21 April 1849
40. Dickens, 1853a, p. 256
41. Dickens, 1850, p. 205
42. Dickens, 1853b, p. 173
43. *Examiner*, 27 January 1849
44. Forster, 1872, p. 435
45. Fielding, 1882, pp. 9–10

Chapter Ten: On Trial

 1. *Morning Chronicle*, 16 and 22 January 1849
 2. *Morning Herald*, 19 February 1849
 3. *Morning Advertiser*, 1 February 1849
 4. *The Times*, 5 February 1849
 5. *The Times*, 5 February 1849
 6. *The Times*, 5 February 1849
 7. *The Times*, 5 February 1849
 8. *Morning Post*, 13 February 1849
 9. *Morning Advertiser*, 31 January 1849
10. *Gentleman's Magazine*, September 1855, pp. 324–5
11. *Morning Post*, 18 November 1848; *Satirist*, 27 January 1849
12. *Morning Chronicle*, 28 February 1849
13. *Morning Chronicle*, 28 February 1849
14. *Morning Chronicle*, 28 February 1849
15. The London Archives, HOBG/138, minutes, 26 January 1849
16. *The Times*, 16 January 1849; *Morning Chronicle*, 16 January 1849
17. *Morning Chronicle*, 2 February 1849; *The Times*, 15 February 1849; *Daily News*, 3 March 1849
18. *Daily News*, 16 February 1849; *The Times*, 16 February 1849; *Morning Herald*, 19 February 1849; *Morning Post*, 26 February 1849
19. *Daily News*, 27 February 1849; *Examiner*, 3 March 1849
20. *Examiner*, 19 August 1848; *Gloucester Journal*, 12 August 1848; *Wilts and Gloucestershire Standard*, 15 August 1848
21. *Examiner*, 19 August 1848
22. Ballantine, 1882, i, pp. 11–12
23. National Portrait Gallery: D32829, lithograph after Robert Samuel Ennis Gallon, c. 1852
24. *Fraser's Magazine*, September 1847, pp. 310–11
25. *Morning Chronicle*, 14 April 1849
26. *Morning Chronicle*, 16 April 1849
27. *Morning Chronicle*, 14 and 16 April 1849
28. *Morning Chronicle*, 16 April 1849; *Bengal Catholic Herald*, 16 June 1849; *Morning Post*, 17 April 1849

29. *Morning Chronicle*, 16 April 1849
30. *Daily News*, 16 April 1849
31. *Daily News*, 14 April 1849
32. oldbaileyonline.org/record/t18490409-919?text=drouet
33. Robinson, 1889, p. 75; *Illustrated London News*, 13 April 1844
34. *Daily News*, 14 April 1849; *Morning Post*, 14 April
35. *Morning Chronicle*, 14 April 1849
36. *Daily News*, 14 April 1849; *Morning Chronicle*, 14 April 1849
37. *Morning Chronicle*, 16 April 1849
38. *Morning Chronicle*, 16 April 1849
39. *Morning Chronicle*, 16 April 1849
40. *Examiner*, 21 April 1849
41. *Morning Chronicle*, 16 April 1849
42. *Daily News*, 16 April 1849
43. *Justice of the Peace*, 21 April 1849
44. *Morning Chronicle*, 16 April 1849
45. *Lancet*, 21 April 1849, p. 435
46. Sprigge, 1897, pp. 404–13
47. *Lancet*, 21 April 1849, p. 435

Chapter Eleven: New Homes

1. The London Archives, HOBG/138, minutes, 27 February 1849; report, 14 March 1849
2. The National Archives, MH 12/7288, appointments, 24 May 1849; letter, 1 June 1849
3. The National Archives, MH 12/7289, letters, 20 May, 16 June 1849
4. The National Archives, MH 12/7289, minutes, 4 June 1849; letter, 7 June 1849
5. The National Archives, MH 12/7289, letter, 16 June 1849
6. The National Archives, MH 12/7289, letters, 11 and 19 July, 6 and 23 August, 19 October 1849; The London Archives, HOBG/139, minutes, 5 and 12 December 1849, 2 and 16 January 1850
7. The London Archives, CHBG/007, minutes, 29 and 31 January, 7, 14 and 21 February, 14 and 15 March, 16 May 1849; CHBG/158/003, letter, 17 May 1849
8. The London Archives, P92/MRY/299, minutes, 3 April 1849
9. The London Archives, CHBG/007, minutes, 14 and 19 February 1849; The National Archives, MH 12/6989, letter, 15 February 1849
10. The London Archives, CHBG/007, minutes, 19 February 1849
11. The London Archives, CHBG/007, minutes, 25 and 31 January, 7, 21 and 28 February 1849
12. The London Archives, CHBG/158/003, letter, 16 October 1849
13. The London Archives, CHBG/007, minutes, 28 February, 2 May 1849
14. The London Archives, CHBG/007, minutes, 1 March, 23 May 1849
15. The London Archives, CHBG/007, minutes, 4 July 1849
16. The London Archives, CHBG/007, minutes, 28 March 1849
17. The National Archives, HO 107/1474, Exeter Street
18. The London Archives, CHBG/007, minutes, 4 and 11 April, 18 July 1849
19. The London Archives, FBG/003, letters, 7, 8 and 31 January 1849; minutes, 22 February 1849
20. The London Archives, FBG/003, letters, 8, 17 and 24 January, 8 February, 8 and 15 March 1849

21. The London Archives, FBG/003, letters, 31 January, 5 and 15 February 1849
22. The London Archives, FBG/003, letters, 15, 22 and 28 February 1849
23. The London Archives, STBG/SG/003, minutes, 9, 12, 22, 23 and 26 January, 2 and 9 February, 16 March 1849
24. The London Archives, STBG/SG/003, minutes, 26 February, 20 July 1849 (with additional punctuation)
25. *Morning Post*, 12 January 1849; *Canterbury Journal*, 13 January 1849
26. General Register Office, death certificate, Mary Ann Doddington, 8 January 1849
27. *Morning Post*, 12 January 1849; *Canterbury Journal*, 13 January 1849
28. The National Archives, MH 12/12521, minutes, 19 January 1849; report, 16 February 1849; letter, 10 March 1849
29. The London Archives, P92/MRY/299, letters, 9 and 17 May 1849
30. The London Archives, P92/MRY/299, report 21 May 1849; letters 24 May, 5 June 1849
31. The London Archives, WEBG/ST/011, minutes, 13 and 27 March 1849
32. The National Archives, MH 12/7837, letter 10 January 1849; The London Archives, WEBG/ST/011, minutes, 6 February 1849
33. The London Archives, WEBG/ST/011, reports, 16 and 22 January 1849
34. The London Archives, WEBG/ST/011, report, 22 January 1849; *Morning Chronicle*, 12 January 1849
35. The London Archives, WEBG/ST/011, report, 11 January 1849; General Register Office, death certificate, Margaret Kingham, 11 January 1849
36. *Morning Chronicle*, 12 January 1849
37. The National Archives, MH 12/7837, letter, 12 March 1849
38. The London Archives, WEBG/ST/011, minutes, 11 and 17 April, 1 May 1849
39. The London Archives, WEBG/ST/011, minutes, 24 April 1849
40. The London Archives, WEBG/ST/011, letter, 30 January 1849; minutes, 3 July 1849
41. The London Archives, WEBG/ST/012, minutes, 13 November 1849
42. The National Archives, MH 12/7837, letter, 22 March 1849; The London Archives, WEBG/ST/011, minutes, 8 June 1849
43. The National Archives, MH 12/7837, letter 9 June 1849; memorial, 25 June 1849
44. The London Archives, WEBG/ST/011, minutes, 8 and 12 June 1849
45. The National Archives, MH 12/7837, report, 28 June 1849
46. The London Archives, WEBG/ST/011, minutes, 3 July 1849
47. The National Archives, MH 12/7837, letter, 7 July 1849
48. The National Archives, MH 12/7837, letter, 2 August 1849
49. The London Archives, WEBG/ST/012, letter, 28 August 1849

Chapter Twelve: After Surrey Hall
1. *Evening Mail*, 18 April 1849
2. *West of England Conservative*, 28 March 1850
3. *West of England Conservative*, 28 March 1850
4. *Examiner*, 30 March 1850
5. *Daily News*, 16 April 1849
6. *Morning Chronicle*, 7 March 1849
7. *The Times*, 16 and 21 April 1849
8. The London Archives, WEBG/ST/011, minutes, 12 June 1849
9. Wandsworth Heritage Service, TP/1/1/4, minutes, 15 February, 23 March, 10 and 17 May, 15 June 1849

10. Dixon, 1850, p. 47

11. Brasier, 1850, pp. 6–11

12. Brasier, 1850, pp. 14–17

13. The National Archives, HO 107/1629, Cliff Terrace

14. Coleridge, 1873, i, p. 283 and ii, pp. 122, 229, 420

15. Coleridge, 1873, ii, pp. 134–5, 229–30

16. General Register Office, death certificate, Maria Drouet, 4 October 1848

17. *Bell's*, 4 February 1849

18. The National Archives, PROB 11/2097/252

19. *Canterbury Journal*, 21 July 1849

20. Knight, 1847, p. 152

21. General Register Office, death certificate, Bartholomew Peter Drouet, 19 July 1849

22. *Canterbury Journal*, 28 July 1849

23. Deceased Online: South Metropolitan Cemetery, burial register, 12 October 1848, 27 July 1849

24. *The Times*, 23 July; *Satirist*, 28 July 1849

25. The London Archives, WEBG/ST/011, minutes, 6 March 1849

26. *Morning Chronicle*, 17 January 1849; The London Archives, HOBG/138, minutes, 26 January 1849

27. Ancestry: St Mary, Hampton, marriage register, Henry Seymour Conway and Miriam Drouet, 21 January 1847; The National Archives, HO 107/1579, Upper Tooting

28. The National Archives, HO 107/1566, Deverell Street

29. The National Archives, RG 9/363, Stockwell Park Road

30. Ancestry: St George the Martyr, Borough High Street, marriage register, William Drouet and Hannah Copping, 9 February 1845; *Kentish Independent*, 15 January 1848

31. Murray, 1854, p. 11

32. The London Archives, WEBG/SM/038/004, 20 February to 5 March 1853; General Register Office, death certificate, William Charles Drouet, 17 December 1858

33. Post Office London Directory, 1858

34. Ancestry: freedom admission papers, William Leonard Drouet, 12 September 1848

35. General Register Office, death certificate, William Leonard Drouet, 28 November 1869

36. *Morning Advertiser*, 7 June 1856 and 16 January 1857; General Register Office, death certificate, Richard Drouet, 16 December 1867

37. *Era*, 3 August 1851

38. The National Archives, MH 12/12456, letter, 20 January 1836

39. The National Archives, MH 12/12109, letters, 15 December 1848, 6 January 1849

40. *Morning Advertiser*, 26 July 1851

41. The National Archives, J 77/14/D49; *Saint James's Chronicle*, 23 November 1861

42. The National Archives, J 77/14/D49; *Saint James's Chronicle*, 23 November 1861

43. *Law Times*, 29 September 1849

44. The London Archives, P95/NIC/112

45. *Morning Advertiser*, 13 March 1850

46. *Illustrated London News*, 27 April 1850

47. Wandsworth Heritage Service, TP/1/1/4, minutes, 23 May 1850; *Illustrated London News*, 27 April 1850

48. Hurley, 1947, p. 24

49. The National Archives, ED 103/30/25

50. The National Archives, ED 103/30/25

51. Brookfield, 1859, p. 16

52. Hurley, 1947, pp. 24–5
53. London Picture Archive: Garratt Lane, The Old Vestry Hall, 1887
54. *Lloyd's*, 29 July 1906; *South Western Star*, 3 August 1906

Epilogue
1. *Hampshire Telegraph*, 27 January 1849
2. *Illustrated London News*, 23 November 1850
3. *Morning Chronicle*, 20 January 1849
4. *East Kent Gazette*, 31 October 1868
5. *Maidstone Journal*, 15 October 1889; *Templar*, 28 May 1874
6. The National Archives, RG 11/865, Spital Street
7. *Daily Mirror*, 27 July 1989

Select Bibliography

Archive Sources
General Register Office
Guildhall Library
Hampshire Record Office
The London Archives
The National Archives
Surrey History Centre
Wandsworth Heritage Service

Directories and Guides
Bradshaw, *Railway Guide*
London and Provincial Medical Directory
Pigot, J. & Co., *Surrey Directory*
Post Office London Directory
The Royal Kalendar

Acts of Parliament
1767 Jonas Hanway's Act
1834 Poor Law Amendment Act
1844 Poor Law Amendment Act

Reports and Government Publications
Brookfield, W. H., *Tabulated Reports on Schools Inspected in the Counties of Kent, Surrey, and Sussex, and in the Channel Islands* (Longman, London, 1859)
General Register Office, *Report on the Mortality of Cholera in England, 1848–49* (HMSO, London, 1852)
Glen, William Cunningham, *The General Consolidated Order Issued by the Poor Law Commissioners on the 24th July, 1847 etc.* (Shaw & Sons, London, 1847)
Glen, William Cunningham, *The Nuisances Removal and Diseases Prevention Acts, 1848 & 1849* (Shaw & Sons, London, 1849)
Local Government Board, *Third Annual Report*, appendix B (HMSO, London, 1874)
Lovick, Thomas, *Report upon the Sanitary Condition of the United Parishes of St. Andrew Holborn, Above the Bars, and St. George the Martyr* (HMSO, London, 1848)
Poor Law Board, *Metropolitan Workhouse Infirmaries, etc.* (HMSO, London, 1866)
Poor Law Commissioners, *Report from His Majesty's Commissioners for Inquiring into the Administration and Practical Operation of the Poor Laws*, appendix A, part 3 (HMSO, London, 1834)
Registrar-General, *Weekly Return of Births and Deaths in London* (HMSO, London, 1854)

Printed Sources

Alcock, Nathanael, *A Treatise on Cholera* (John Churchill, London, 1849)

Amidon, Lynne A., *An Illustrated History of the Royal Free Hospital* (Royal Free Hospital, London, 1996)

Arnold, Catharine, *Necropolis: London and Its Dead* (Simon & Schuster, London, 2006)

Ballantine, William, *Some Experiences of a Barrister's Life* (Richard Bentley & Son, London, 1882)

Baly, William and William W. Gull, *Reports on Epidemic Cholera* (John Churchill, London, 1854)

Beames, Thomas, *The Rookeries of London: Past, Present and Prospective* (Thomas Bosworth, London, 1850)

Behlmer, George K., 'Grave Doubts: Victorian Medicine, Moral Panic, and the Signs of Death', *Journal of British Studies*, vol. 42, no. 2 (April 2003), pp. 206–35

Bligh, Eric, *Tooting Corner* (Secker & Warburg, London, 1946)

Brasier, W. C., publ., *New Margate, Ramsgate, and Broadstairs Guide* (W. C. Brasier, Margate, 1850)

Brayley, Edward Wedlake, *A Topographical History of Surrey*, vol. 3. (G. Willis, London, 1850)

Brice, A. W. C., '"A Truly British Judge": Another Article by Dickens', *The Dickensian*, vol. 66, no. 360 (January 1970), pp. 30–5

Brice, A. W. C. and K. J. Fielding, 'Dickens and the Tooting Disaster', *Victorian Studies*, vol. 12, no. 2 (December 1968), pp. 227–44

British and Foreign School Society, *A Handbook to the Borough Road Schools* (British and Foreign School Society, London, 1854)

Burgess, Henry, *The Duty of the State to Its Infant Poor. A Letter to Lord John Russell, Occasioned by the Recent Disclosures Respecting the Infant Poor at Tooting* (C. Cox, London, 1849)

Burney, Ian A., *Bodies of Evidence: Medicine and the Politics of the English Inquest, 1830–1926* (Johns Hopkins University Press, Baltimore, 2000)

Clarke, H. G. & Co., publ., *London As It Is Today: Where to Go, and What to See, during the Great Exhibition* (H. G. Clarke, London, 1851)

Cochrane, Charles, *The Journal of a Tour* (Simpkin and Marshall, London, 1830)

Coleridge, Edith, ed., *Memoir and Letters of Sara Coleridge* (Henry S. King, London, 1873)

Curle, B. R., 'Mr Drouet's Establishment at Tooting: An Essay in Victorian Child Welfare', *Surrey Archaeological Collections*, vol. 66 (1969), pp. 87–98

Dickens, Charles, *Bleak House* (Bradbury and Evans, London, 1853a)

Dickens, Charles, 'Home for Homeless Women', *Household Words*, vol. 7, no. 161 (23 April 1853b), pp. 169–75

Dickens, Charles, *Oliver Twist* (Richard Bentley, London, 1838)

Dickens, Charles, 'A Walk in the Workhouse', *Household Words*, vol. 1, no. 9 (25 May 1850), pp. 204–7

Diprose, John, *Some Account of the Parish of Saint Clement Danes (Westminster) Past and Present* (Diprose and Bateman, London, 1868)

Dixon, C. D., publ., *The Visitors' New Guide (Historical and Descriptive,) to the Isle of Thanet* (C. D. Dixon, Margate, 1850)

Doré, Gustave and Blanchard Jerrold, *London: A Pilgrimage* (Grant & Co., London, 1872)

Fielding, C. H., *A Hand-Book of Higham: or The Curiosities of a Country Parish* (W. T. Wildish, Rochester, 1882)

Fisher, Yvonne King, *Coroners in London and Middlesex, c. 1820–1888* (PhD thesis, Open University, 2020)

Forster, John, *The Life of Charles Dickens* (Chapman and Hall, London, 1872 etc.)

Foss, Edward, *A Biographical Dictionary of the Judges of England etc.* (John Murray, London, 1870)

Foster, Joseph, *Men-at-the-Bar* (Hazell, Watson and Viney Ltd, 1885)

Glen, William Cunningham, ed., *Shaws' Union Officers' Manual of Duties* (Shaw & Sons, London, 1846)

Gull, William W., *Report on the Morbid Anatomy, Pathology, and Treatment, of Epidemic Cholera* (John Churchill, London, 1854)

Harris, Edmund, *The Rogue Goths: R. L. Roumieu, Joseph Peacock and Bassett Keeling* (Liverpool University Press, Liverpool, 2024)

Helmstadter, Carol and Judith Godden, *Nursing Before Nightingale, 1815–1899* (Ashgate Publishing Limited, Farnham, 2011)

Higginbotham, Peter, *The Workhouse Encyclopaedia* (The History Press, Stroud, 2012)

Hurley, A. J., *Days That are Gone* (A. J. Hurley Ltd., London, 1947)

Jeanneret, Henry, *Epidemic Cholera, Diarrhoea and Dysentery* (George Philip & Son, London, 1857)

Knight, Charles, *Knight's Cyclopaedia of London* (Charles Knight, London, 1851)

Knight, Charles, publ., *The Land We Live In*, vol. 1 (Charles Knight, London, 1847)

A Late Relieving Officer, *The Poor Laws Unmasked: Being a General Exposition of Our Workhouse Institutions* (Thomas Day, London, 1859)

Lee, Anthony and John Robinson and Janet Robinson, *Margate Through Time* (Amberley Publishing, Stroud, 2012)

Levinge, Edward P., *The Justices' Manual* (Edward J. Milliken, Dublin, 1853)

Lewis, Samuel, *The History and Topography of the Parish of Saint Mary, Islington, in the County of Middlesex* (J. H. Jackson, London, 1842)

Lewis, Samuel, *Islington As It Was and As It Is* (J. H. Jackson, London, 1854)

Lock Asylum, *An Account of the Institution of the Lock Asylum, for the Reception of Penitent Female Patients, When Discharged from the Lock Hospital* (B. Meredith, London, 1810)

Low, Sampson, *The Charities of London* (Sampson Low, London, 1850)

Mayhew, Henry, *London Labour and the London Poor* (Griffin, Bohn & Co., London, 1861 edition)

Measom, George, *The Official Illustrated Guide to the South-Eastern Railway and All Its Branches* (Reed and Pardon, London, 1853)

Morden, W. E., *The History of Tooting-Graveney, Surrey* (Edmund Seale, London, 1897)

Morris, G. A. and S. A., *A History of St Nicholas, Tooting Parish Church*, (G. A. and S. A. Morris, Tooting, 1984)

Murray, John, publ., *The Annual Subscription Charities and Public Societies in London* (John Murray, London, 1823)

Murray, John, publ., *A Handbook for Travellers in France* (John Murray, London, 1854)

Pettigrew, T. J., *The Pauper Farming System* (T. Rodd, London, 1836)

Ritch, Alistair, *Sickness in the Workhouse: Poor Law Medical Care in Provincial England, 1834–1914* (University of Rochester Press, Rochester, NY, 2019)

Robinson, Serjeant, *Bench and Bar: Reminiscences of One of the Last of an Ancient Race* (Hurst and Blackett, London, 1889)

Rogers, Joseph, M.D., *Reminiscences of a Workhouse Medical Officer* (T. Fisher Unwin, London, 1889)

Romero Ruiz, Maria Isabel, 'Fallen Women and the London Lock Hospital Laws and By-Laws of 1840 (Revised 1848)', *Journal of English Studies*, vol. 8 (2010), pp. 141–58

Shapter, Thomas, *The History of the Cholera in Exeter in 1832* (John Churchill, London, 1849)
Slater, Michael, *Dickens' Journalism*, vol. 2 (J. M. Dent, London, 1996)
Sprigge, S. Squire, *The Life and Times of Thomas Wakley* (Longmans, Green & Co., London, 1897)
Stanley, Dorothy, *The Autobiography of Sir Henry Morton Stanley, G.C.B.* (Sampson Low & Co., London, 1909)
Storey, Graham and K. J. Fielding, eds., *The Letters of Charles Dickens*, vol. 5 (Oxford University Press, Oxford, 1980)
Thomas, Amanda J., *Cholera: The Victorian Plague* (Pen & Sword Books Ltd, Barnsley, 2015)
Thornbury, Walter, *Old and New London*, vol. 2 (Cassell, Petter & Galpin, London, 1878)
Whorton, James C., *The Arsenic Century: How Victorian Britain was Poisoned at Home, Work, and Play* (Oxford University Press, Oxford, 2010)
Wood, Peter, *Poverty and the Workhouse in Victorian Britain* (Alan Sutton, Stroud, 1991)

Newspapers / Journals
Ancient Balham and Tooting
Annual Register
Bell's Life in London
Bengal Catholic Herald
British Medical Journal
Builder
Canterbury Journal
Daily Mirror
Daily News
Derby Mercury
Dover Telegraph
Durham Chronicle
East Kent Gazette
Edinburgh Medical and Surgical Journal
Era
Essex Herald
Evening Mail
Examiner
Fraser's Magazine for Town and Country
Gentleman's Magazine
Globe
Gloucester Journal
Hampshire Chronicle
Hampshire Telegraph
Household Words
Illustrated London News
John Bull
Journal of Health
Justice of the Peace
Kentish Independent
Lancet
Law Chronicle
Law Times

Leicestershire Mercury
Lloyd's Weekly Newspaper
London Journal of Medicine
London Medical Gazette
Maidstone Journal
Manchester Times
Medical Times
Monmouthshire Beacon
Morning Advertiser
Morning Chronicle
Morning Herald
Morning Post
Northern Star
Public Ledger
Ragged School Union Magazine
Retrospect of Practical Medicine and Surgery
Saint James's Chronicle
Salisbury and Winchester Journal
Satirist
South Western Star
Sun
Tait's Edinburgh Magazine
Taunton Courier
Templar
The Times
True Sun
Weekly Chronicle
Weekly Dispatch
West Kent Guardian
West of England Conservative
Wilts and Gloucestershire Standard
Wiltshire Independent
York Herald

Web Sources
ancestry.co.uk
https://blog.nationalarchives.gov.uk/george-sangliers-petitions-two-sides-every-petition
british-history.ac.uk
https://deceasedonline.com
digitalpanopticon.org
findmypast.co.uk
mapco.net/index.htm
https://maps.nls.uk
oldbaileyonline.org
oxforddnb.com
wellcome.org
workhouses.org.uk

Index